Monstres
Volume 5:

My Son the Killer

Joann SfAR, Lewis TRONDHEIM, story
Guest artists: My Son the Killer: BLUTCH
Soldiers of Honor: BEZIAN

color: WALTER

NANTIER · BEALL · MINOUSTCHINE
Publishing inc.
new york

See previews, get exclusives and order from:
NBMPUB.COM

we have over 200 titles available
Catalog upon request
NBM
160 Broadway, Suite 700, East Wing
New York, NY 10038
If ordering by mail add $4 P&H 1st item,
$1 each addt'l

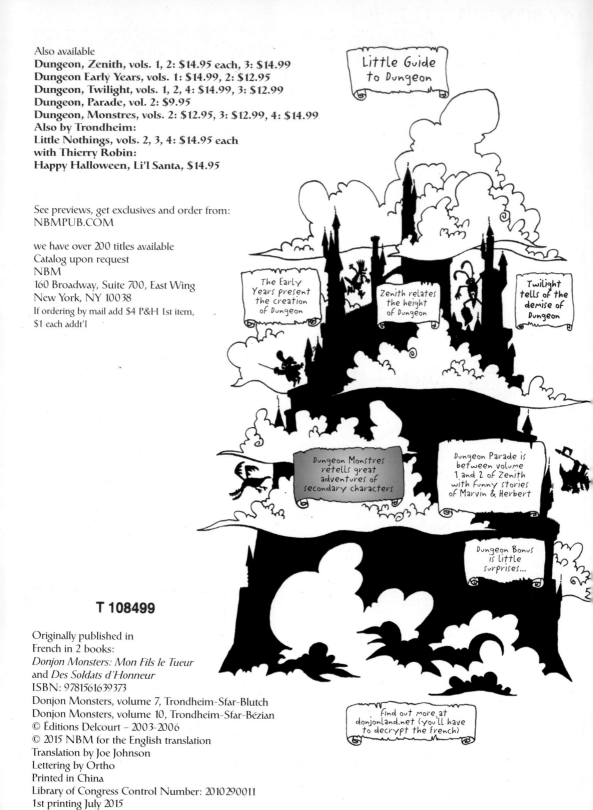

Little Guide to Dungeon

The Early Years present the creation of Dungeon

Zenith relates the height of Dungeon

Twilight tells of the demise of Dungeon

Dungeon Monstres retells great adventures of secondary characters

Dungeon Parade is between volume 1 and 2 of Zenith with funny stories of Marvin & Herbert

Dungeon Bonus is little surprises...

find out more at donjonland.net (you'll have to decrypt the french)

T 108499

Originally published in
French in 2 books:
Donjon Monsters: Mon Fils le Tueur
and *Des Soldats d'Honneur*
ISBN: 9781561639373
Donjon Monsters, volume 7, Trondheim-Sfar-Blutch
Donjon Monsters, volume 10, Trondheim-Sfar-Bézian
© Éditions Delcourt – 2003-2006
© 2015 NBM for the English translation
Translation by Joe Johnson
Lettering by Ortho
Printed in China
Library of Congress Control Number: 2010290011
1st printing July 2015

MY SON THE KILLER

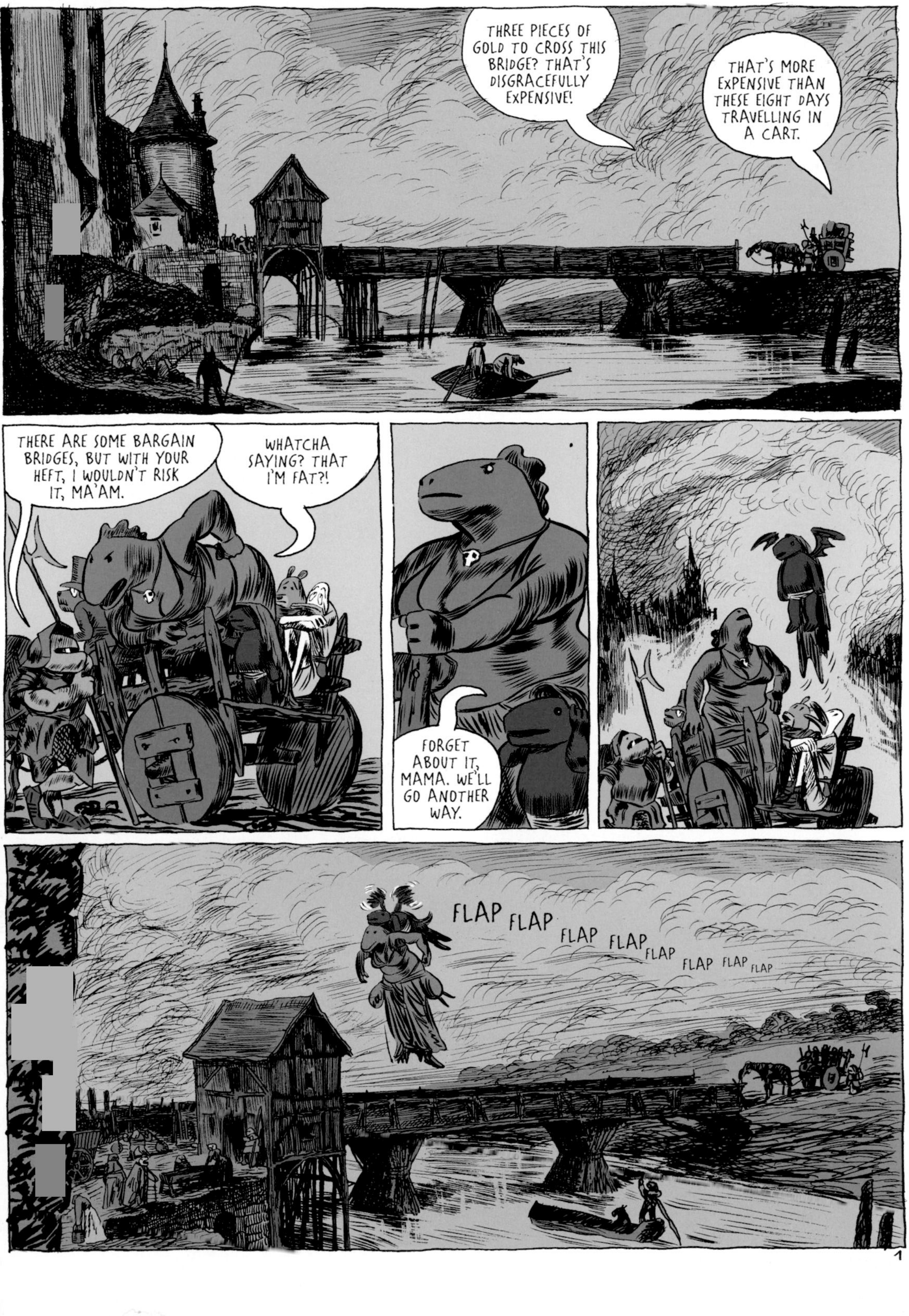

THREE PIECES OF GOLD TO CROSS THIS BRIDGE? THAT'S DISGRACEFULLY EXPENSIVE!
THAT'S MORE EXPENSIVE THAN THESE EIGHT DAYS TRAVELLING IN A CART.
THERE ARE SOME BARGAIN BRIDGES, BUT WITH YOUR HEFT, I WOULDN'T RISK IT, MA'AM.
WHATCHA SAYING? THAT I'M FAT?!
FORGET ABOUT IT, MAMA. WE'LL GO ANOTHER WAY.
FLAP FLAP FLAP FLAP FLAP FLAP FLAP FLAP

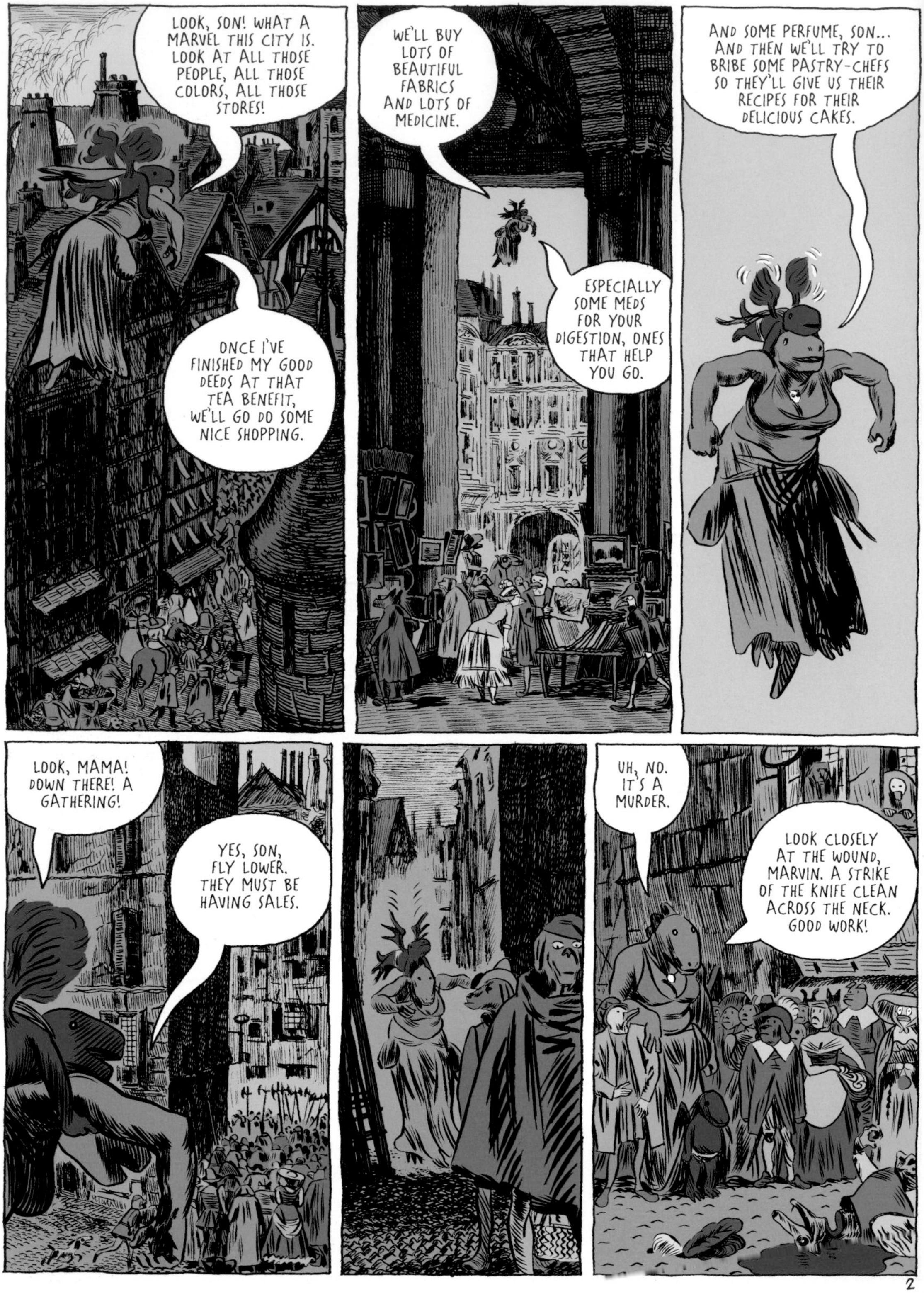
LOOK, SON! WHAT A MARVEL THIS CITY IS. LOOK AT ALL THOSE PEOPLE, ALL THOSE COLORS, ALL THOSE STORES!
ONCE I'VE FINISHED MY GOOD DEEDS AT THAT TEA BENEFIT, WE'LL GO DO SOME NICE SHOPPING.
WE'LL BUY LOTS OF BEAUTIFUL FABRICS AND LOTS OF MEDICINE.
ESPECIALLY SOME MEDS FOR YOUR DIGESTION, ONES THAT HELP YOU GO.
AND SOME PERFUME, SON... AND THEN WE'LL TRY TO BRIBE SOME PASTRY-CHEFS SO THEY'LL GIVE US THEIR RECIPES FOR THEIR DELICIOUS CAKES.
LOOK, MAMA! DOWN THERE! A GATHERING!
YES, SON, FLY LOWER. THEY MUST BE HAVING SALES.
UH, NO. IT'S A MURDER.
LOOK CLOSELY AT THE WOUND, MARVIN. A STRIKE OF THE KNIFE CLEAN ACROSS THE NECK. GOOD WORK!

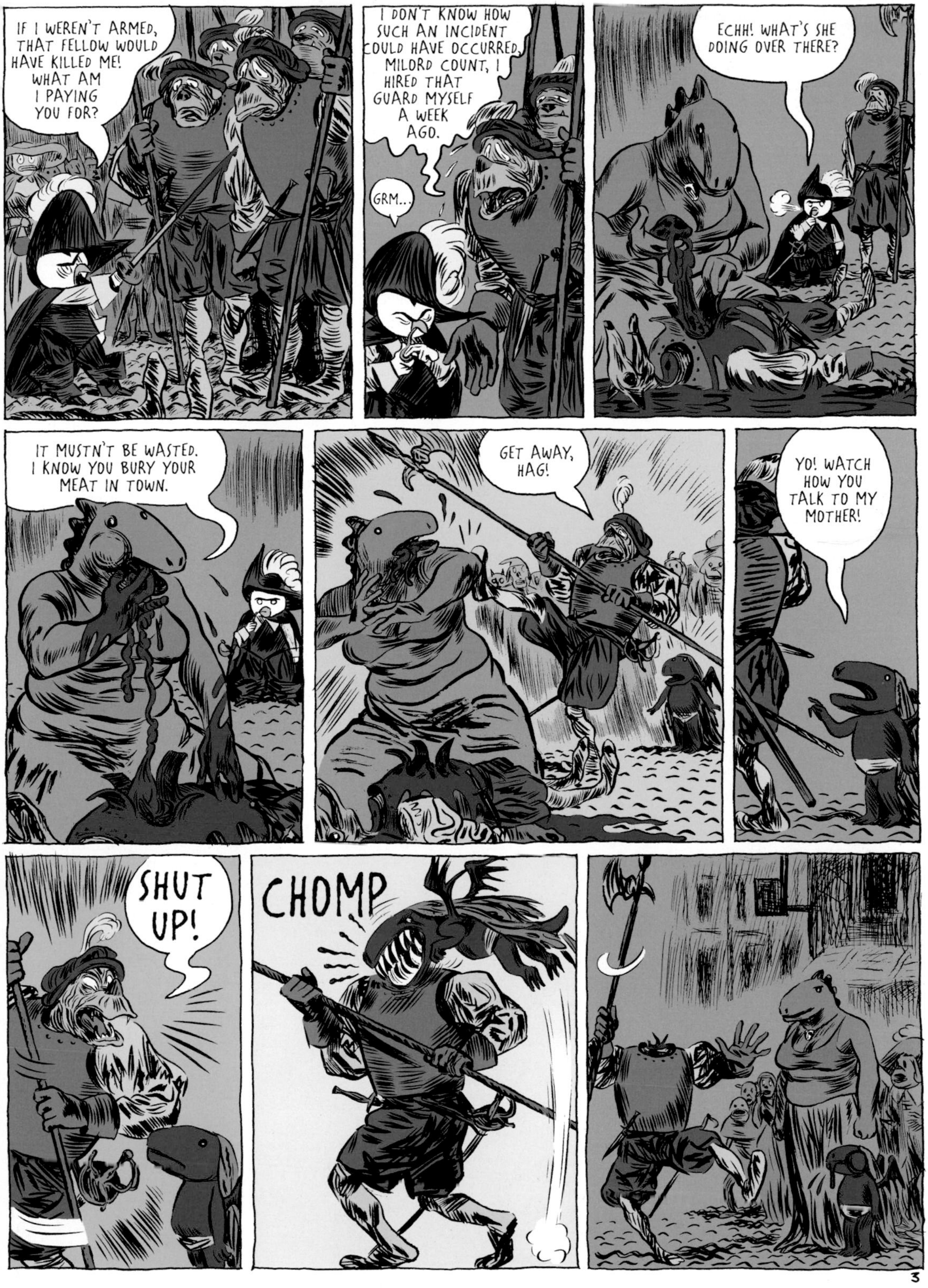
IF I WEREN'T ARMED, THAT FELLOW WOULD HAVE KILLED ME! WHAT AM I PAYING YOU FOR?
I DON'T KNOW HOW SUCH AN INCIDENT COULD HAVE OCCURRED, MILORD COUNT, I HIRED THAT GUARD MYSELF A WEEK AGO.
GRM...
ECHH! WHAT'S SHE DOING OVER THERE?
IT MUSTN'T BE WASTED. I KNOW YOU BURY YOUR MEAT IN TOWN.
GET AWAY, HAG!
YO! WATCH HOW YOU TALK TO MY MOTHER!
SHUT UP!
CHOMP

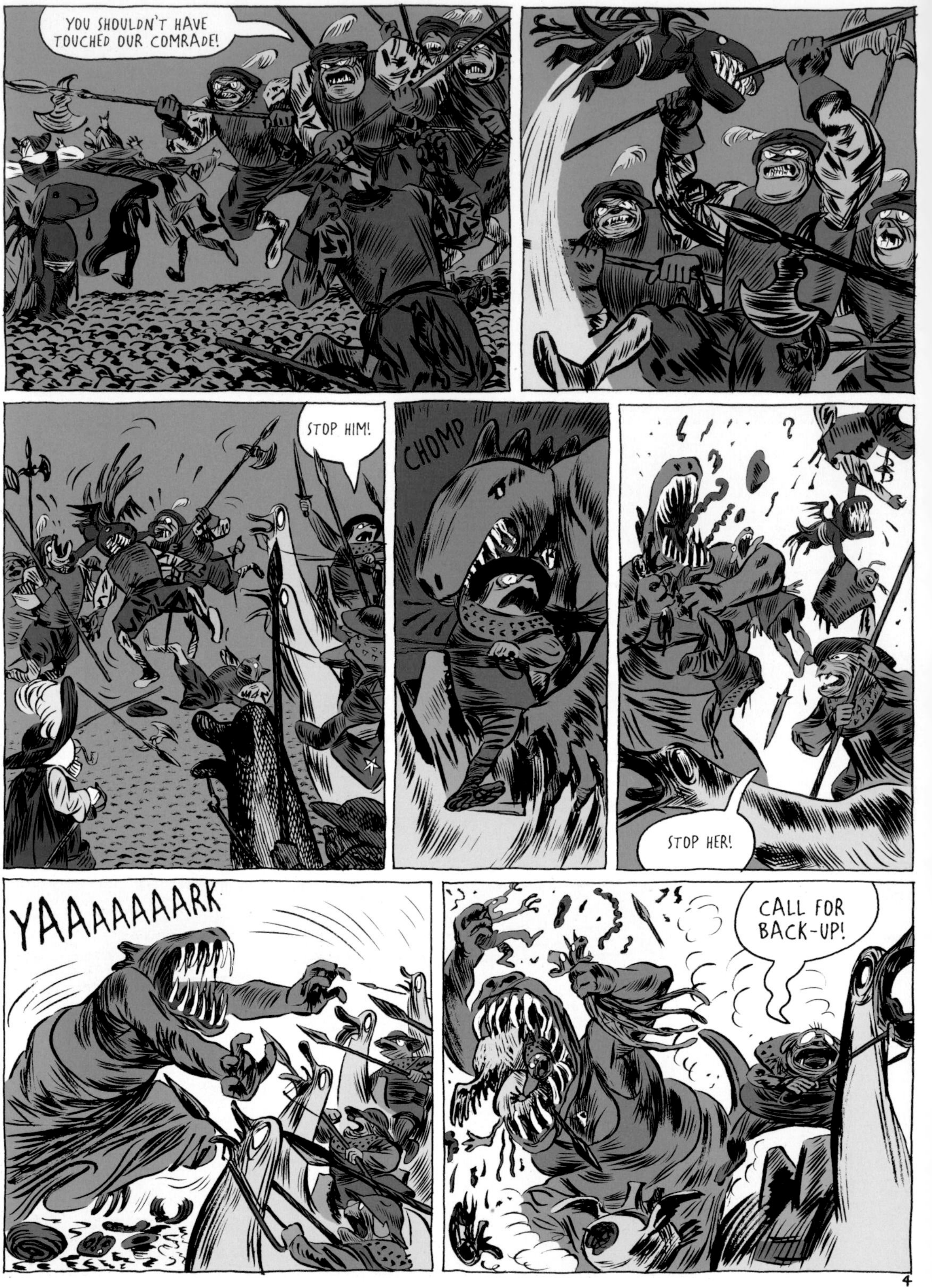
YOU SHOULDN'T HAVE TOUCHED OUR COMRADE!
STOP HIM!
CHOMP
?
STOP HER!
YAAAAAAARK
CALL FOR BACK-UP!

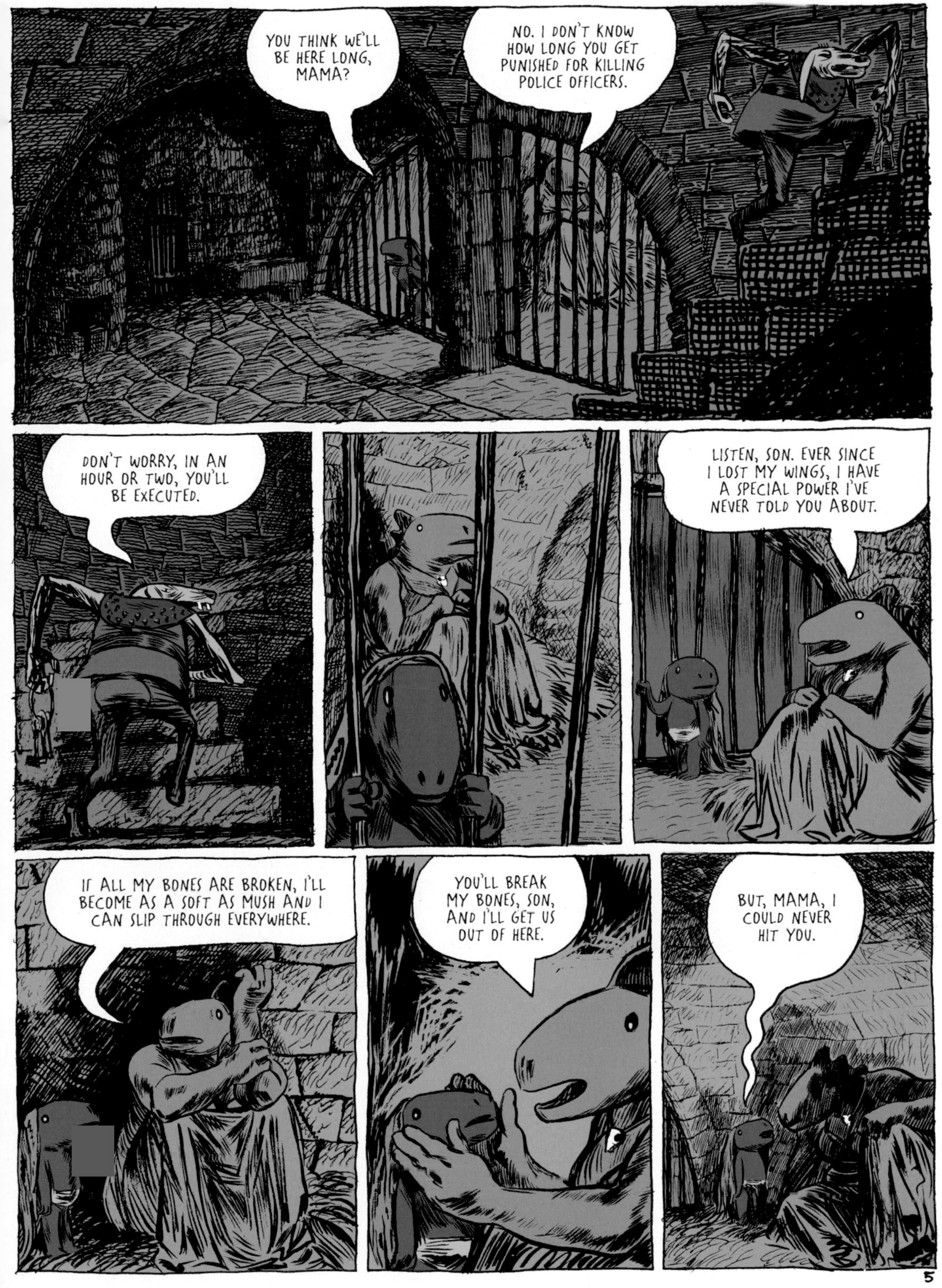
YOU THINK WE'LL BE HERE LONG, MAMA?
NO. I DON'T KNOW HOW LONG YOU GET PUNISHED FOR KILLING POLICE OFFICERS.
DON'T WORRY, IN AN HOUR OR TWO, YOU'LL BE EXECUTED.
LISTEN, SON. EVER SINCE I LOST MY WINGS, I HAVE A SPECIAL POWER I'VE NEVER TOLD YOU ABOUT.
IF ALL MY BONES ARE BROKEN, I'LL BECOME AS A SOFT AS MUSH AND I CAN SLIP THROUGH EVERYWHERE.
YOU'LL BREAK MY BONES, SON, AND I'LL GET US OUT OF HERE.
BUT, MAMA, I COULD NEVER HIT YOU.

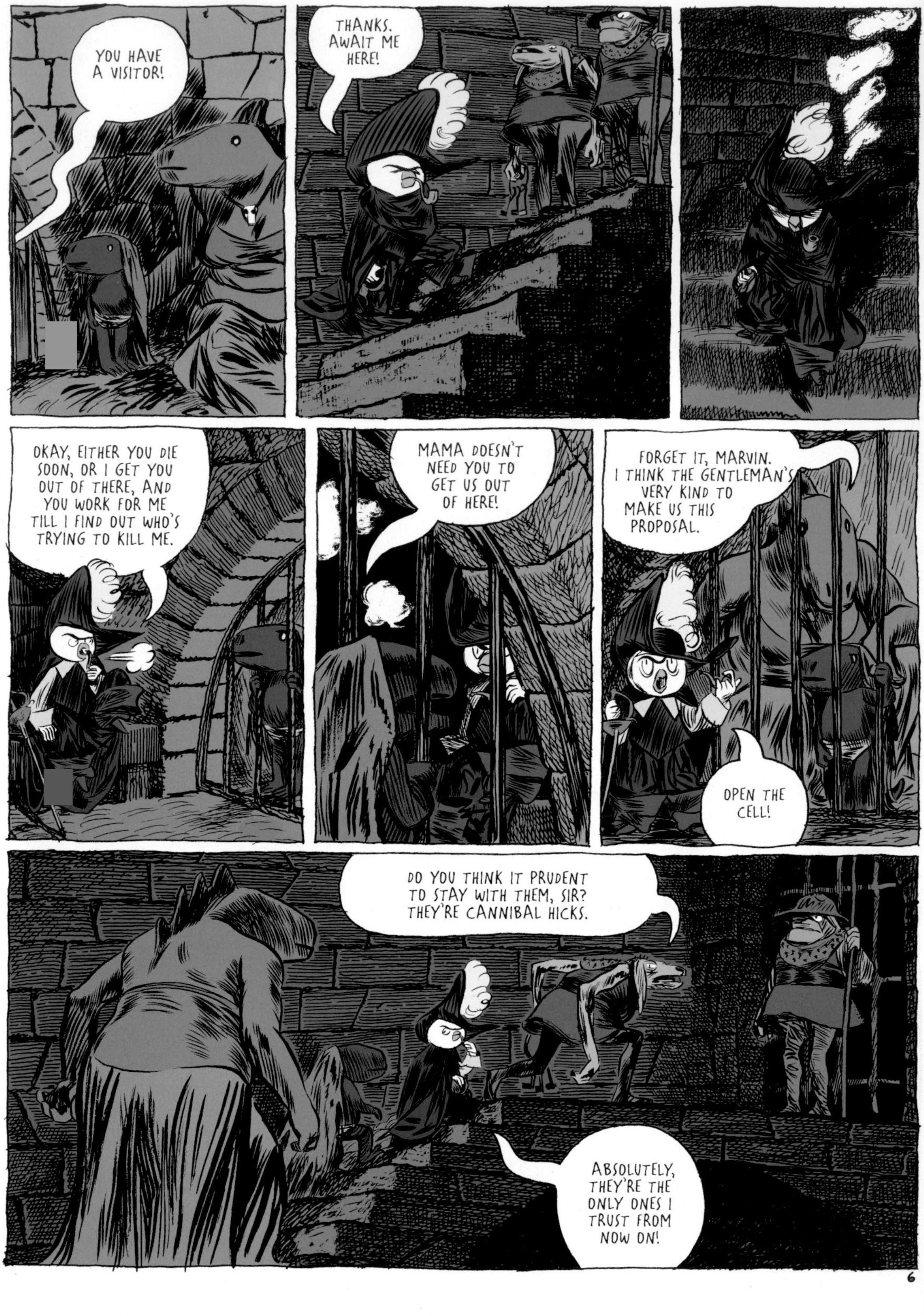
YOU HAVE A VISITOR!
THANKS. AWAIT ME HERE!
OKAY, EITHER YOU DIE SOON, OR I GET YOU OUT OF THERE, AND YOU WORK FOR ME TILL I FIND OUT WHO'S TRYING TO KILL ME.
MAMA DOESN'T NEED YOU TO GET US OUT OF HERE!
FORGET IT, MARVIN. I THINK THE GENTLEMAN'S VERY KIND TO MAKE US THIS PROPOSAL.
OPEN THE CELL!
DO YOU THINK IT PRUDENT TO STAY WITH THEM, SIR? THEY'RE CANNIBAL HICKS.
ABSOLUTELY, THEY'RE THE ONLY ONES I TRUST FROM NOW ON!

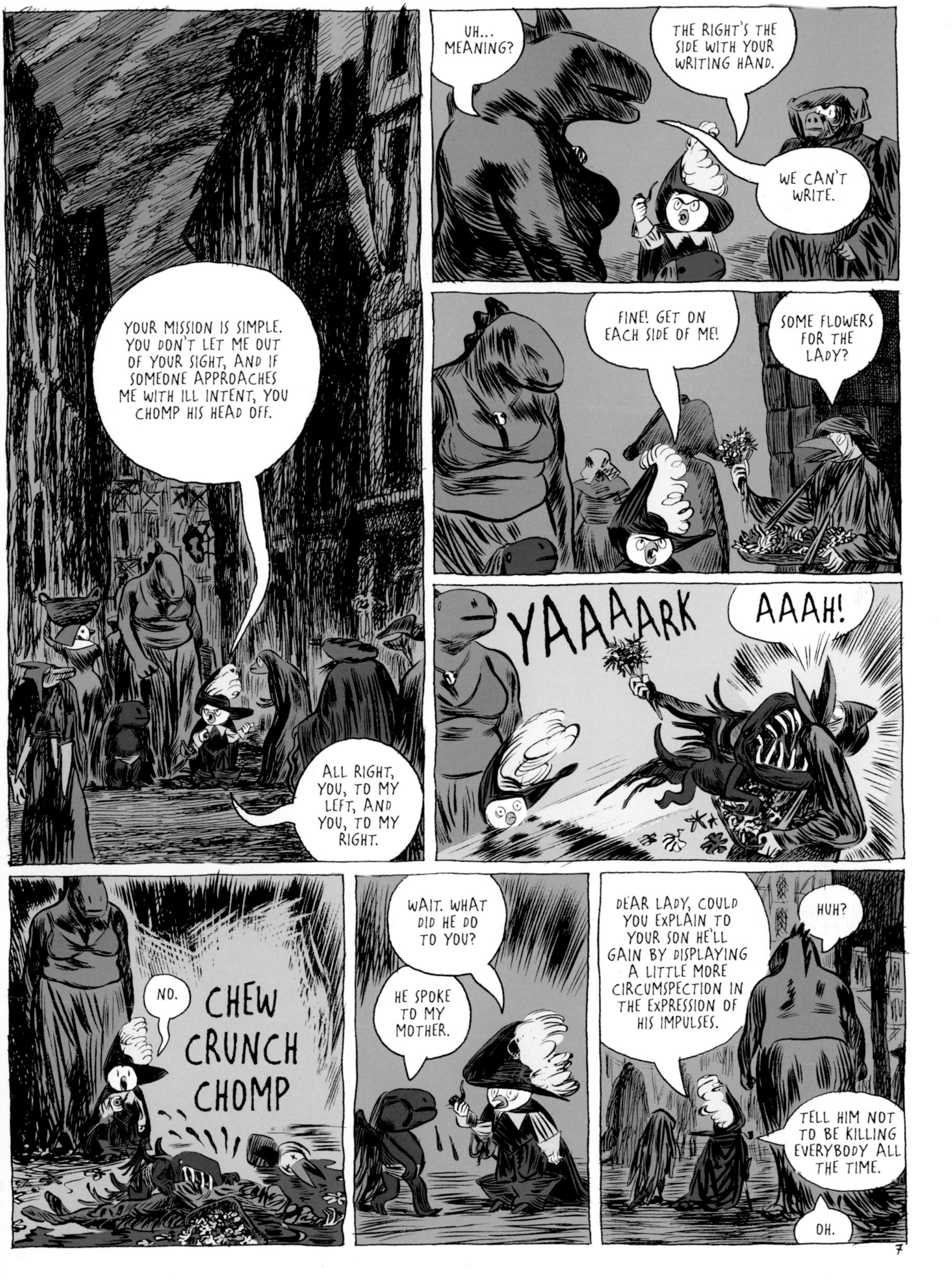
YOUR MISSION IS SIMPLE. YOU DON'T LET ME OUT OF YOUR SIGHT, AND IF SOMEONE APPROACHES ME WITH ILL INTENT, YOU CHOMP HIS HEAD OFF.
ALL RIGHT, YOU, TO MY LEFT, AND YOU, TO MY RIGHT.
UH... MEANING?
THE RIGHT'S THE SIDE WITH YOUR WRITING HAND.
WE CAN'T WRITE.
FINE! GET ON EACH SIDE OF ME!
SOME FLOWERS FOR THE LADY?
YAAAARK
AAAH!
NO.
CHEW CRUNCH CHOMP
WAIT. WHAT DID HE DO TO YOU?
HE SPOKE TO MY MOTHER.
DEAR LADY, COULD YOU EXPLAIN TO YOUR SON HE'LL GAIN BY DISPLAYING A LITTLE MORE CIRCUMSPECTION IN THE EXPRESSION OF HIS IMPULSES.
HUH?
TELL HIM NOT TO BE KILLING EVERYBODY ALL THE TIME.
OH.

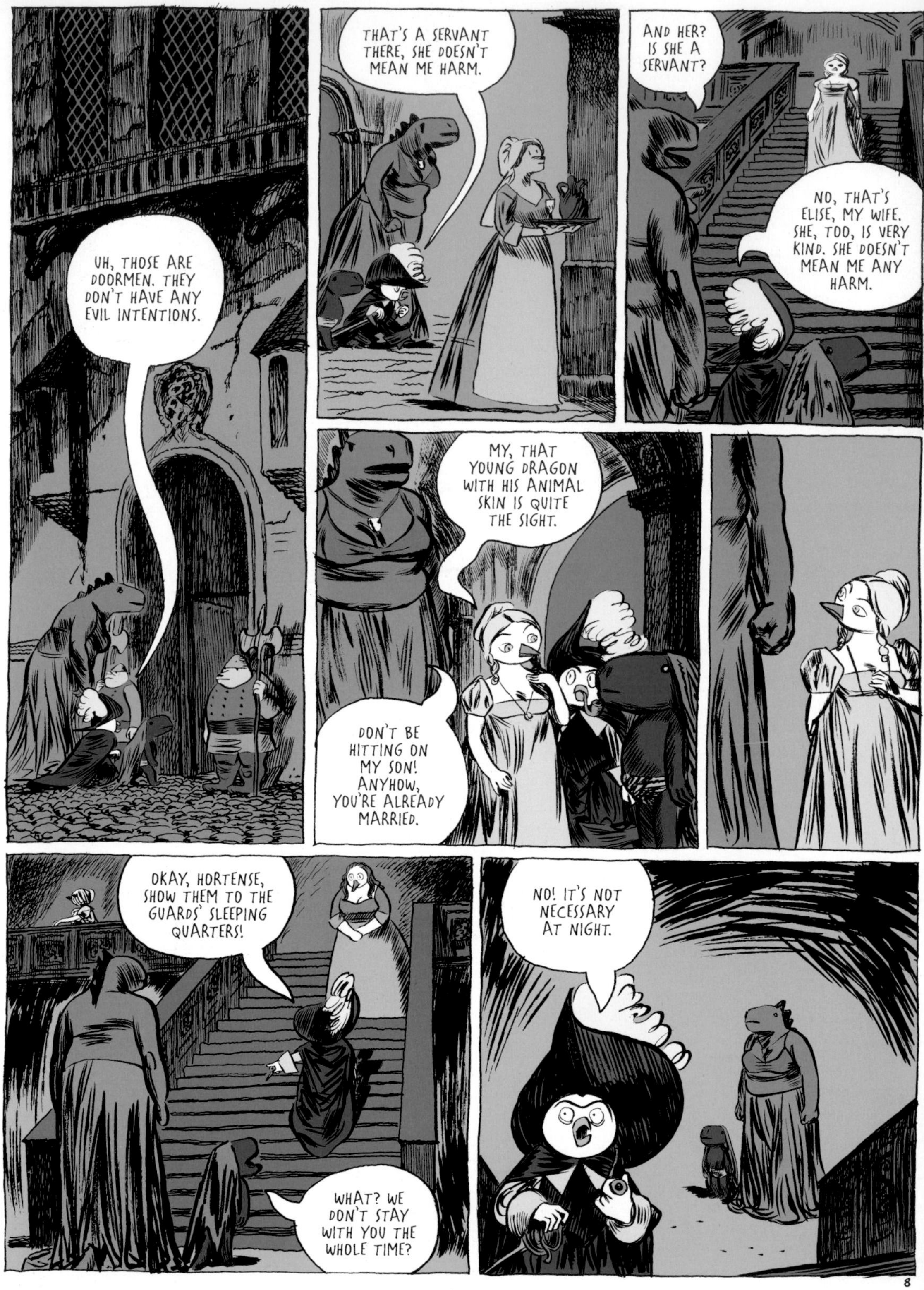
UH, THOSE ARE DOORMEN. THEY DON'T HAVE ANY EVIL INTENTIONS.
THAT'S A SERVANT THERE, SHE DOESN'T MEAN ME HARM.
AND HER? IS SHE A SERVANT?
NO, THAT'S ELISE, MY WIFE. SHE, TOO, IS VERY KIND. SHE DOESN'T MEAN ME ANY HARM.
MY, THAT YOUNG DRAGON WITH HIS ANIMAL SKIN IS QUITE THE SIGHT.
DON'T BE HITTING ON MY SON! ANYHOW, YOU'RE ALREADY MARRIED.
OKAY, HORTENSE, SHOW THEM TO THE GUARDS' SLEEPING QUARTERS!
WHAT? WE DON'T STAY WITH YOU THE WHOLE TIME?
NO! IT'S NOT NECESSARY AT NIGHT.

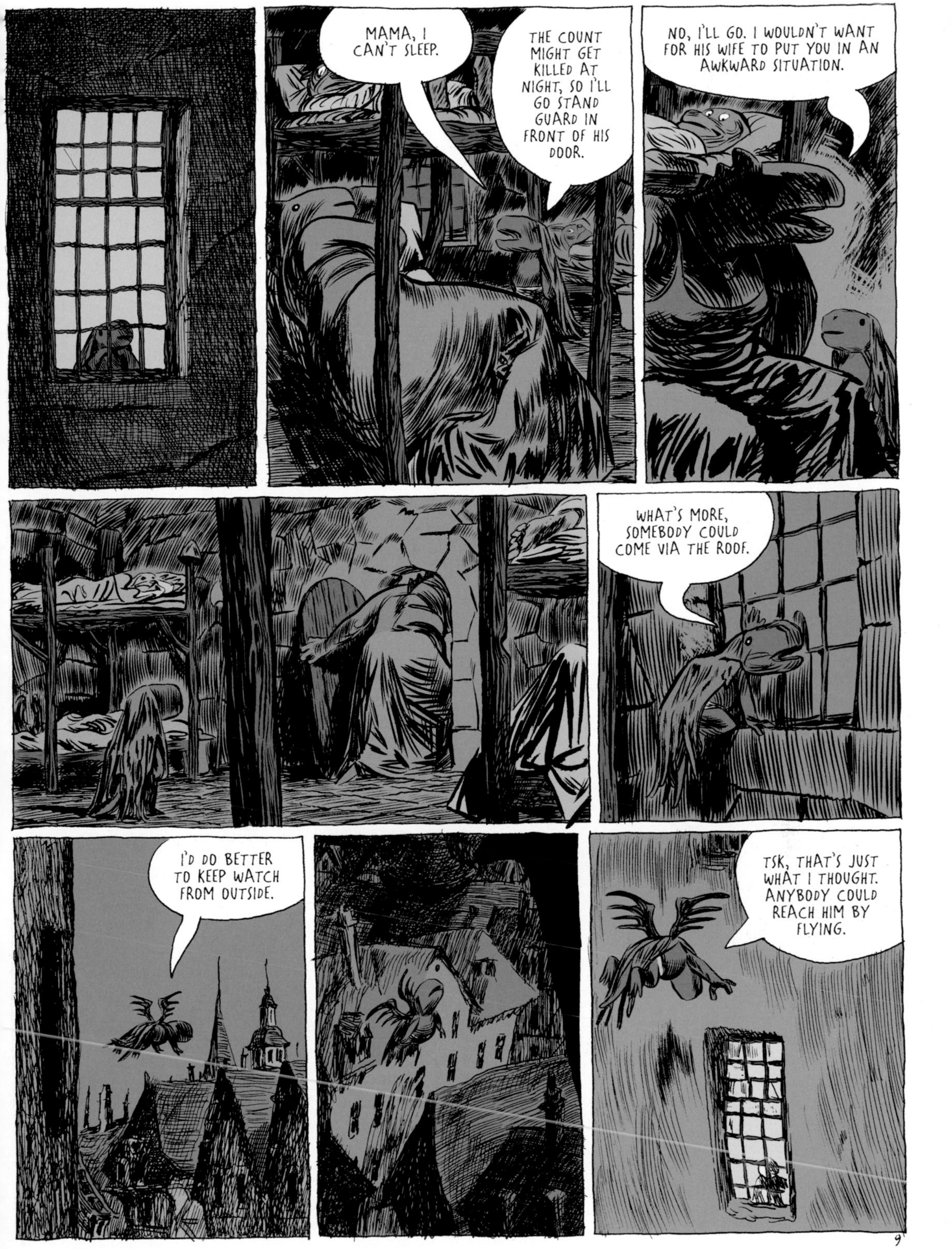
MAMA, I CAN'T SLEEP.
THE COUNT MIGHT GET KILLED AT NIGHT, SO I'LL GO STAND GUARD IN FRONT OF HIS DOOR.
NO, I'LL GO. I WOULDN'T WANT FOR HIS WIFE TO PUT YOU IN AN AWKWARD SITUATION.
WHAT'S MORE, SOMEBODY COULD COME VIA THE ROOF.
I'D DO BETTER TO KEEP WATCH FROM OUTSIDE.
TSK, THAT'S JUST WHAT I THOUGHT. ANYBODY COULD REACH HIM BY FLYING.

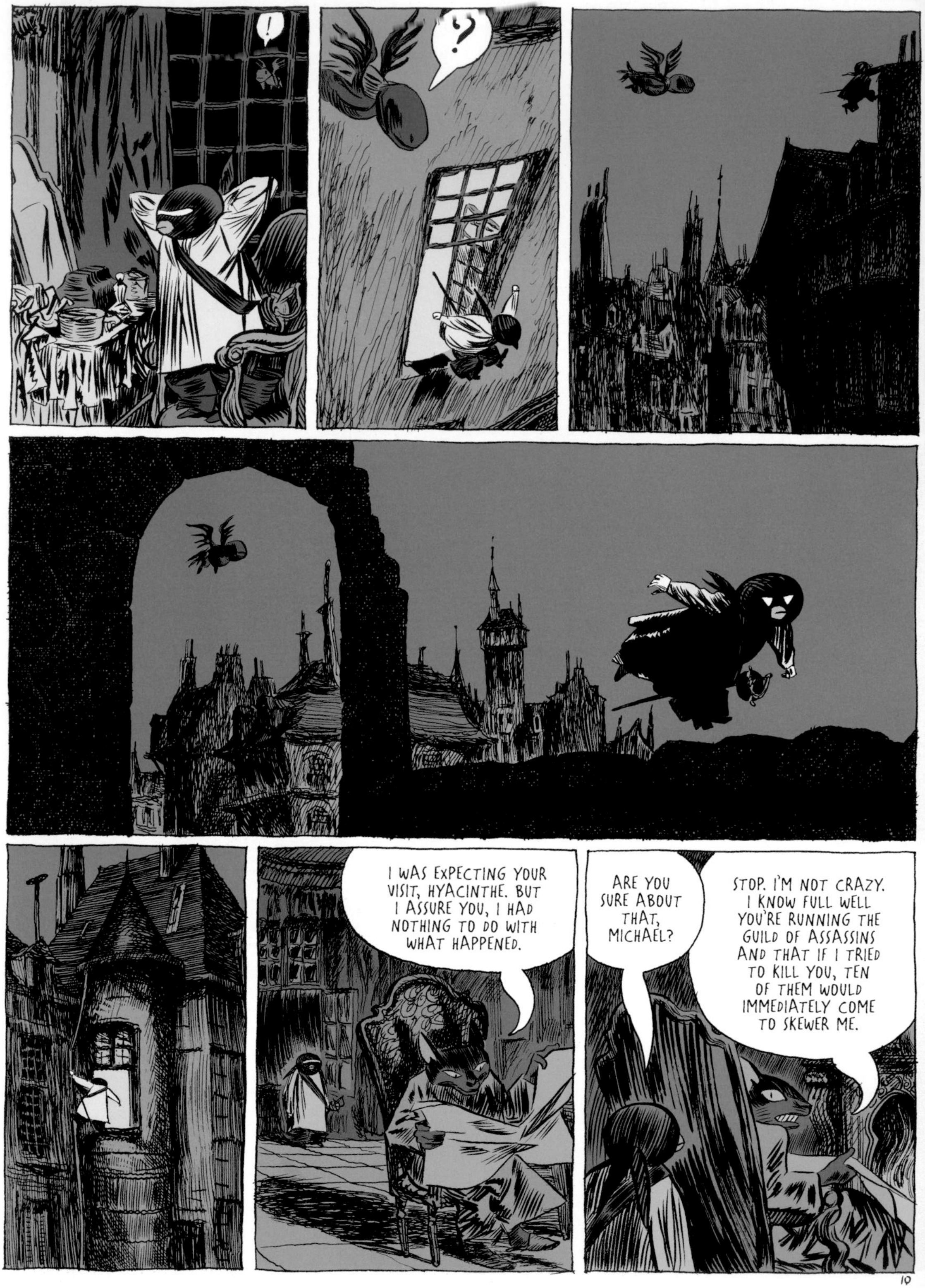
!
?
I WAS EXPECTING YOUR VISIT, HYACINTHE. BUT I ASSURE YOU, I HAD NOTHING TO DO WITH WHAT HAPPENED.
ARE YOU SURE ABOUT THAT, MICHAEL?
STOP. I'M NOT CRAZY. I KNOW FULL WELL YOU'RE RUNNING THE GUILD OF ASSASSINS AND THAT IF I TRIED TO KILL YOU, TEN OF THEM WOULD IMMEDIATELY COME TO SKEWER ME.

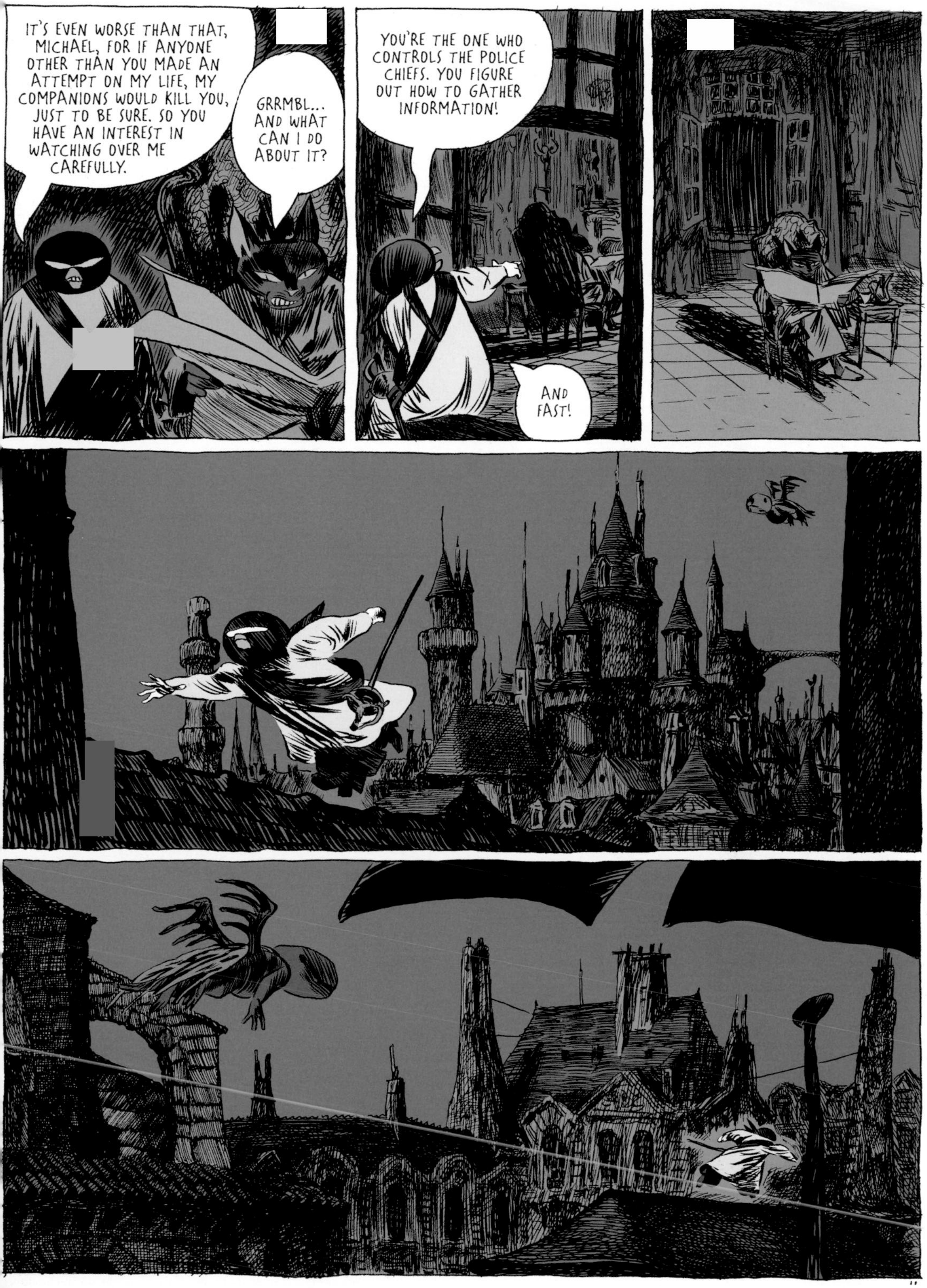
IT'S EVEN WORSE THAN THAT, MICHAEL, FOR IF ANYONE OTHER THAN YOU MADE AN ATTEMPT ON MY LIFE, MY COMPANIONS WOULD KILL YOU, JUST TO BE SURE. SO YOU HAVE AN INTEREST IN WATCHING OVER ME CAREFULLY.
GRRMBL... AND WHAT CAN I DO ABOUT IT?
YOU'RE THE ONE WHO CONTROLS THE POLICE CHIEFS. YOU FIGURE OUT HOW TO GATHER INFORMATION!
AND FAST!

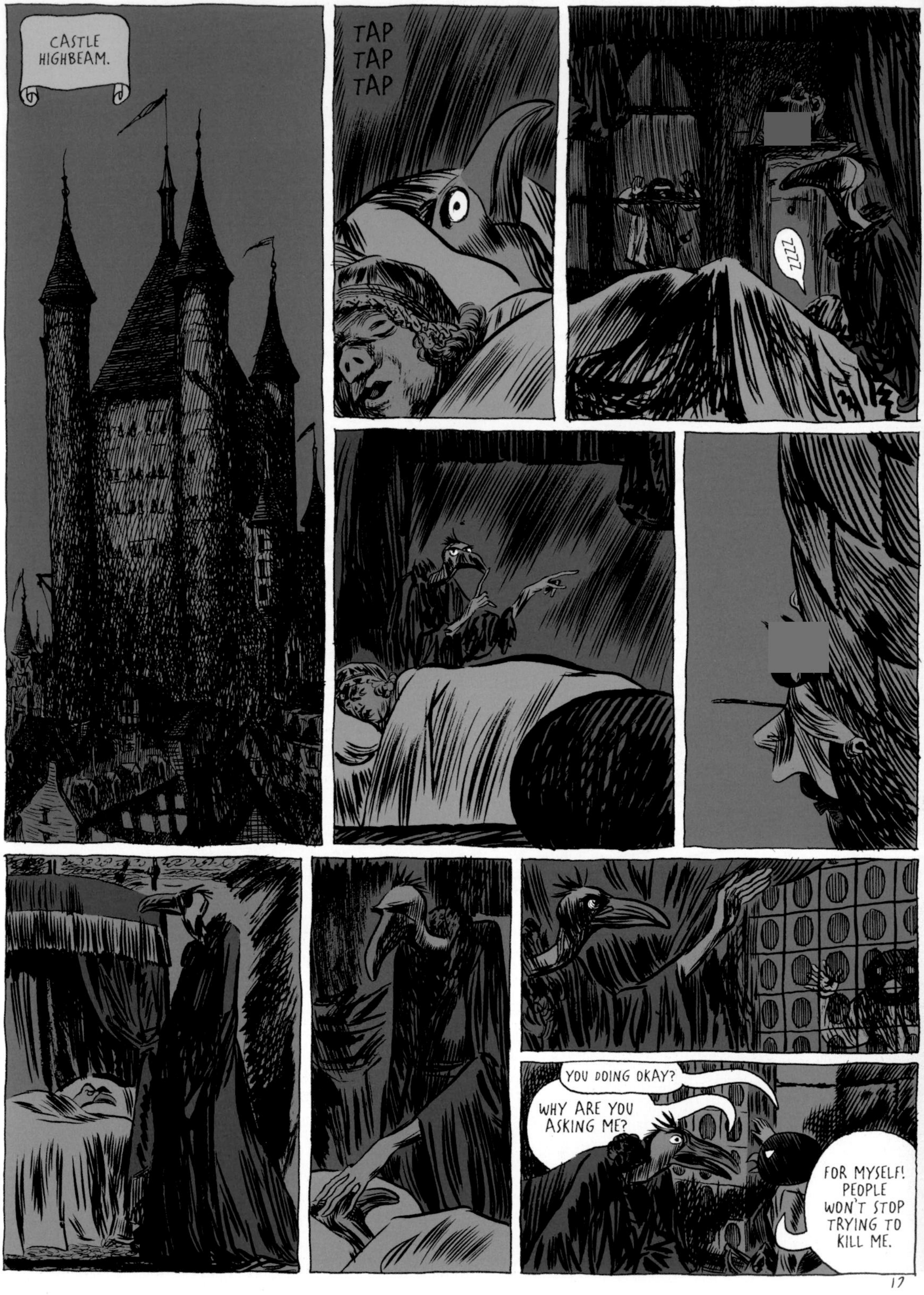
CASTLE HIGHBEAM.
TAP
TAP
TAP
ZZZZ
YOU DOING OKAY?
WHY ARE YOU ASKING ME?
FOR MYSELF! PEOPLE WON'T STOP TRYING TO KILL ME.

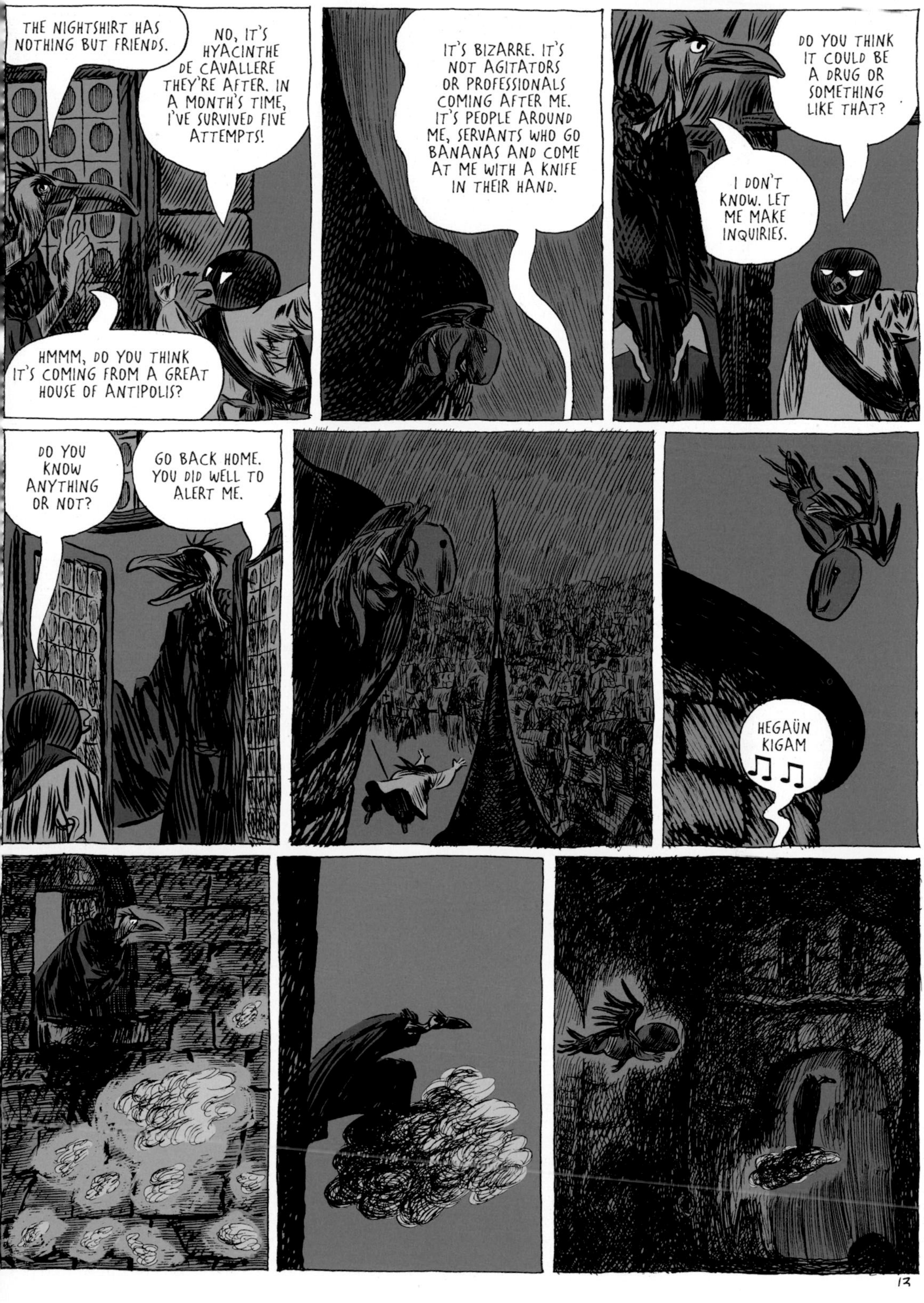

THE NIGHTSHIRT HAS NOTHING BUT FRIENDS.
NO, IT'S HYACINTHE DE CAVALLERE THEY'RE AFTER. IN A MONTH'S TIME, I'VE SURVIVED FIVE ATTEMPTS!
HMMM, DO YOU THINK IT'S COMING FROM A GREAT HOUSE OF ANTIPOLIS?
IT'S BIZARRE. IT'S NOT AGITATORS OR PROFESSIONALS COMING AFTER ME. IT'S PEOPLE AROUND ME, SERVANTS WHO GO BANANAS AND COME AT ME WITH A KNIFE IN THEIR HAND.
DO YOU THINK IT COULD BE A DRUG OR SOMETHING LIKE THAT?
I DON'T KNOW. LET ME MAKE INQUIRIES.
DO YOU KNOW ANYTHING OR NOT?
GO BACK HOME. YOU DID WELL TO ALERT ME.
HEGAÜN KIGAM ♫ ♫

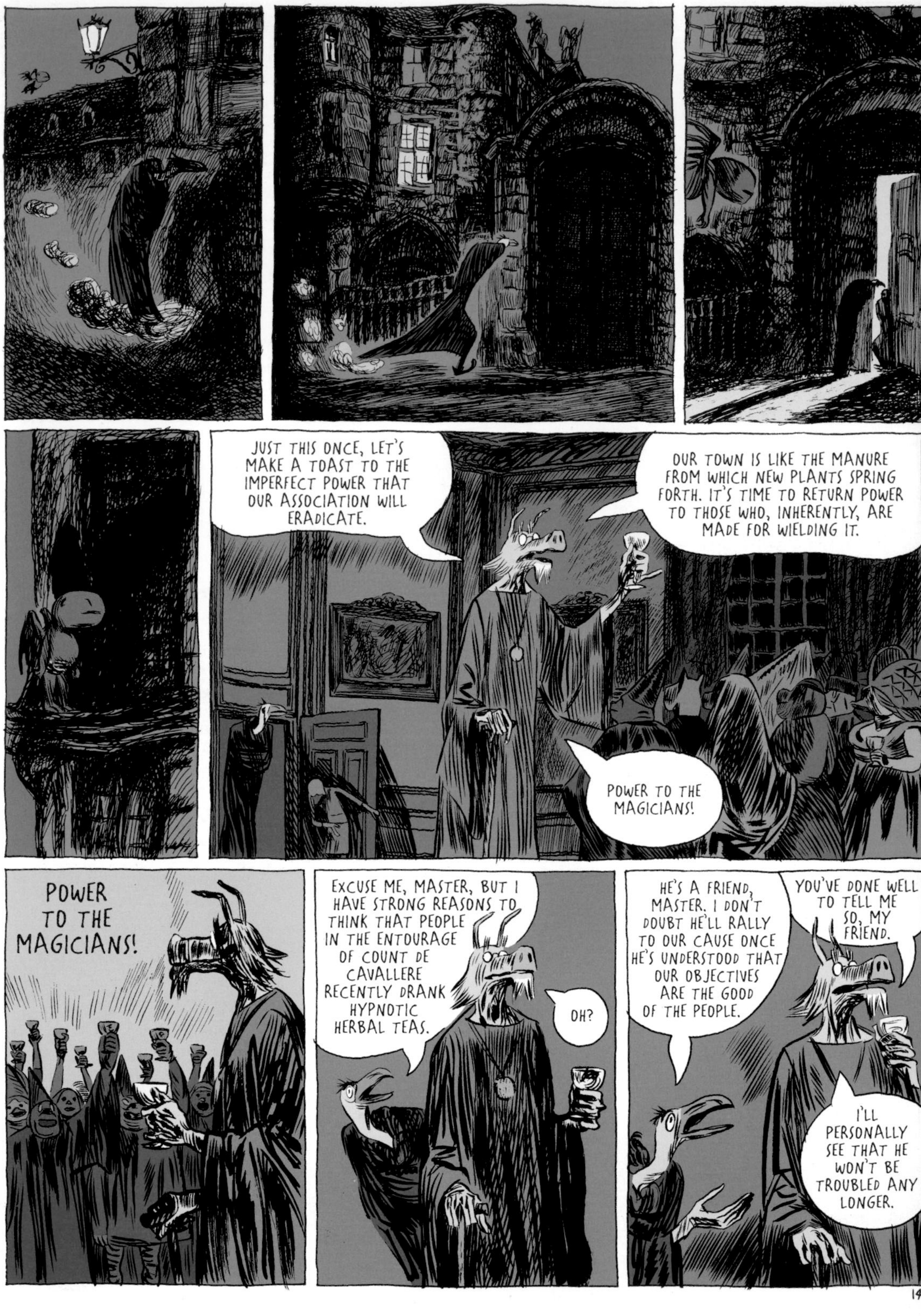

JUST THIS ONCE, LET'S MAKE A TOAST TO THE IMPERFECT POWER THAT OUR ASSOCIATION WILL ERADICATE.
OUR TOWN IS LIKE THE MANURE FROM WHICH NEW PLANTS SPRING FORTH. IT'S TIME TO RETURN POWER TO THOSE WHO, INHERENTLY, ARE MADE FOR WIELDING IT.
POWER TO THE MAGICIANS!
POWER TO THE MAGICIANS!
EXCUSE ME, MASTER, BUT I HAVE STRONG REASONS TO THINK THAT PEOPLE IN THE ENTOURAGE OF COUNT DE CAVALLERE RECENTLY DRANK HYPNOTIC HERBAL TEAS.
OH?
HE'S A FRIEND, MASTER. I DON'T DOUBT HE'LL RALLY TO OUR CAUSE ONCE HE'S UNDERSTOOD THAT OUR OBJECTIVES ARE THE GOOD OF THE PEOPLE.
YOU'VE DONE WELL TO TELL ME SO, MY FRIEND.
I'LL PERSONALLY SEE THAT HE WON'T BE TROUBLED ANY LONGER.

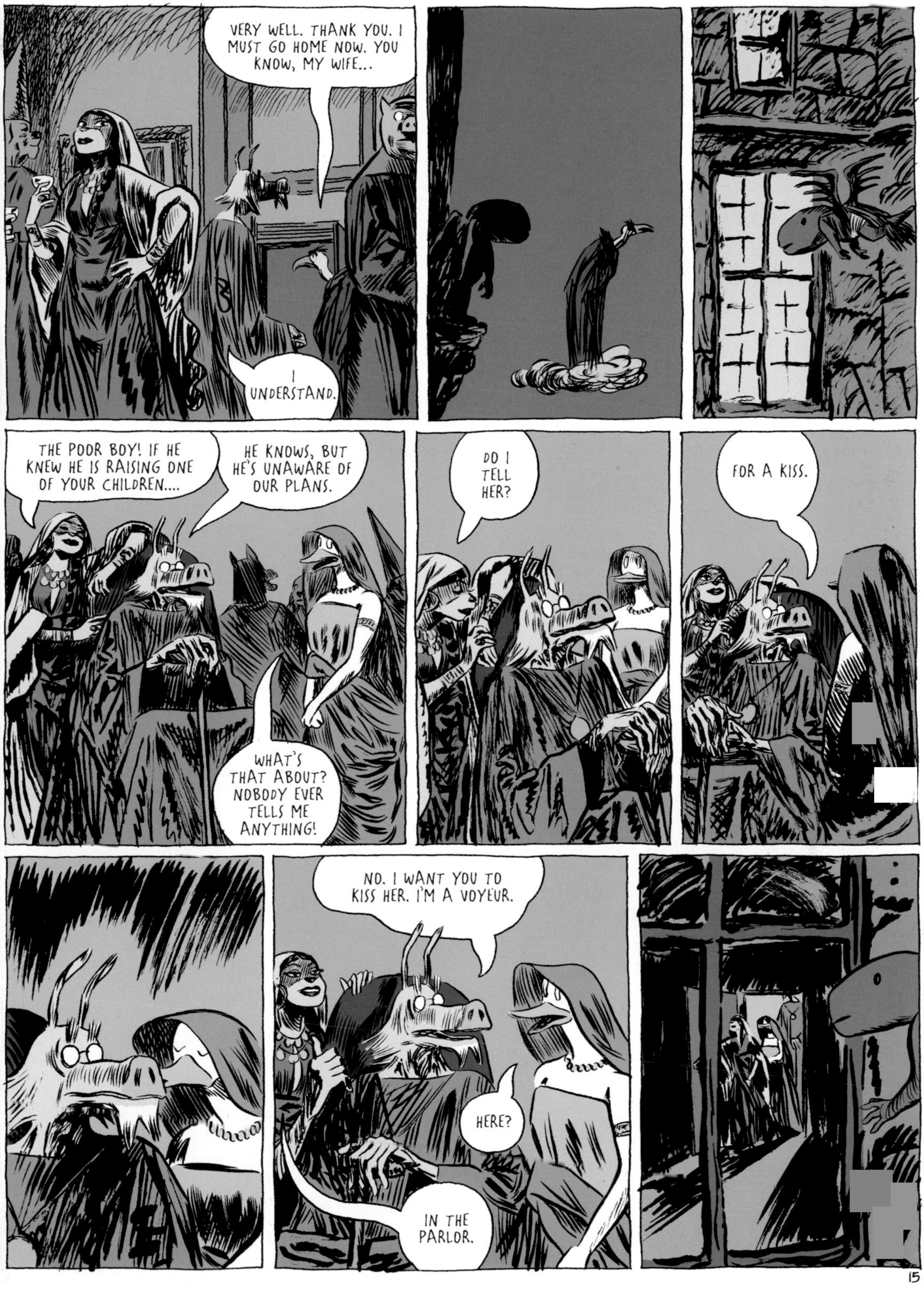
VERY WELL. THANK YOU. I MUST GO HOME NOW. YOU KNOW, MY WIFE...
I UNDERSTAND.
THE POOR BOY! IF HE KNEW HE IS RAISING ONE OF YOUR CHILDREN....
HE KNOWS, BUT HE'S UNAWARE OF OUR PLANS.
WHAT'S THAT ABOUT? NOBODY EVER TELLS ME ANYTHING!
DO I TELL HER?
FOR A KISS.
NO. I WANT YOU TO KISS HER. I'M A VOYEUR.
HERE?
IN THE PARLOR.

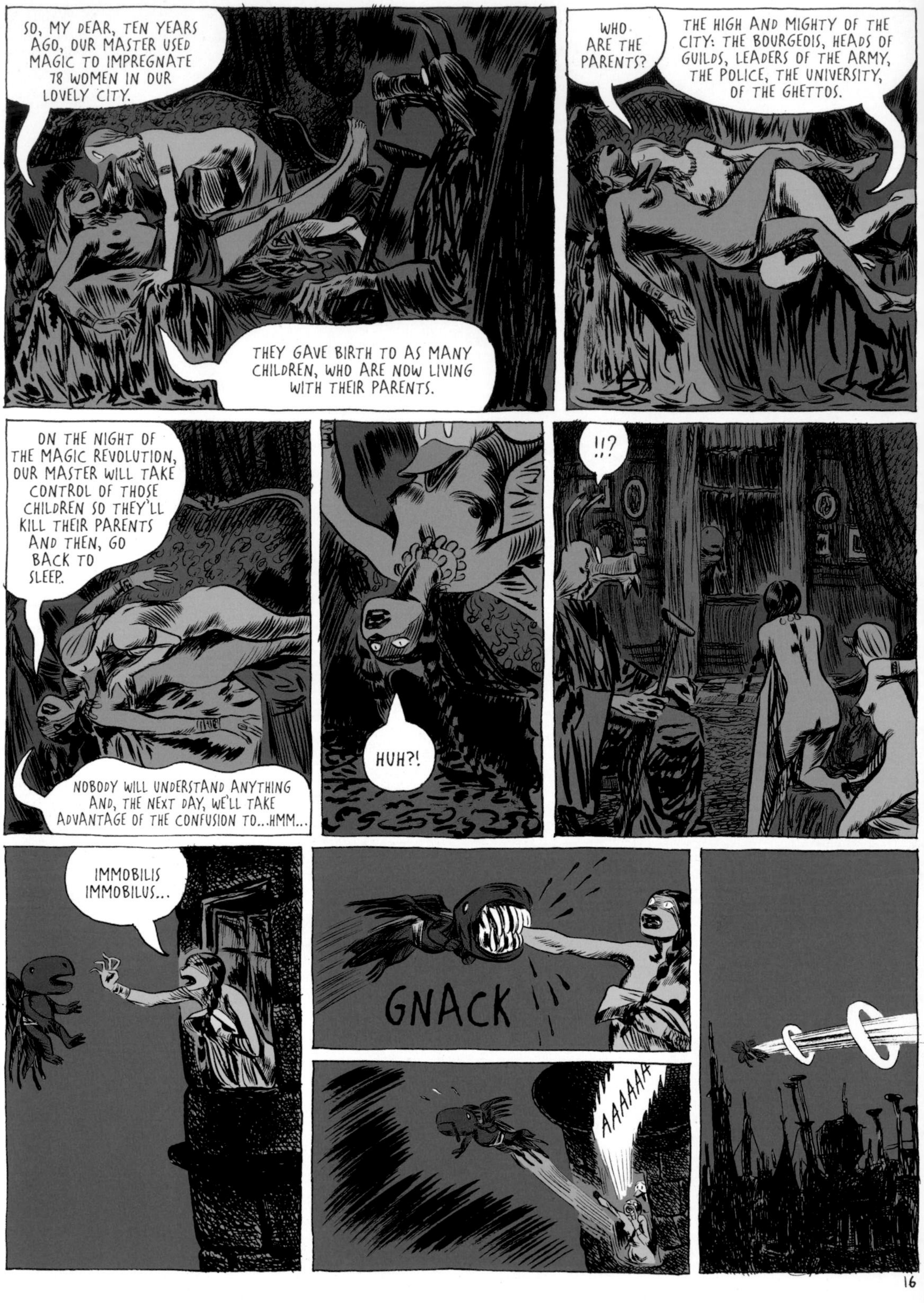
SO, MY DEAR, TEN YEARS AGO, OUR MASTER USED MAGIC TO IMPREGNATE 78 WOMEN IN OUR LOVELY CITY.
THEY GAVE BIRTH TO AS MANY CHILDREN, WHO ARE NOW LIVING WITH THEIR PARENTS.
WHO ARE THE PARENTS?
THE HIGH AND MIGHTY OF THE CITY: THE BOURGEOIS, HEADS OF GUILDS, LEADERS OF THE ARMY, THE POLICE, THE UNIVERSITY, OF THE GHETTOS.
ON THE NIGHT OF THE MAGIC REVOLUTION, OUR MASTER WILL TAKE CONTROL OF THOSE CHILDREN SO THEY'LL KILL THEIR PARENTS AND THEN, GO BACK TO SLEEP.
NOBODY WILL UNDERSTAND ANYTHING AND, THE NEXT DAY, WE'LL TAKE ADVANTAGE OF THE CONFUSION TO...HMM...
HUH?!
!!?
IMMOBILIS IMMOBILUS...
GNACK
AAAAAA

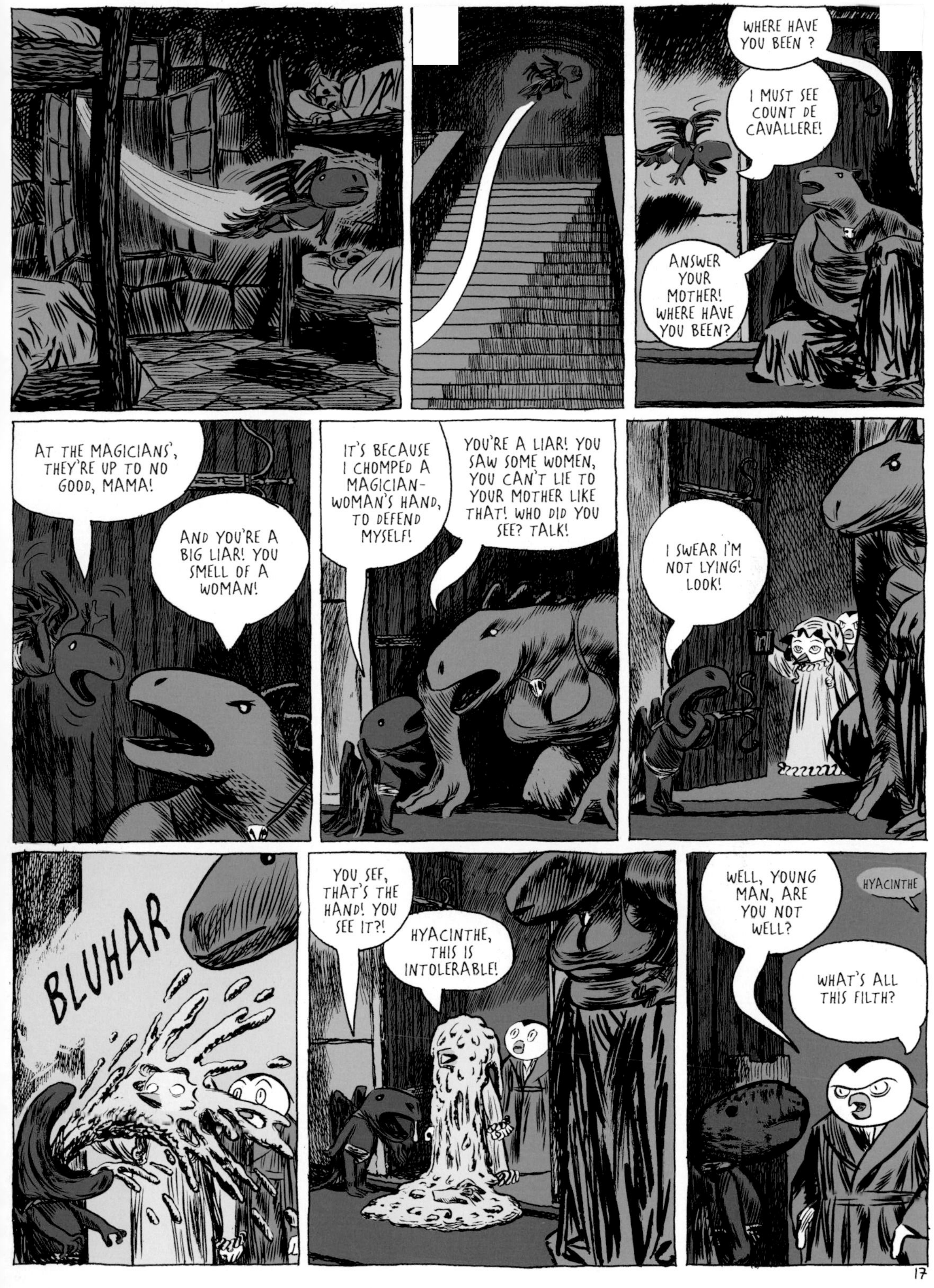
WHERE HAVE YOU BEEN ?
I MUST SEE COUNT DE CAVALLERE!
ANSWER YOUR MOTHER! WHERE HAVE YOU BEEN?
AT THE MAGICIANS', THEY'RE UP TO NO GOOD, MAMA!
AND YOU'RE A BIG LIAR! YOU SMELL OF A WOMAN!
IT'S BECAUSE I CHOMPED A MAGICIAN-WOMAN'S HAND, TO DEFEND MYSELF!
YOU'RE A LIAR! YOU SAW SOME WOMEN, YOU CAN'T LIE TO YOUR MOTHER LIKE THAT! WHO DID YOU SEE? TALK!
I SWEAR I'M NOT LYING! LOOK!
BLUHAR
YOU SEF, THAT'S THE HAND! YOU SEE IT?!
HYACINTHE, THIS IS INTOLERABLE!
WELL, YOUNG MAN, ARE YOU NOT WELL?
HYACINTHE
WHAT'S ALL THIS FILTH?

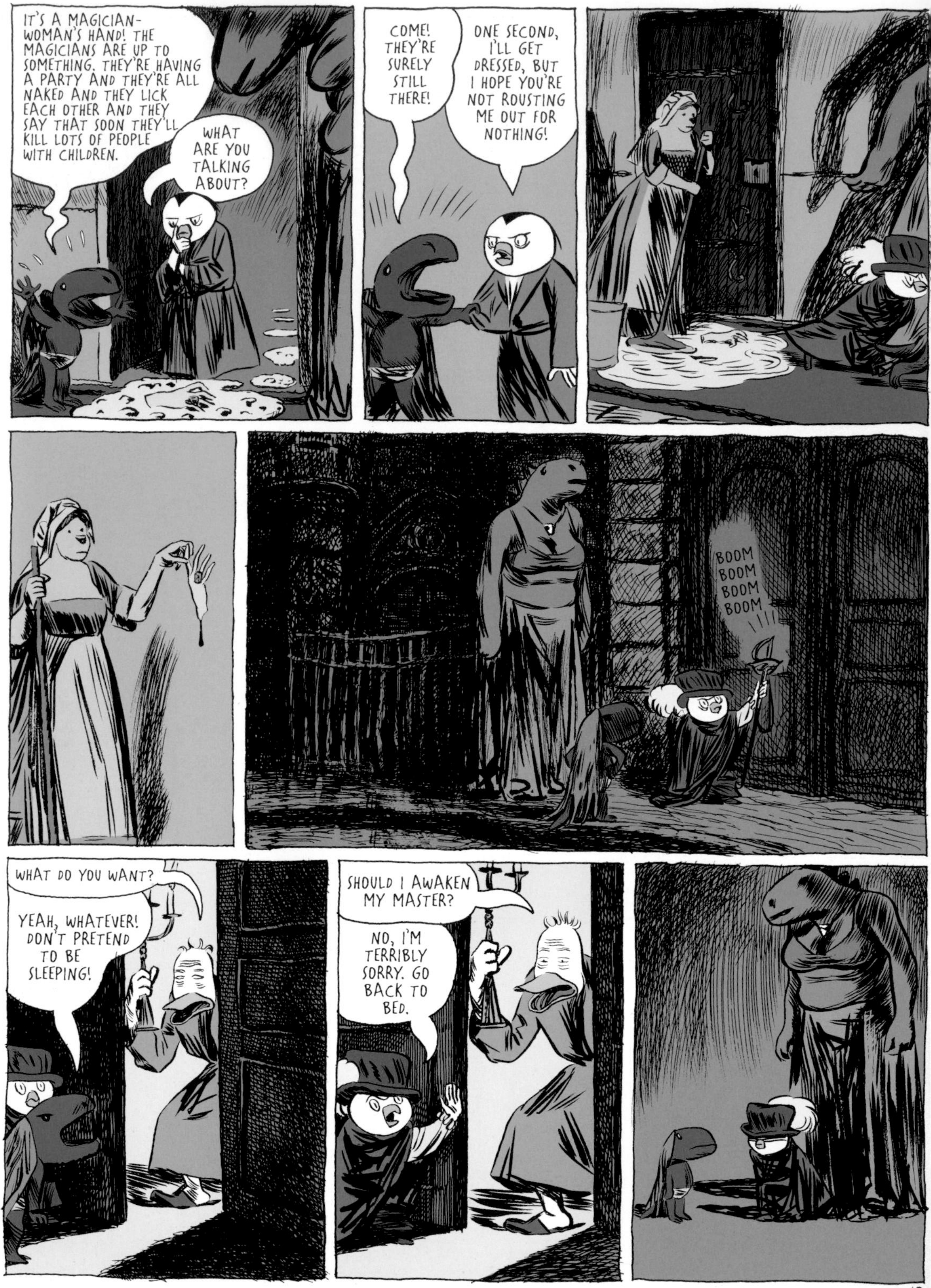
IT'S A MAGICIAN-WOMAN'S HAND! THE MAGICIANS ARE UP TO SOMETHING. THEY'RE HAVING A PARTY AND THEY'RE ALL NAKED AND THEY LICK EACH OTHER AND THEY SAY THAT SOON THEY'LL KILL LOTS OF PEOPLE WITH CHILDREN.
WHAT ARE YOU TALKING ABOUT?
COME! THEY'RE SURELY STILL THERE!
ONE SECOND, I'LL GET DRESSED, BUT I HOPE YOU'RE NOT ROUSTING ME OUT FOR NOTHING!
BOOM BOOM BOOM BOOM
WHAT DO YOU WANT?
YEAH, WHATEVER! DON'T PRETEND TO BE SLEEPING!
SHOULD I AWAKEN MY MASTER?
NO, I'M TERRIBLY SORRY. GO BACK TO BED.

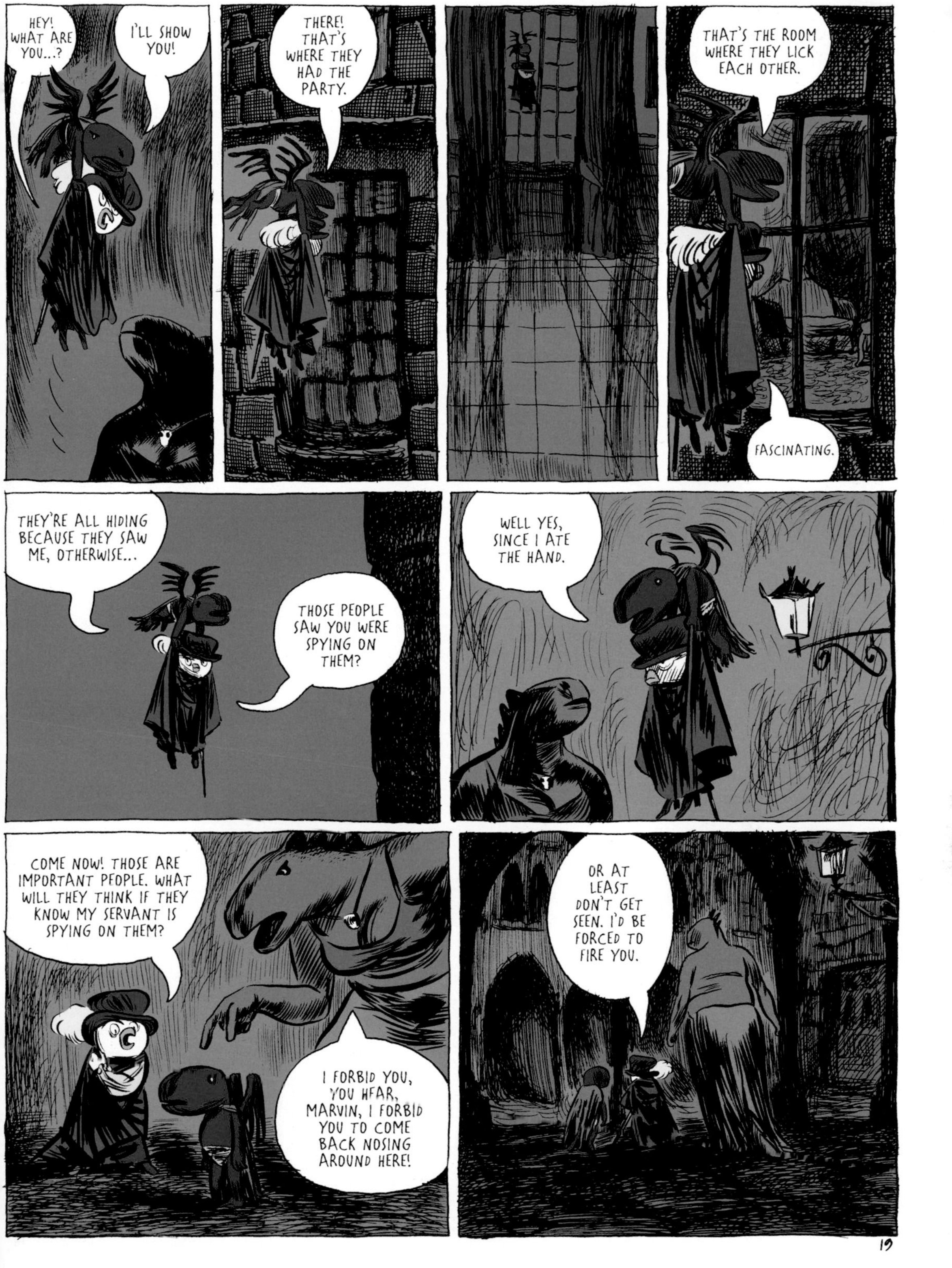
HEY! WHAT ARE YOU...?
I'LL SHOW YOU!
THERE! THAT'S WHERE THEY HAD THE PARTY.
THAT'S THE ROOM WHERE THEY LICK EACH OTHER.
FASCINATING.
THEY'RE ALL HIDING BECAUSE THEY SAW ME, OTHERWISE...
THOSE PEOPLE SAW YOU WERE SPYING ON THEM?
WELL YES, SINCE I ATE THE HAND.
COME NOW! THOSE ARE IMPORTANT PEOPLE. WHAT WILL THEY THINK IF THEY KNOW MY SERVANT IS SPYING ON THEM?
I FORBID YOU, YOU HEAR, MARVIN, I FORBID YOU TO COME BACK NOSING AROUND HERE!
OR AT LEAST DON'T GET SEEN. I'D BE FORCED TO FIRE YOU.

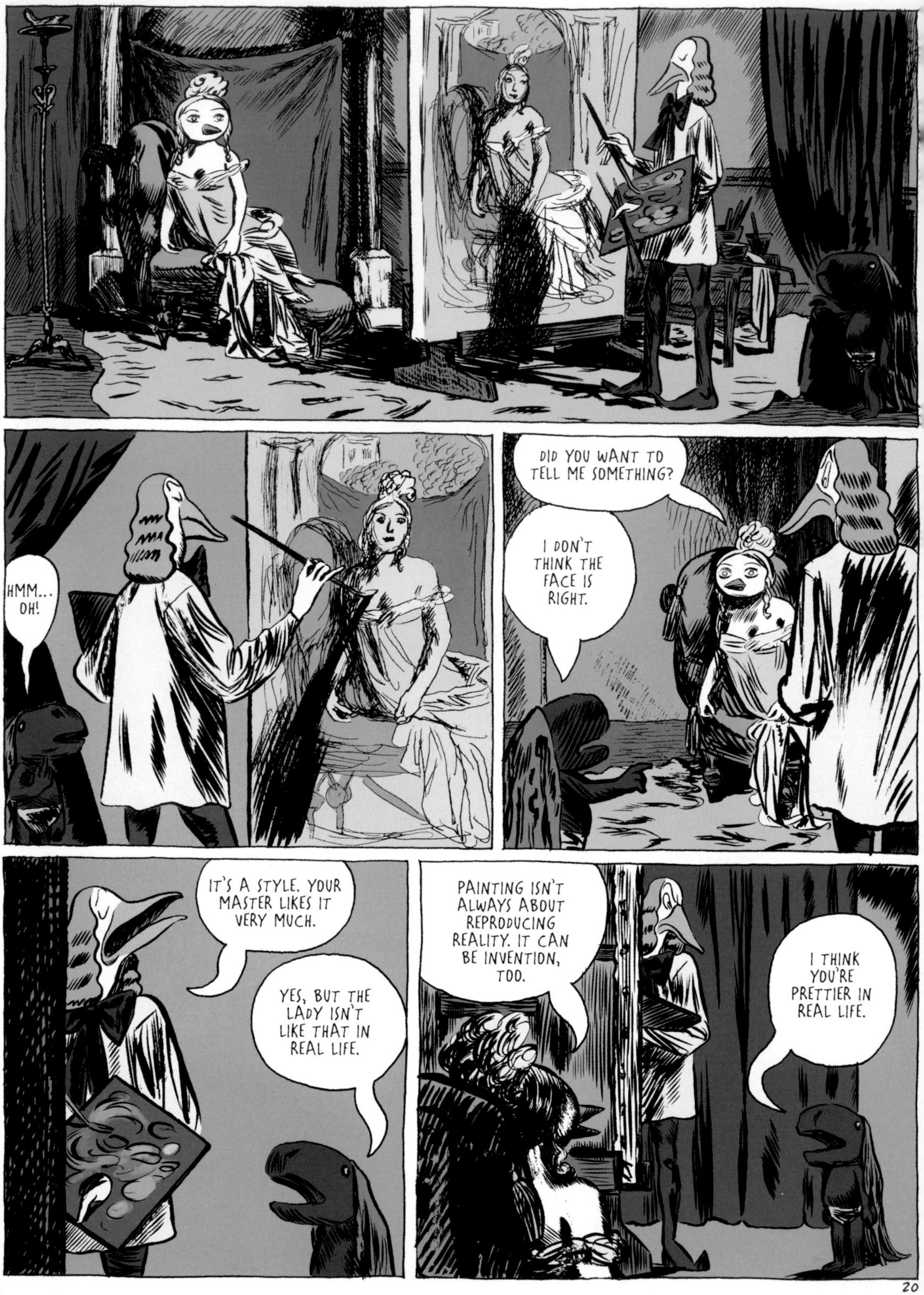
HMM... OH!
DID YOU WANT TO TELL ME SOMETHING?
I DON'T THINK THE FACE IS RIGHT.
IT'S A STYLE. YOUR MASTER LIKES IT VERY MUCH.
YES, BUT THE LADY ISN'T LIKE THAT IN REAL LIFE.
PAINTING ISN'T ALWAYS ABOUT REPRODUCING REALITY. IT CAN BE INVENTION, TOO.
I THINK YOU'RE PRETTIER IN REAL LIFE.

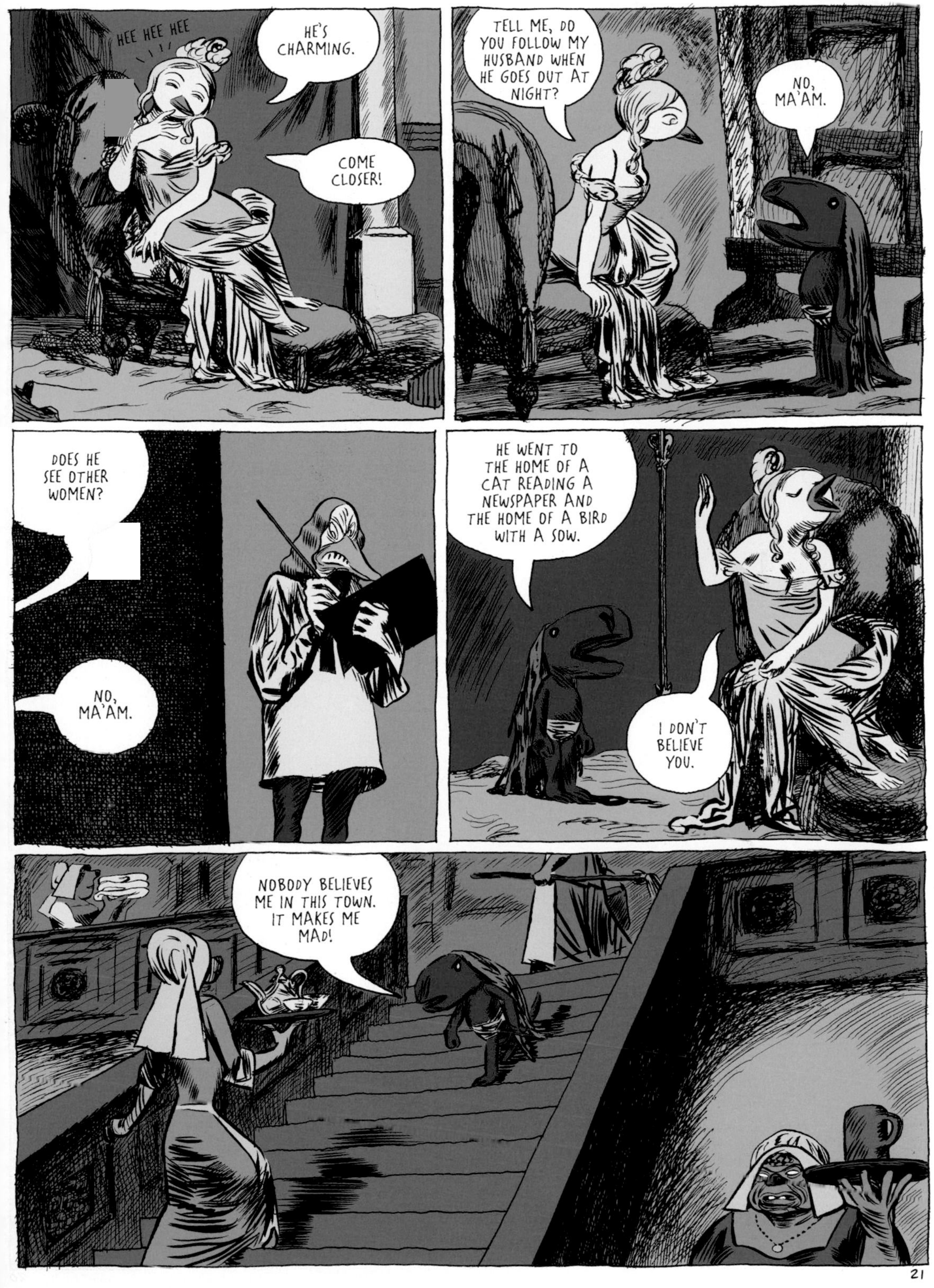
HEE HEE HEE
HE'S CHARMING.
COME CLOSER!
TELL ME, DO YOU FOLLOW MY HUSBAND WHEN HE GOES OUT AT NIGHT?
NO, MA'AM.
DOES HE SEE OTHER WOMEN?
NO, MA'AM.
HE WENT TO THE HOME OF A CAT READING A NEWSPAPER AND THE HOME OF A BIRD WITH A SOW.
I DON'T BELIEVE YOU.
NOBODY BELIEVES ME IN THIS TOWN. IT MAKES ME MAD!

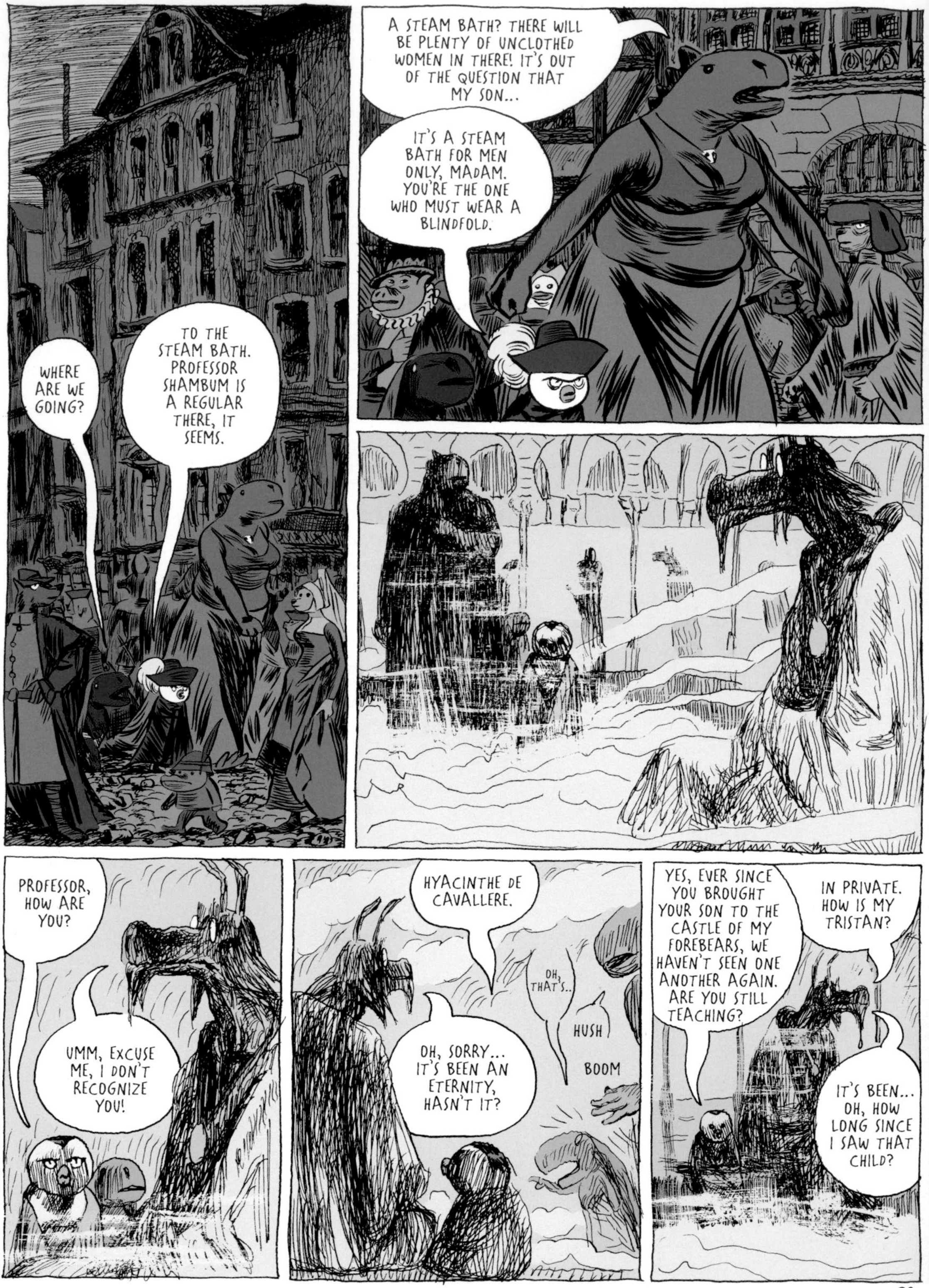

WHERE ARE WE GOING?
TO THE STEAM BATH. PROFESSOR SHAMBUM IS A REGULAR THERE, IT SEEMS.
A STEAM BATH? THERE WILL BE PLENTY OF UNCLOTHED WOMEN IN THERE! IT'S OUT OF THE QUESTION THAT MY SON...
IT'S A STEAM BATH FOR MEN ONLY, MADAM. YOU'RE THE ONE WHO MUST WEAR A BLINDFOLD.
PROFESSOR, HOW ARE YOU?
UMM, EXCUSE ME, I DON'T RECOGNIZE YOU!
HYACINTHE DE CAVALLERE.
OH, THAT'S...
HUSH
BOOM
OH, SORRY... IT'S BEEN AN ETERNITY, HASN'T IT?
YES, EVER SINCE YOU BROUGHT YOUR SON TO THE CASTLE OF MY FOREBEARS, WE HAVEN'T SEEN ONE ANOTHER AGAIN. ARE YOU STILL TEACHING?
IN PRIVATE. HOW IS MY TRISTAN?
IT'S BEEN... OH, HOW LONG SINCE I SAW THAT CHILD?

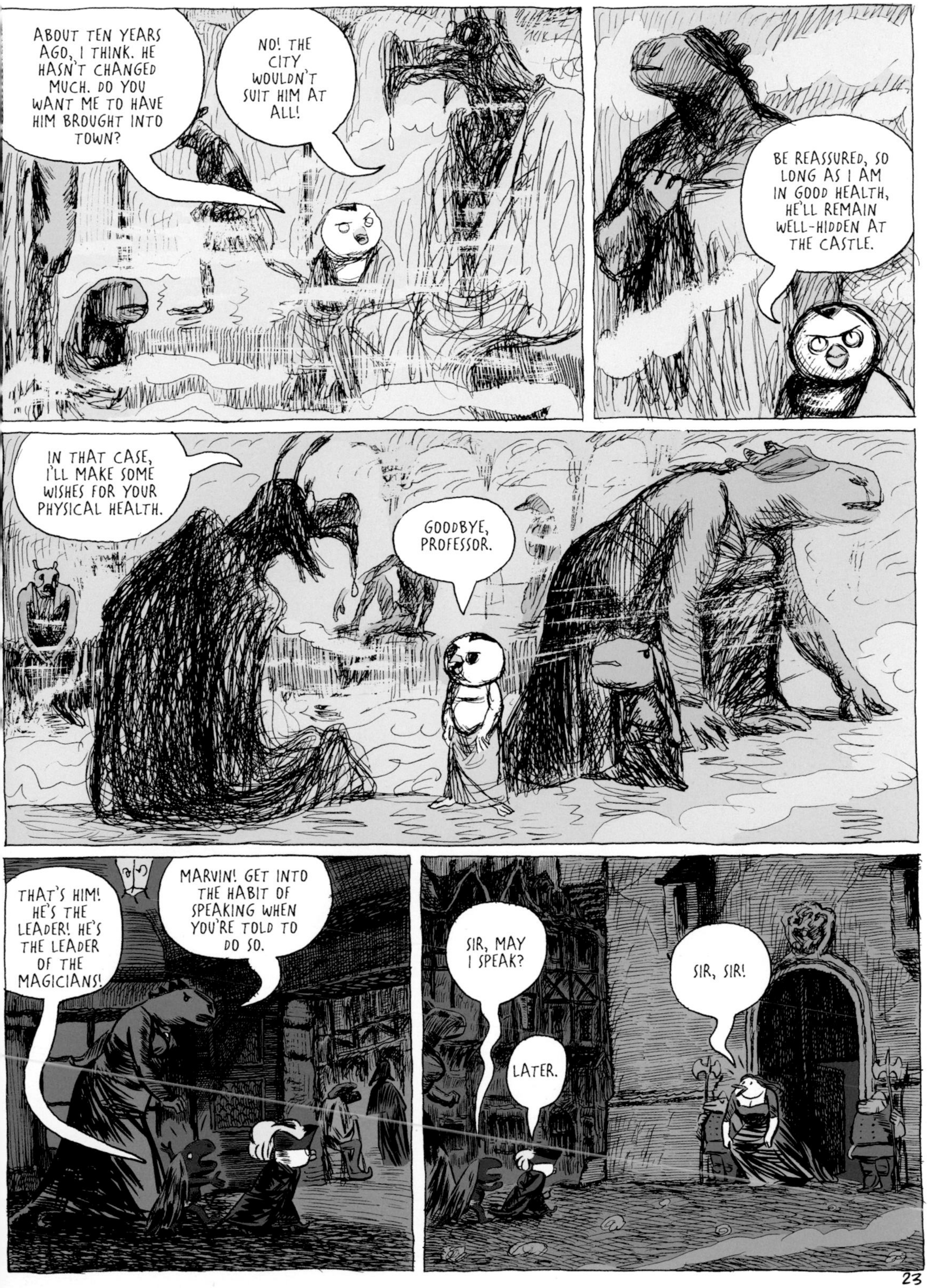
ABOUT TEN YEARS AGO, I THINK. HE HASN'T CHANGED MUCH. DO YOU WANT ME TO HAVE HIM BROUGHT INTO TOWN?
NO! THE CITY WOULDN'T SUIT HIM AT ALL!
BE REASSURED, SO LONG AS I AM IN GOOD HEALTH, HE'LL REMAIN WELL-HIDDEN AT THE CASTLE.
IN THAT CASE, I'LL MAKE SOME WISHES FOR YOUR PHYSICAL HEALTH.
GOODBYE, PROFESSOR.
THAT'S HIM! HE'S THE LEADER! HE'S THE LEADER OF THE MAGICIANS!
MARVIN! GET INTO THE HABIT OF SPEAKING WHEN YOU'RE TOLD TO DO SO.
SIR, MAY I SPEAK?
LATER.
SIR, SIR!

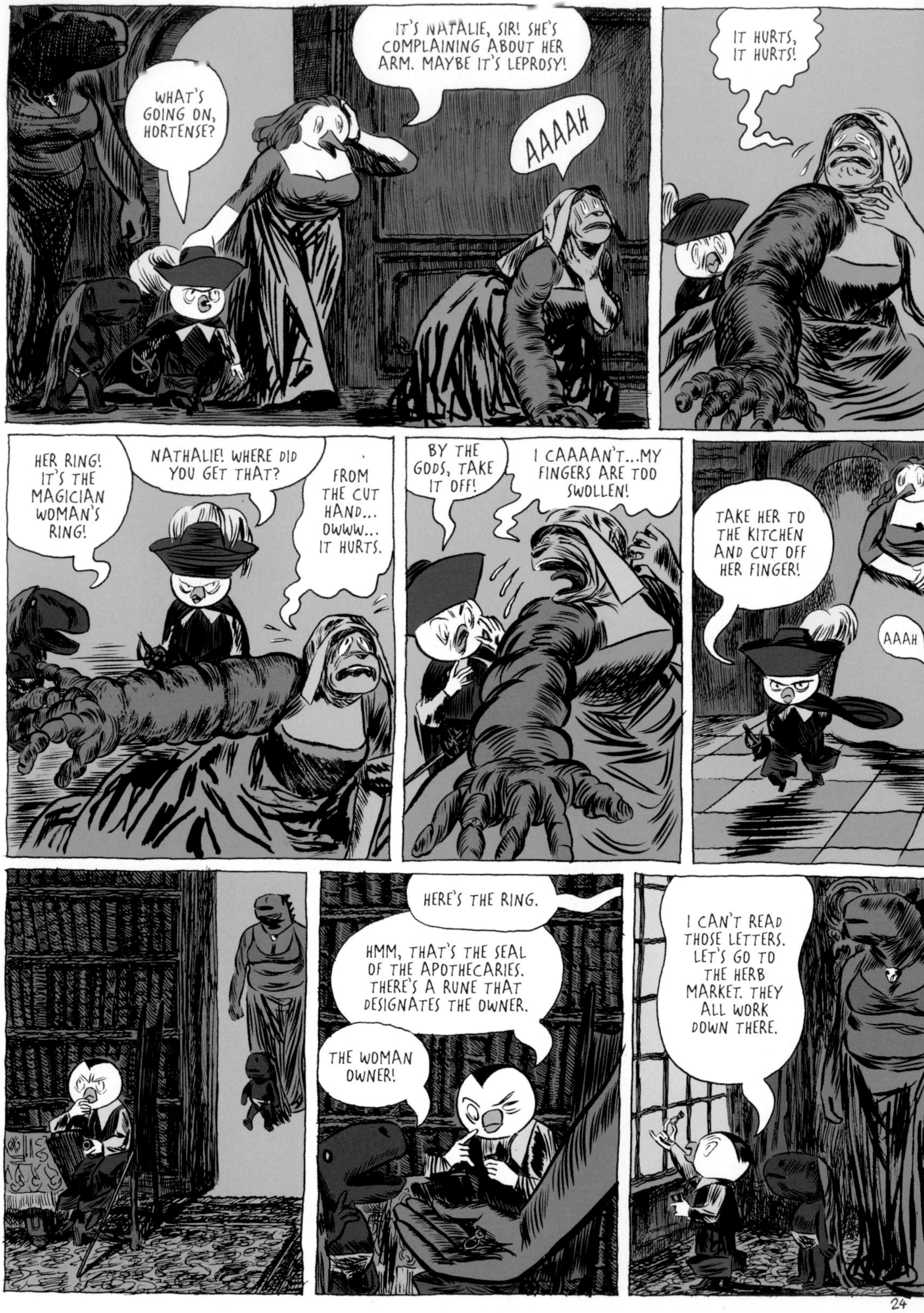
WHAT'S GOING ON, HORTENSE?
IT'S NATALIE, SIR! SHE'S COMPLAINING ABOUT HER ARM. MAYBE IT'S LEPROSY!
AAAAH
IT HURTS, IT HURTS!
HER RING! IT'S THE MAGICIAN WOMAN'S RING!
NATHALIE! WHERE DID YOU GET THAT?
FROM THE CUT HAND... OWWW... IT HURTS.
BY THE GODS, TAKE IT OFF!
I CAAAAN'T...MY FINGERS ARE TOO SWOLLEN!
TAKE HER TO THE KITCHEN AND CUT OFF HER FINGER!
AAAH
HERE'S THE RING.
HMM, THAT'S THE SEAL OF THE APOTHECARIES. THERE'S A RUNE THAT DESIGNATES THE OWNER.
THE WOMAN OWNER!
I CAN'T READ THOSE LETTERS. LET'S GO TO THE HERB MARKET. THEY ALL WORK DOWN THERE.

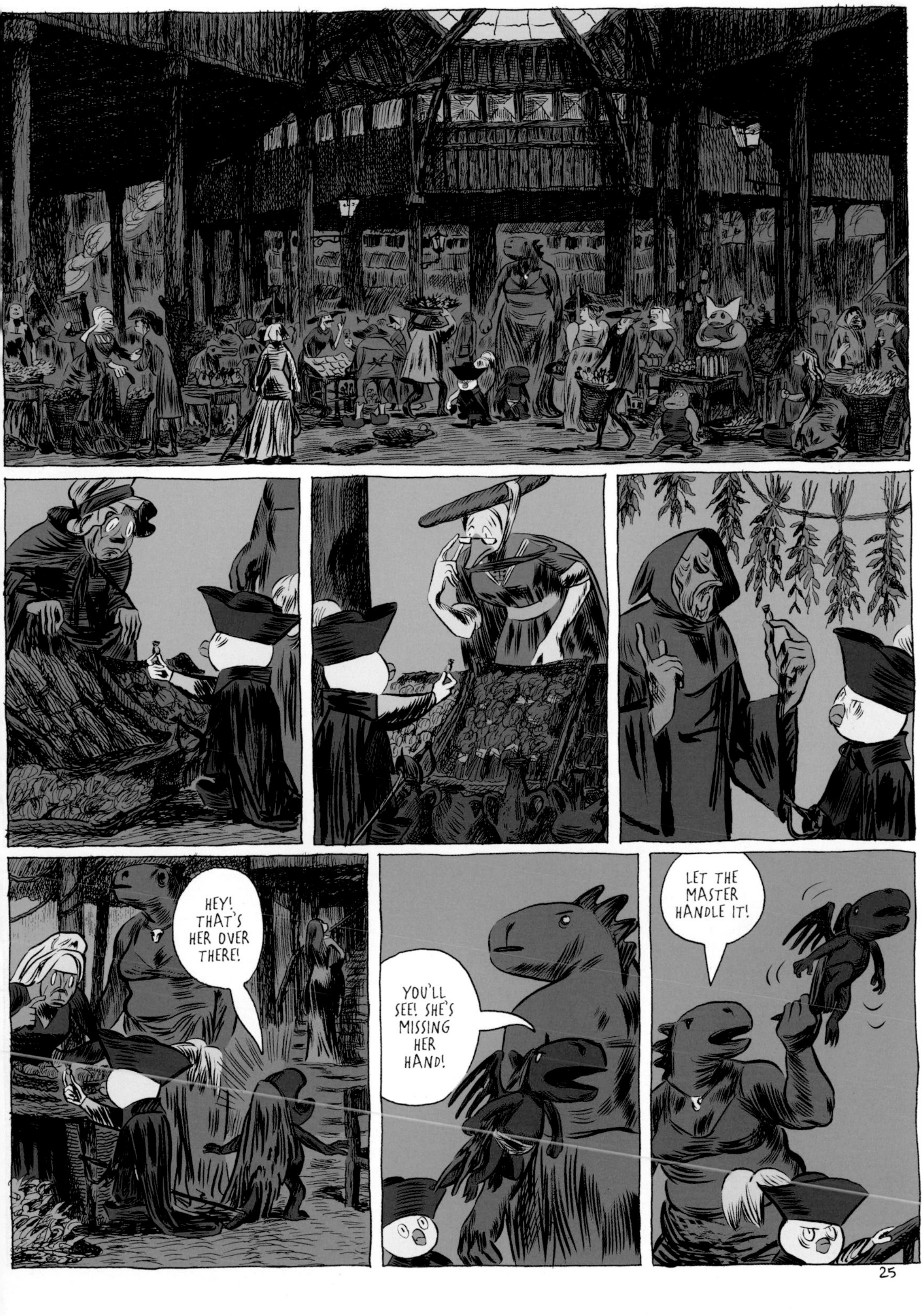
HEY! THAT'S HER OVER THERE!
YOU'LL SEE! SHE'S MISSING HER HAND!
LET THE MASTER HANDLE IT!

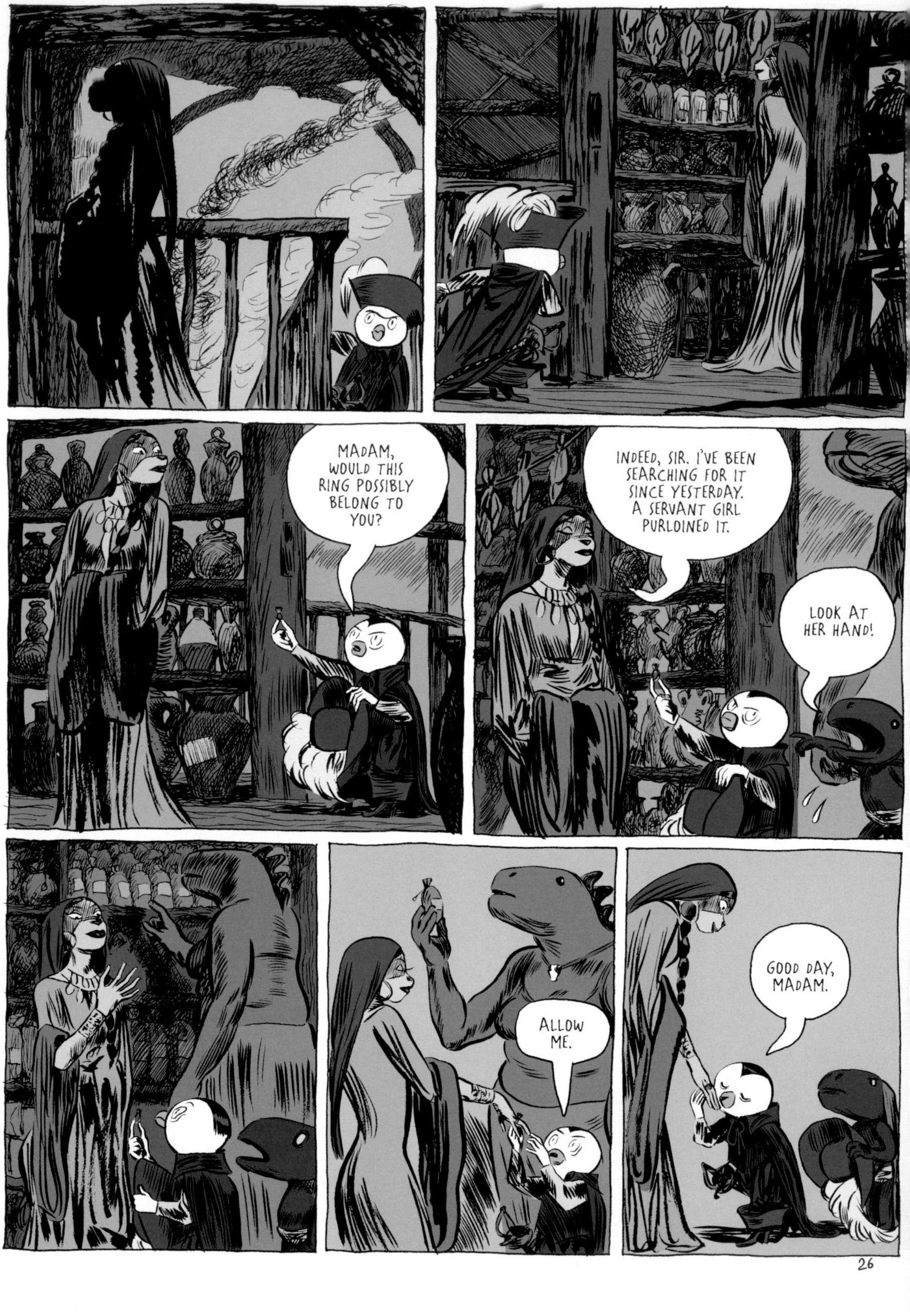
MADAM, WOULD THIS RING POSSIBLY BELONG TO YOU?
INDEED, SIR. I'VE BEEN SEARCHING FOR IT SINCE YESTERDAY. A SERVANT GIRL PURLOINED IT.
LOOK AT HER HAND!
ALLOW ME.
GOOD DAY, MADAM.

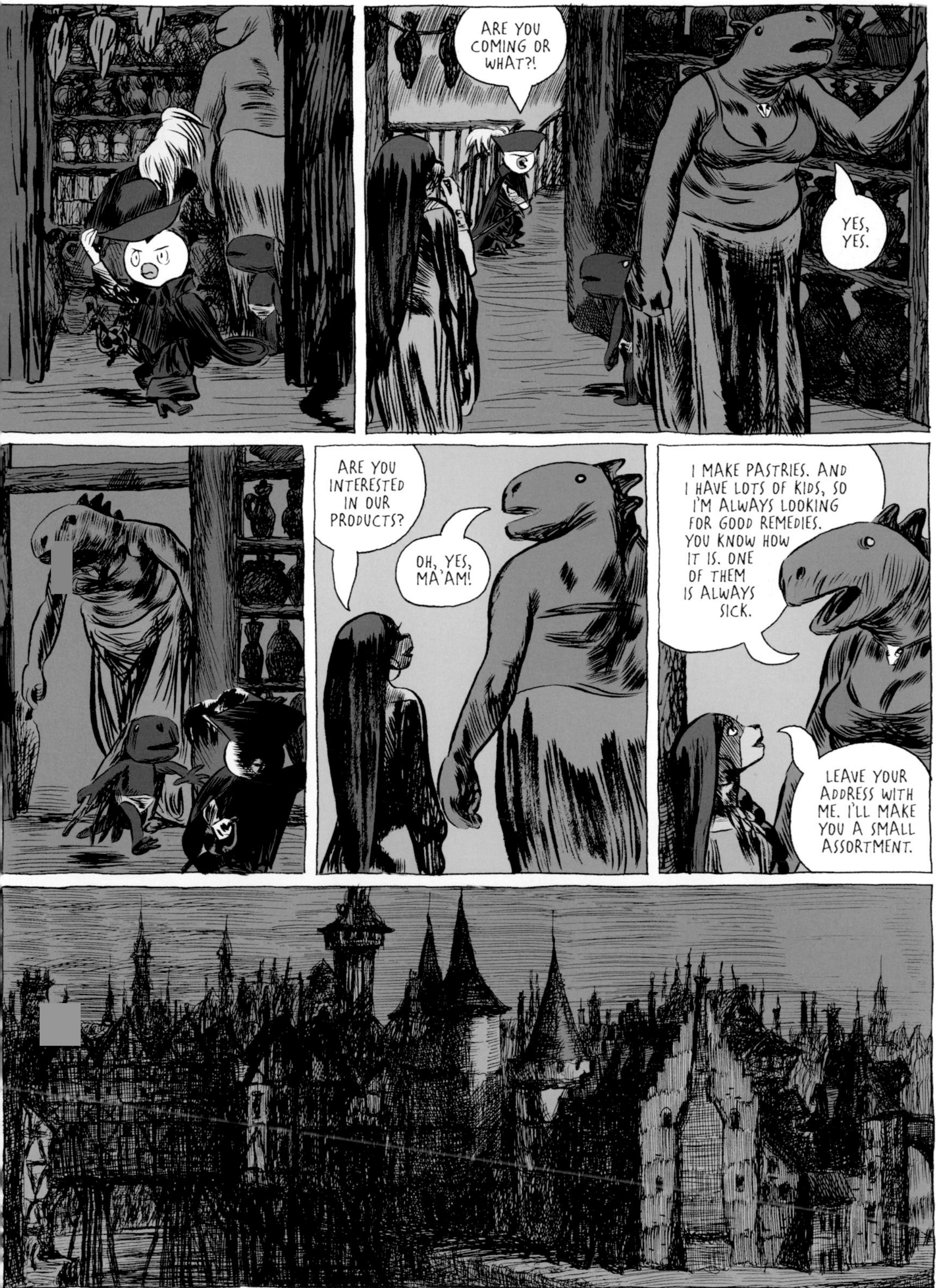
ARE YOU COMING OR WHAT?!
YES, YES.
ARE YOU INTERESTED IN OUR PRODUCTS?
OH, YES, MA'AM!
I MAKE PASTRIES. AND I HAVE LOTS OF KIDS, SO I'M ALWAYS LOOKING FOR GOOD REMEDIES. YOU KNOW HOW IT IS. ONE OF THEM IS ALWAYS SICK.
LEAVE YOUR ADDRESS WITH ME. I'LL MAKE YOU A SMALL ASSORTMENT.

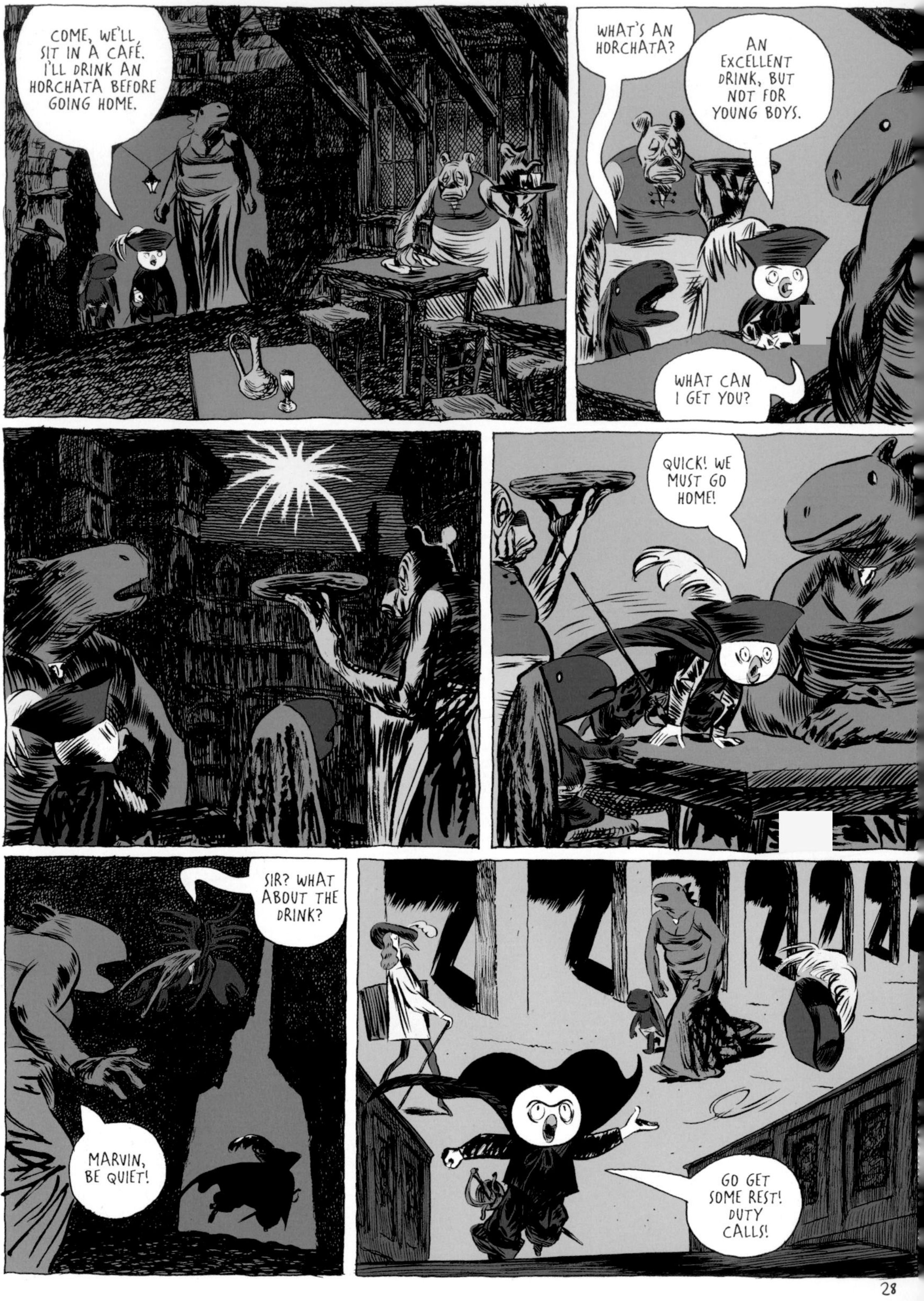
COME, WE'LL SIT IN A CAFÉ. I'LL DRINK AN HORCHATA BEFORE GOING HOME.
WHAT'S AN HORCHATA?
AN EXCELLENT DRINK, BUT NOT FOR YOUNG BOYS.
WHAT CAN I GET YOU?
QUICK! WE MUST GO HOME!
SIR? WHAT ABOUT THE DRINK?
MARVIN, BE QUIET!
GO GET SOME REST! DUTY CALLS!

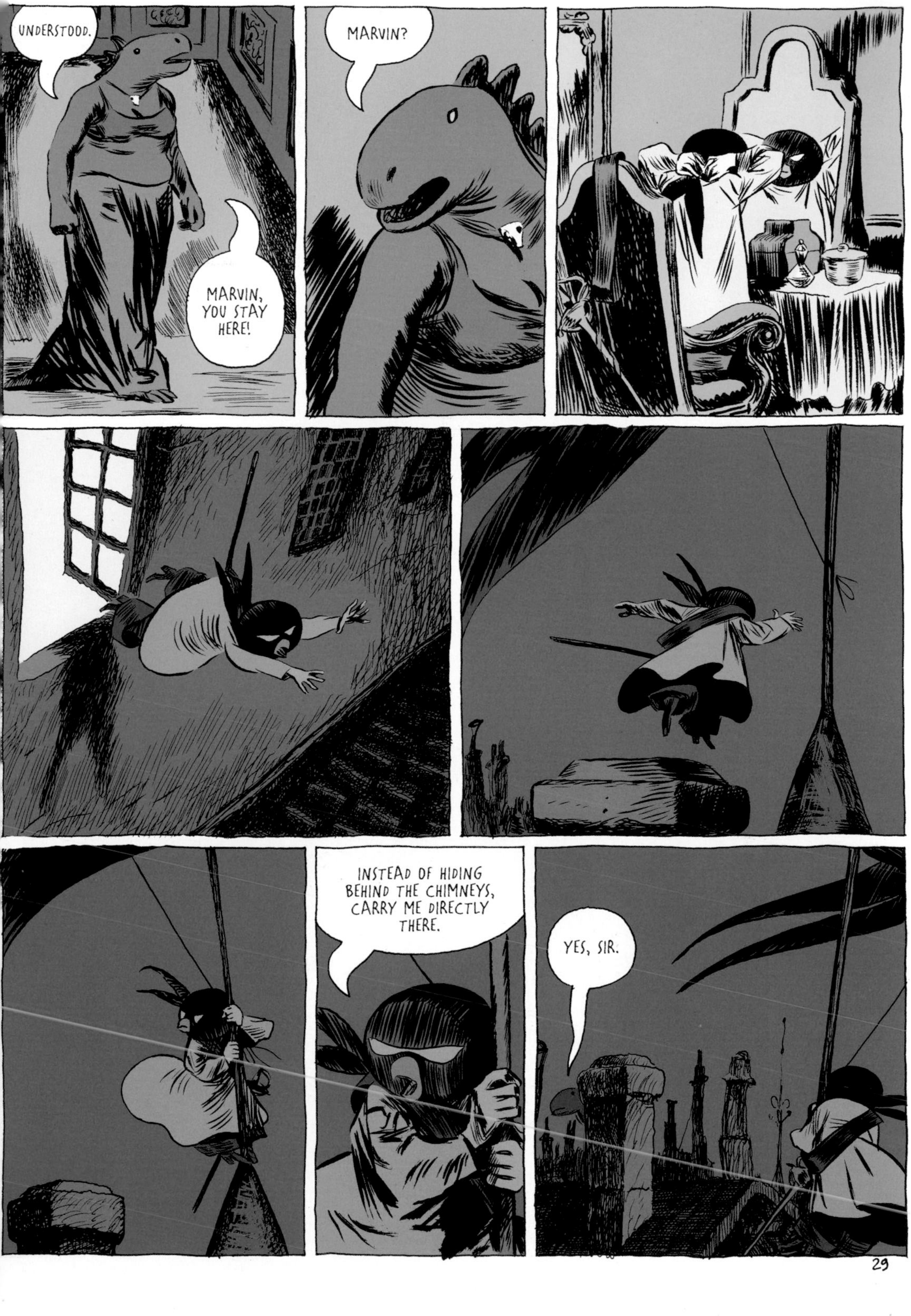
UNDERSTOOD.
MARVIN, YOU STAY HERE!
MARVIN?
INSTEAD OF HIDING BEHIND THE CHIMNEYS, CARRY ME DIRECTLY THERE.
YES, SIR.

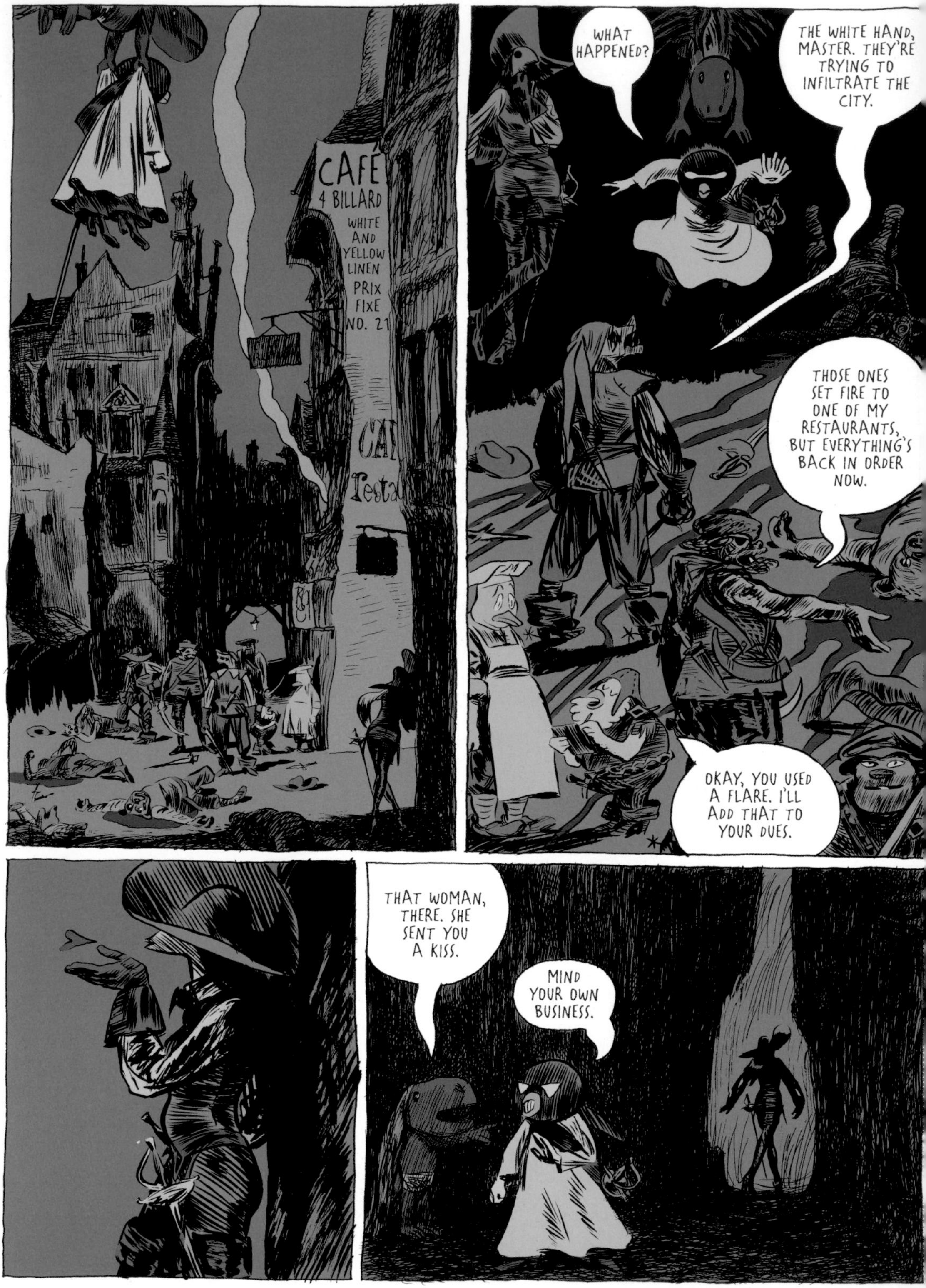
CAFÉ
4 BILLARD
WHITE AND YELLOW LINEN
PRIX FIXE
NO. 21
WHAT HAPPENED?
THE WHITE HAND, MASTER. THEY'RE TRYING TO INFILTRATE THE CITY.
THOSE ONES SET FIRE TO ONE OF MY RESTAURANTS, BUT EVERYTHING'S BACK IN ORDER NOW.
OKAY, YOU USED A FLARE. I'LL ADD THAT TO YOUR DUES.
THAT WOMAN, THERE. SHE SENT YOU A KISS.
MIND YOUR OWN BUSINESS.

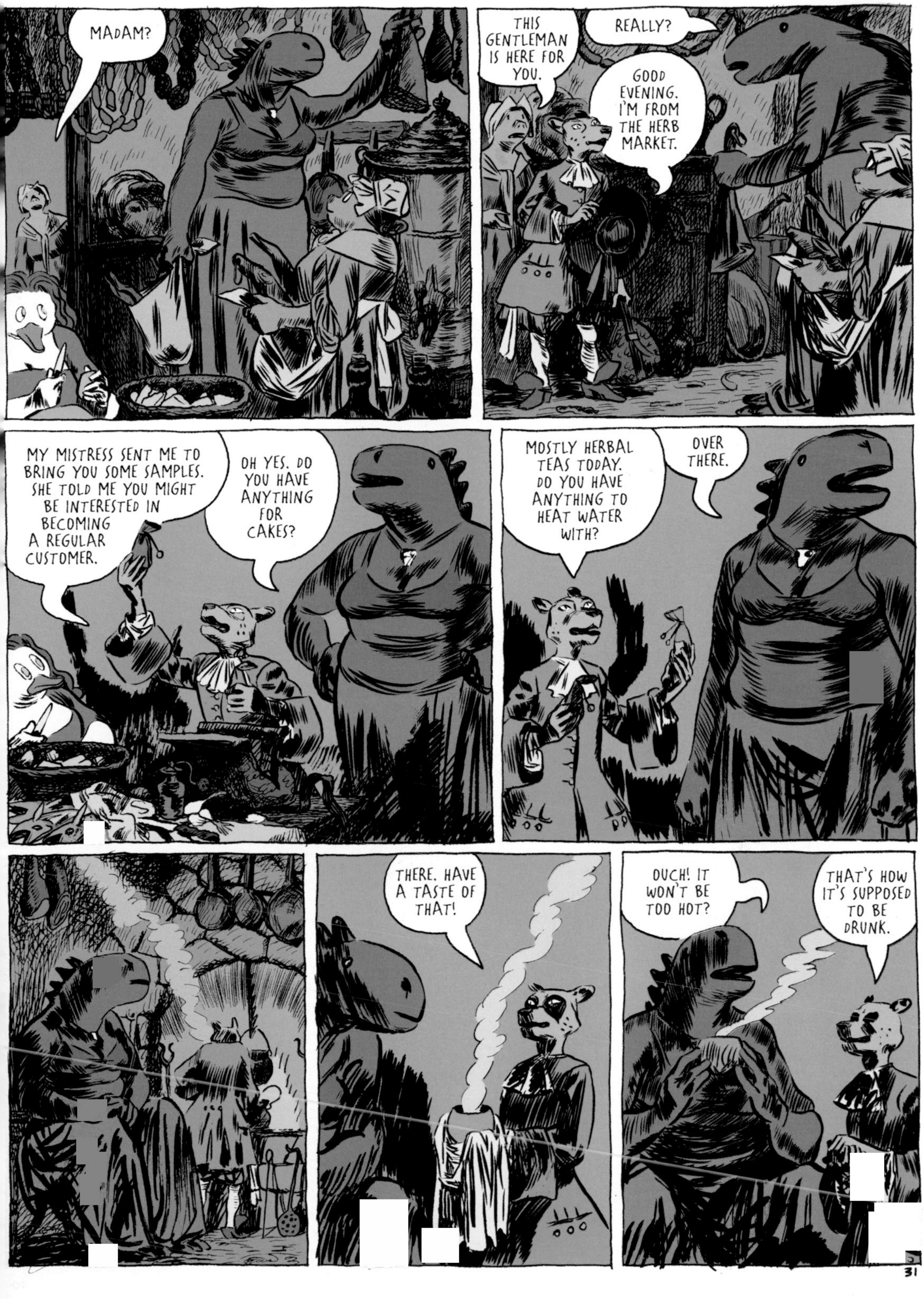
MADAM?
THIS GENTLEMAN IS HERE FOR YOU.
REALLY?
GOOD EVENING. I'M FROM THE HERB MARKET.
MY MISTRESS SENT ME TO BRING YOU SOME SAMPLES. SHE TOLD ME YOU MIGHT BE INTERESTED IN BECOMING A REGULAR CUSTOMER.
OH YES. DO YOU HAVE ANYTHING FOR CAKES?
MOSTLY HERBAL TEAS TODAY. DO YOU HAVE ANYTHING TO HEAT WATER WITH?
OVER THERE.
THERE. HAVE A TASTE OF THAT!
OUCH! IT WON'T BE TOO HOT?
THAT'S HOW IT'S SUPPOSED TO BE DRUNK.

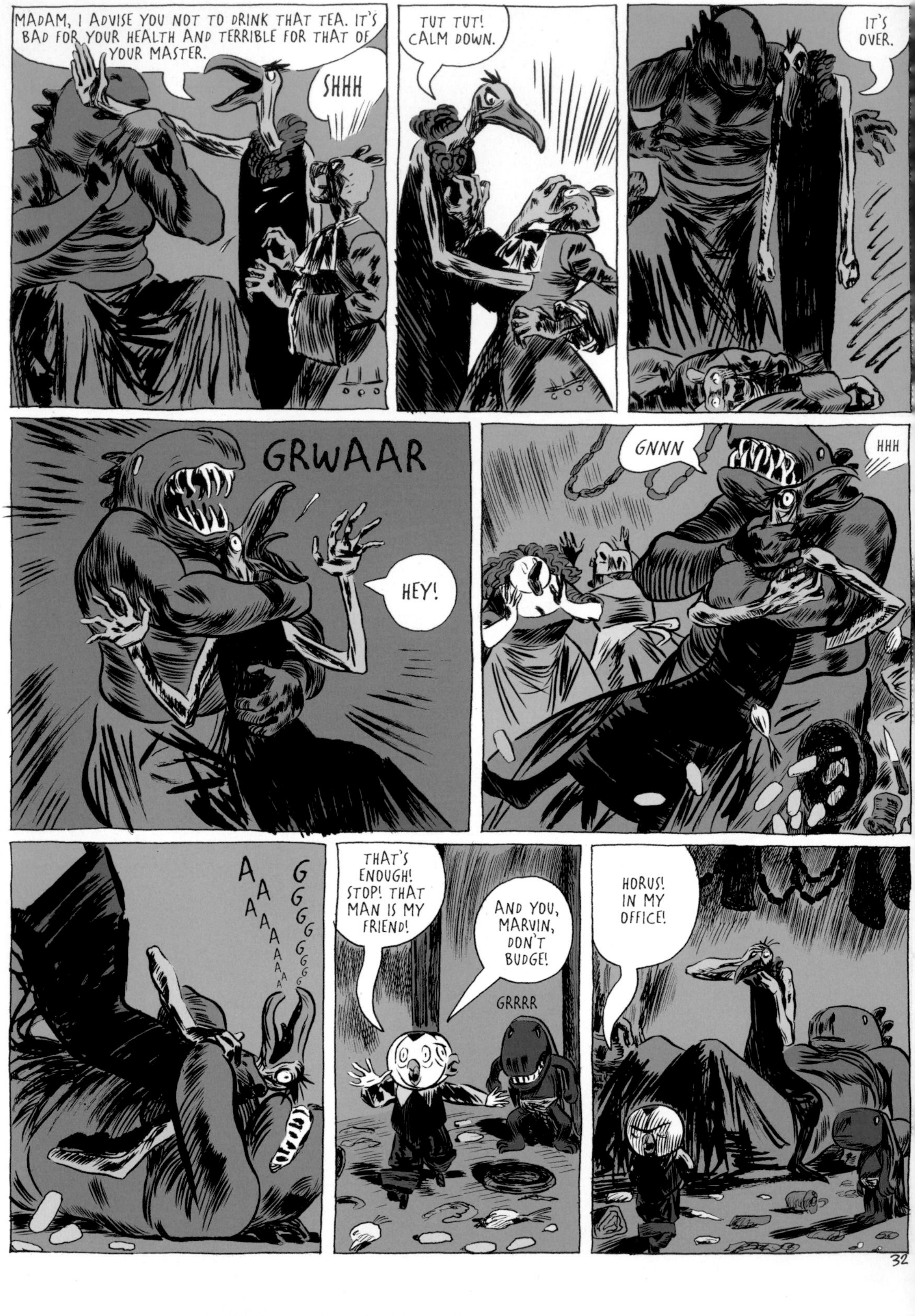
MADAM, I ADVISE YOU NOT TO DRINK THAT TEA. IT'S BAD FOR YOUR HEALTH AND TERRIBLE FOR THAT OF YOUR MASTER.
SHHH
TUT TUT! CALM DOWN.
IT'S OVER.
GRWAAR
HEY!
GNNN
HHH
AAAAAAAAA
GGGGGGGG
THAT'S ENOUGH! STOP! THAT MAN IS MY FRIEND!
AND YOU, MARVIN, DON'T BUDGE!
GRRRR
HORUS! IN MY OFFICE!

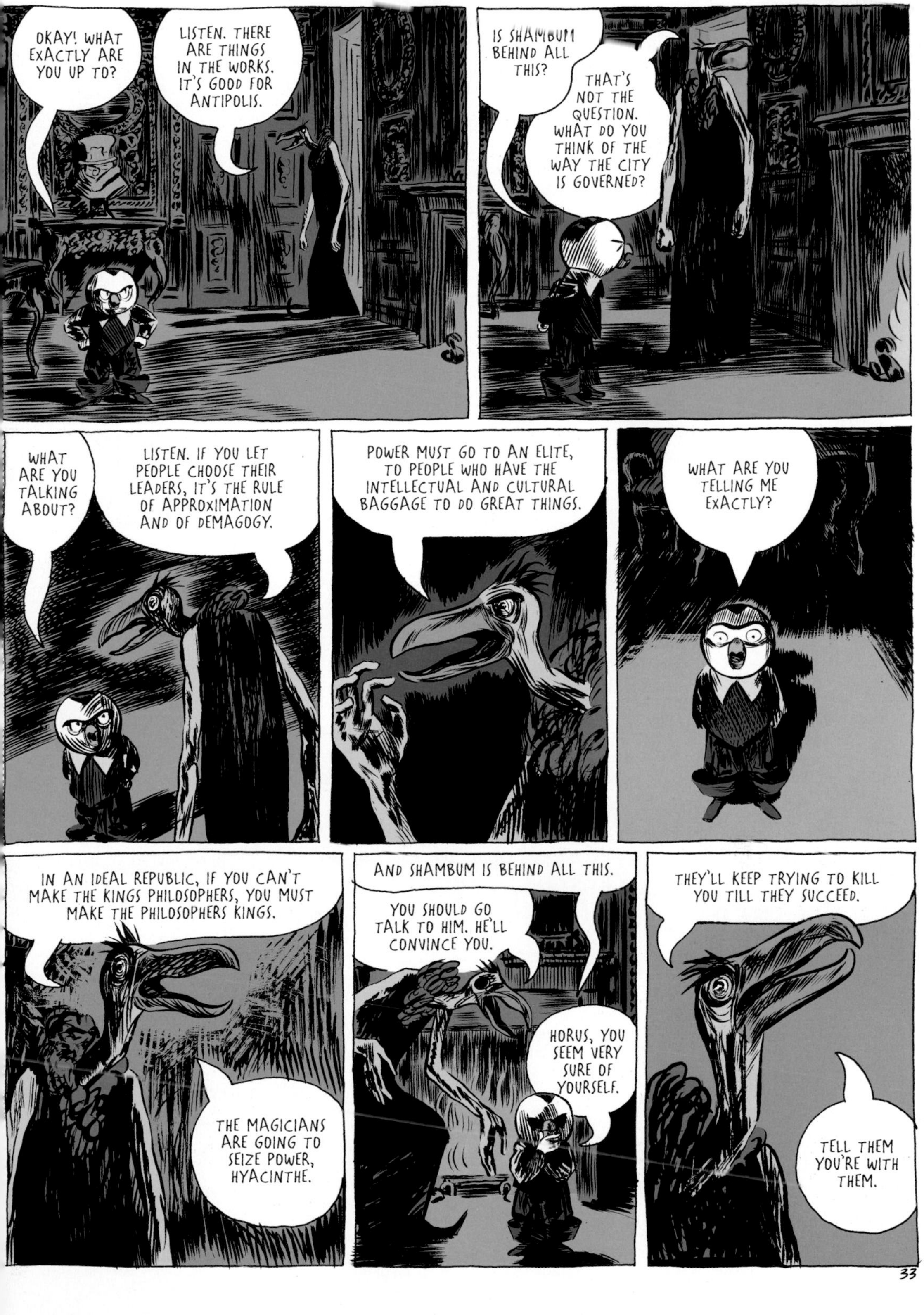
OKAY! WHAT EXACTLY ARE YOU UP TO?
LISTEN. THERE ARE THINGS IN THE WORKS. IT'S GOOD FOR ANTIPOLIS.
IS SHAMBUM BEHIND ALL THIS?
THAT'S NOT THE QUESTION. WHAT DO YOU THINK OF THE WAY THE CITY IS GOVERNED?
WHAT ARE YOU TALKING ABOUT?
LISTEN. IF YOU LET PEOPLE CHOOSE THEIR LEADERS, IT'S THE RULE OF APPROXIMATION AND OF DEMAGOGY.
POWER MUST GO TO AN ELITE, TO PEOPLE WHO HAVE THE INTELLECTUAL AND CULTURAL BAGGAGE TO DO GREAT THINGS.
WHAT ARE YOU TELLING ME EXACTLY?
IN AN IDEAL REPUBLIC, IF YOU CAN'T MAKE THE KINGS PHILOSOPHERS, YOU MUST MAKE THE PHILOSOPHERS KINGS.
THE MAGICIANS ARE GOING TO SEIZE POWER, HYACINTHE.
AND SHAMBUM IS BEHIND ALL THIS.
YOU SHOULD GO TALK TO HIM. HE'LL CONVINCE YOU.
HORUS, YOU SEEM VERY SURE OF YOURSELF.
THEY'LL KEEP TRYING TO KILL YOU TILL THEY SUCCEED.
TELL THEM YOU'RE WITH THEM.

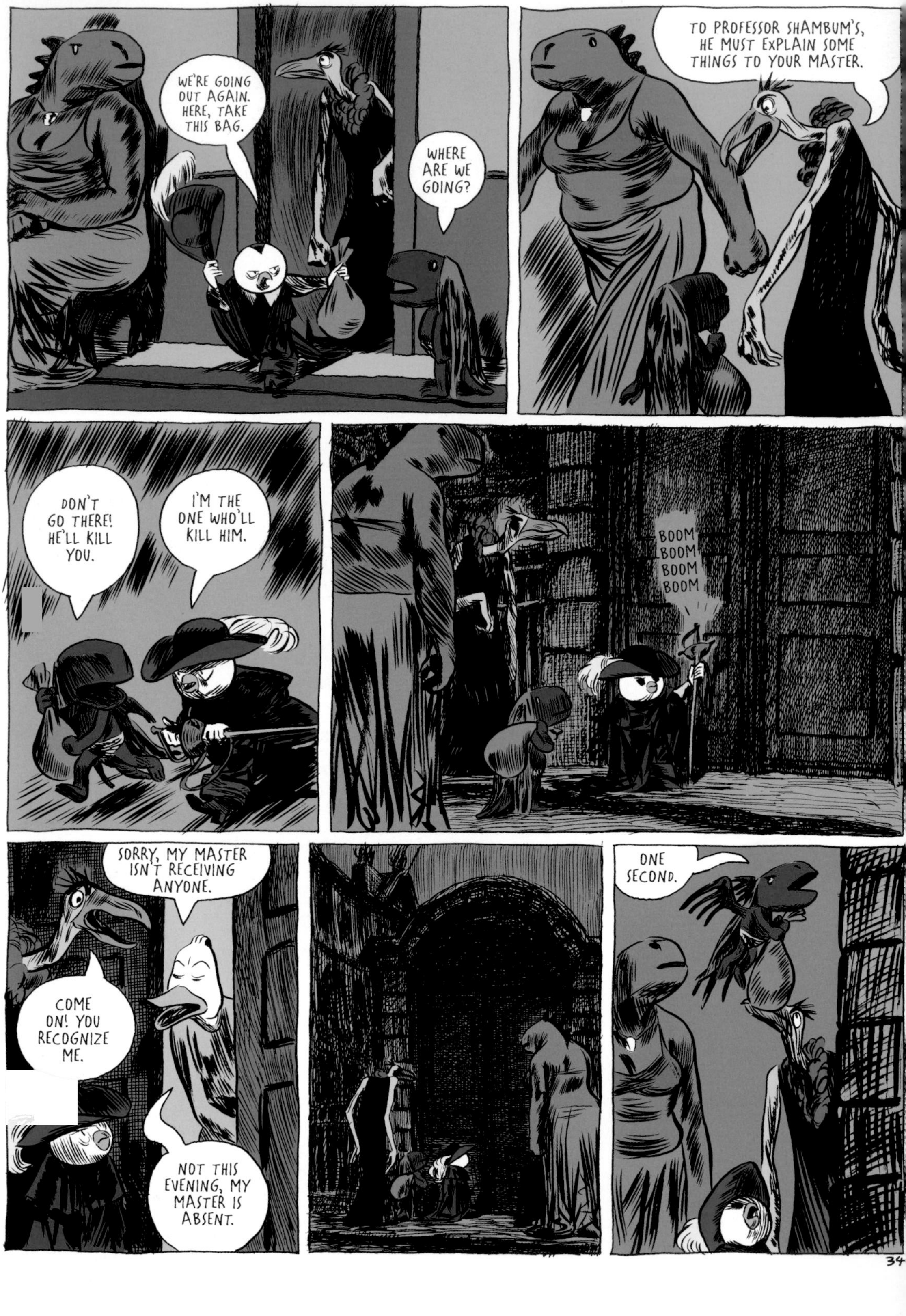
WE'RE GOING OUT AGAIN. HERE, TAKE THIS BAG.
WHERE ARE WE GOING?
TO PROFESSOR SHAMBUM'S, HE MUST EXPLAIN SOME THINGS TO YOUR MASTER.
DON'T GO THERE! HE'LL KILL YOU.
I'M THE ONE WHO'LL KILL HIM.
BOOM BOOM BOOM BOOM
SORRY, MY MASTER ISN'T RECEIVING ANYONE.
COME ON! YOU RECOGNIZE ME.
NOT THIS EVENING, MY MASTER IS ABSENT.
ONE SECOND.

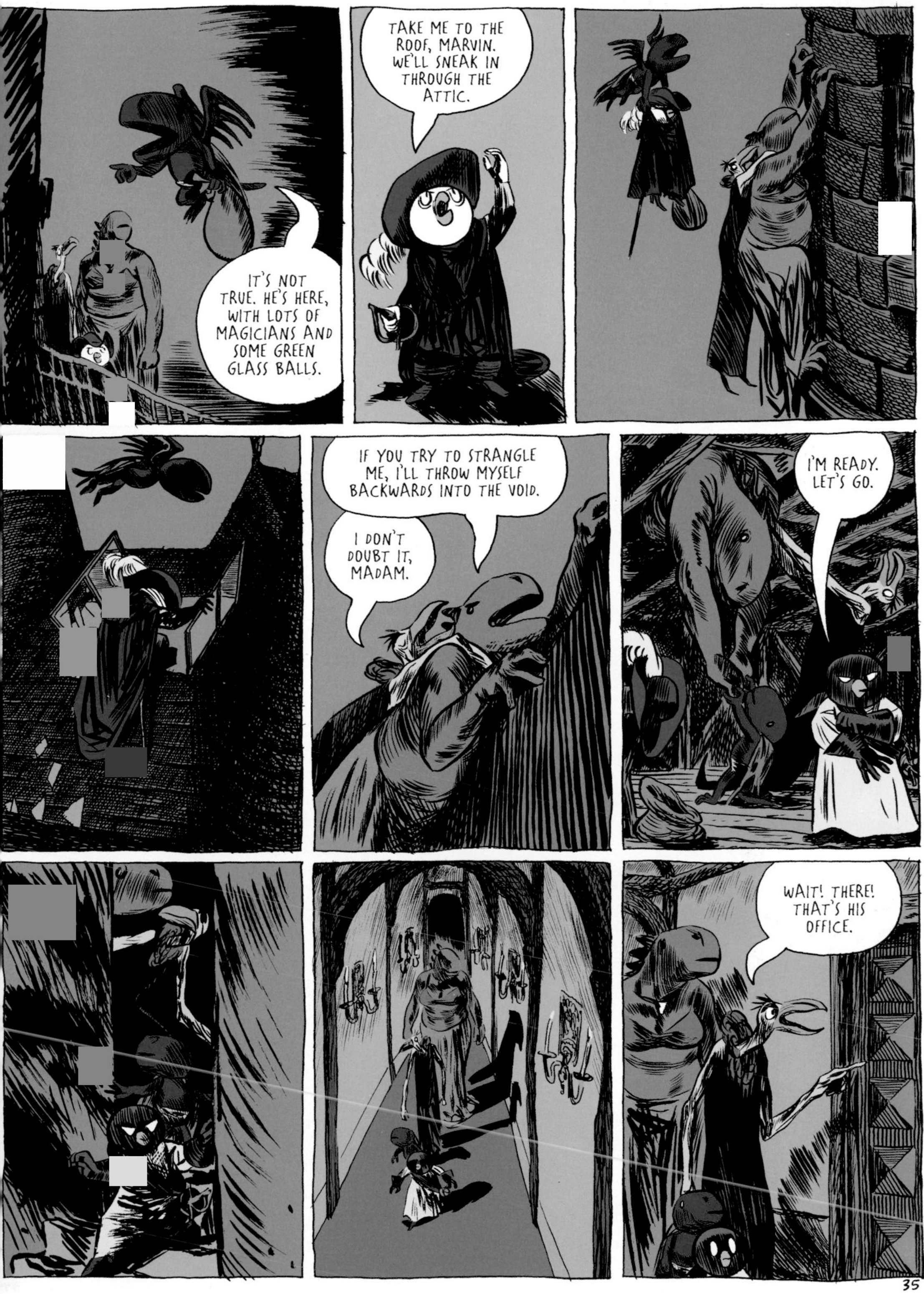
IT'S NOT TRUE. HE'S HERE, WITH LOTS OF MAGICIANS AND SOME GREEN GLASS BALLS.
TAKE ME TO THE ROOF, MARVIN. WE'LL SNEAK IN THROUGH THE ATTIC.
IF YOU TRY TO STRANGLE ME, I'LL THROW MYSELF BACKWARDS INTO THE VOID.
I DON'T DOUBT IT, MADAM.
I'M READY. LET'S GO.
WAIT! THERE! THAT'S HIS OFFICE.

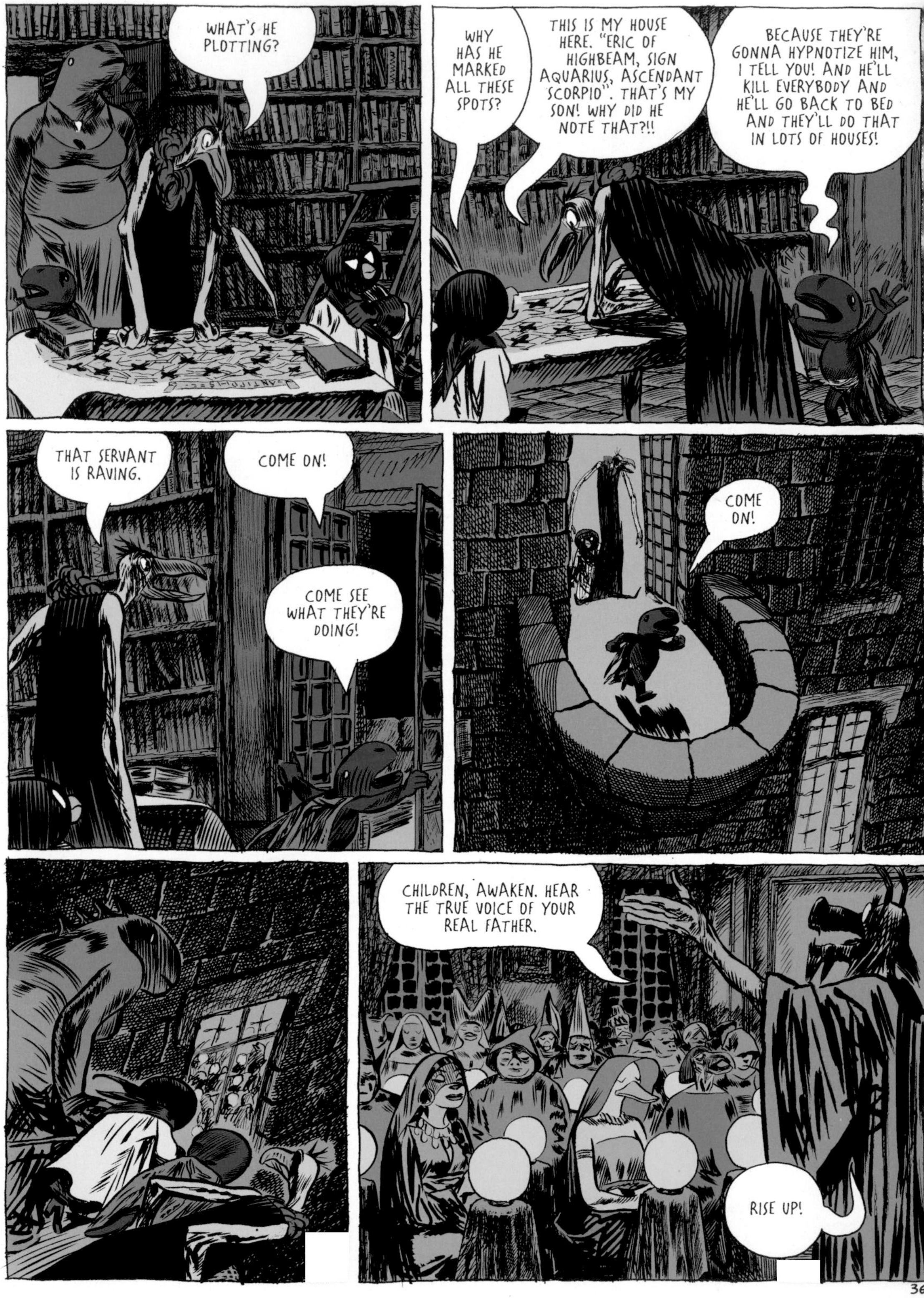
WHAT'S HE PLOTTING?
WHY HAS HE MARKED ALL THESE SPOTS?
THIS IS MY HOUSE HERE. "ERIC OF HIGHBEAM, SIGN AQUARIUS, ASCENDANT SCORPIO". THAT'S MY SON! WHY DID HE NOTE THAT?!!
BECAUSE THEY'RE GONNA HYPNOTIZE HIM, I TELL YOU! AND HE'LL KILL EVERYBODY AND HE'LL GO BACK TO BED AND THEY'LL DO THAT IN LOTS OF HOUSES!
THAT SERVANT IS RAVING.
COME ON!
COME SEE WHAT THEY'RE DOING!
COME ON!
CHILDREN, AWAKEN. HEAR THE TRUE VOICE OF YOUR REAL FATHER.
RISE UP!

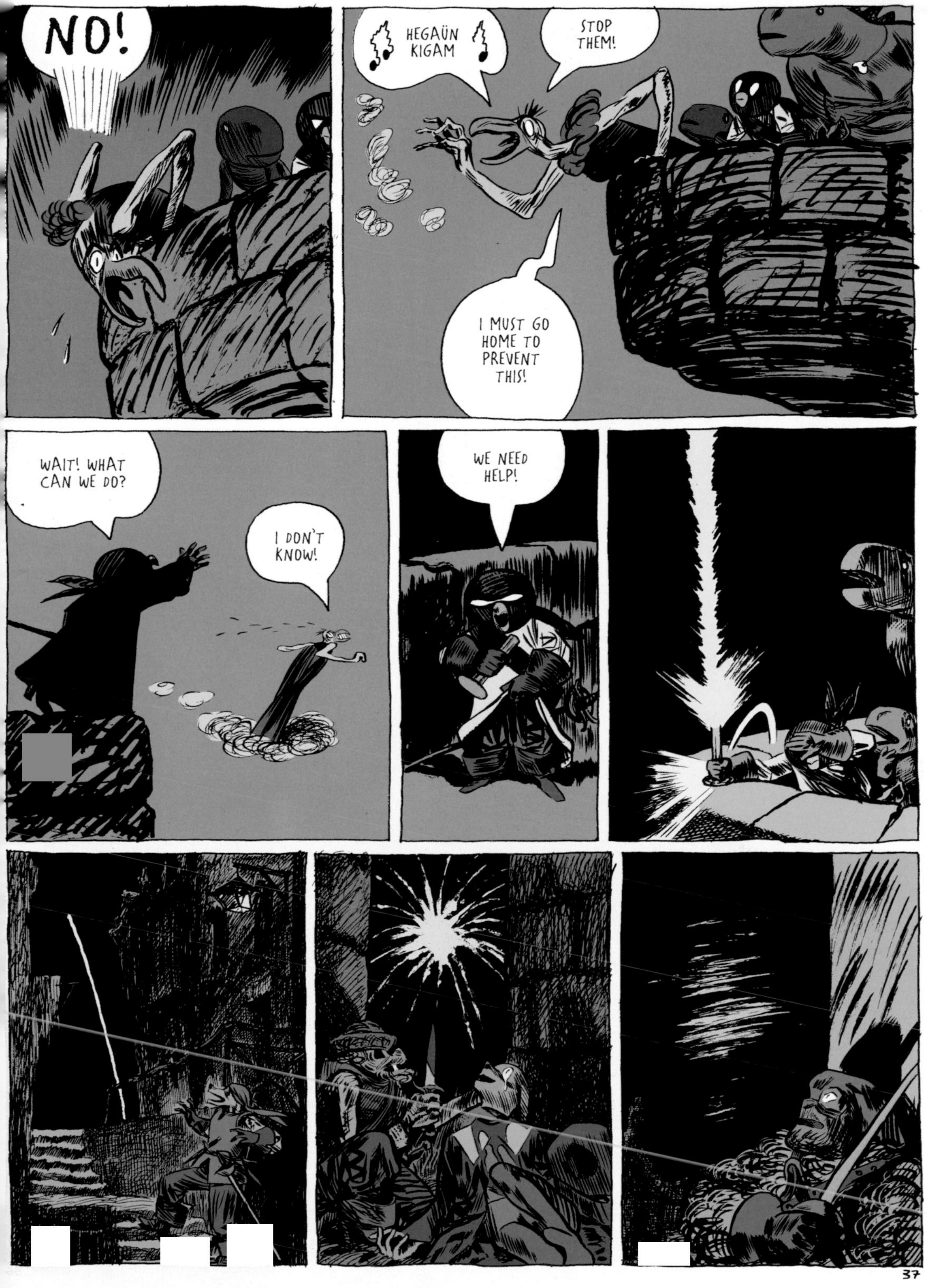
NO!
HEGAÜN KIGAM
STOP THEM!
I MUST GO HOME TO PREVENT THIS!
WAIT! WHAT CAN WE DO?
I DON'T KNOW!
WE NEED HELP!

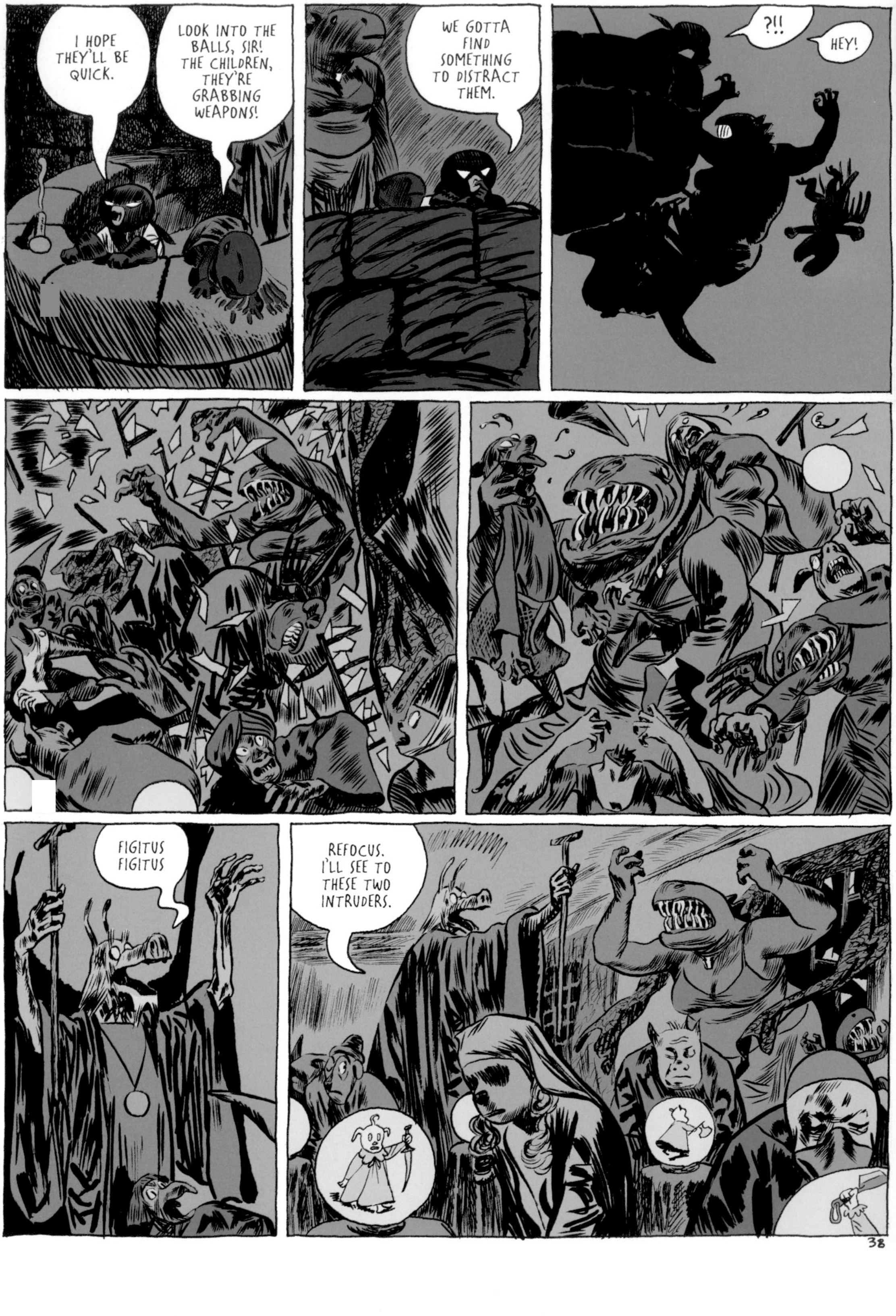
I HOPE THEY'LL BE QUICK.
LOOK INTO THE BALLS, SIR! THE CHILDREN, THEY'RE GRABBING WEAPONS!
WE GOTTA FIND SOMETHING TO DISTRACT THEM.
?!!
HEY!
FIGITUS FIGITUS
REFOCUS. I'LL SEE TO THESE TWO INTRUDERS.

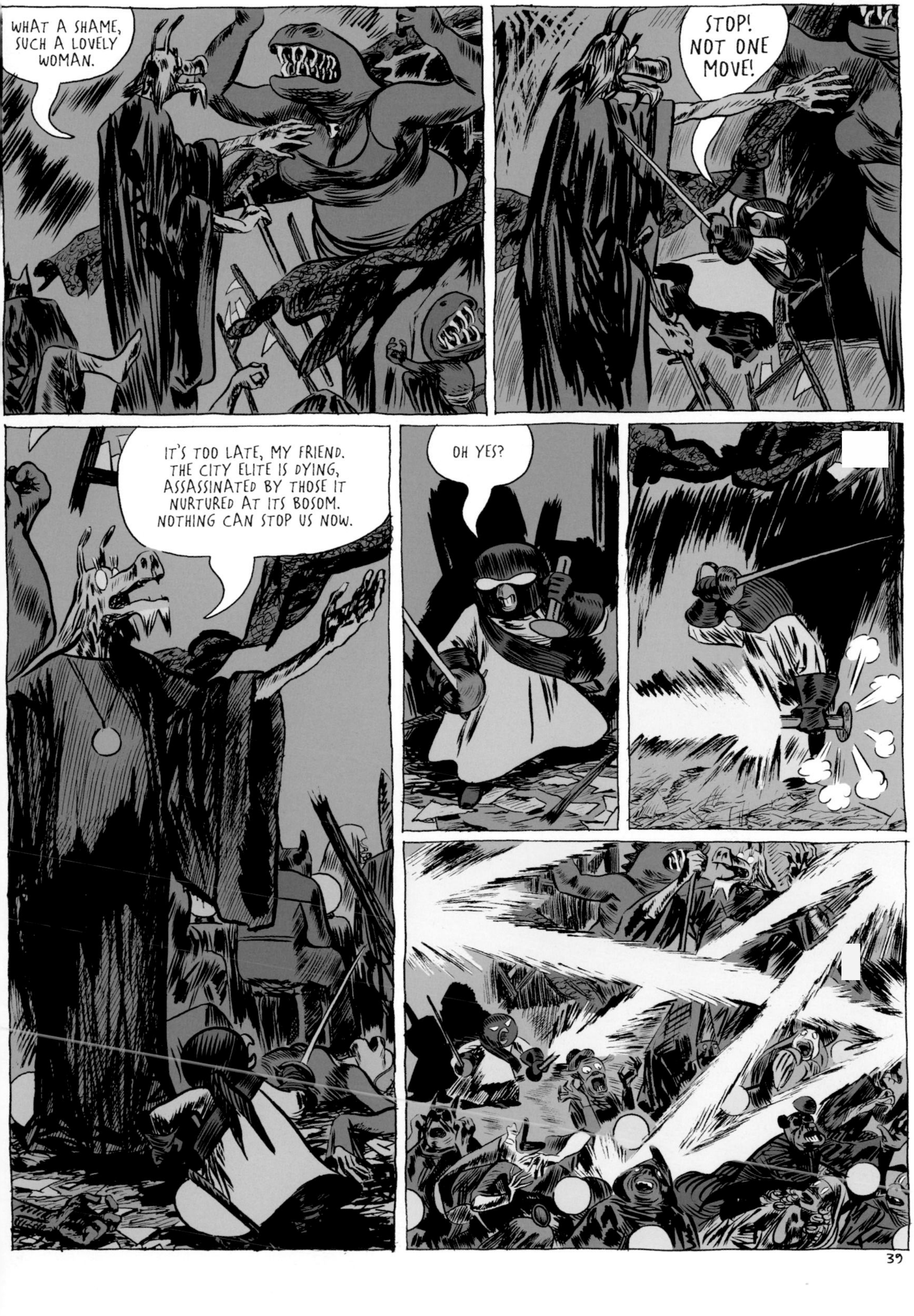
WHAT A SHAME, SUCH A LOVELY WOMAN.
STOP! NOT ONE MOVE!
IT'S TOO LATE, MY FRIEND. THE CITY ELITE IS DYING, ASSASSINATED BY THOSE IT NURTURED AT ITS BOSOM. NOTHING CAN STOP US NOW.
OH YES?

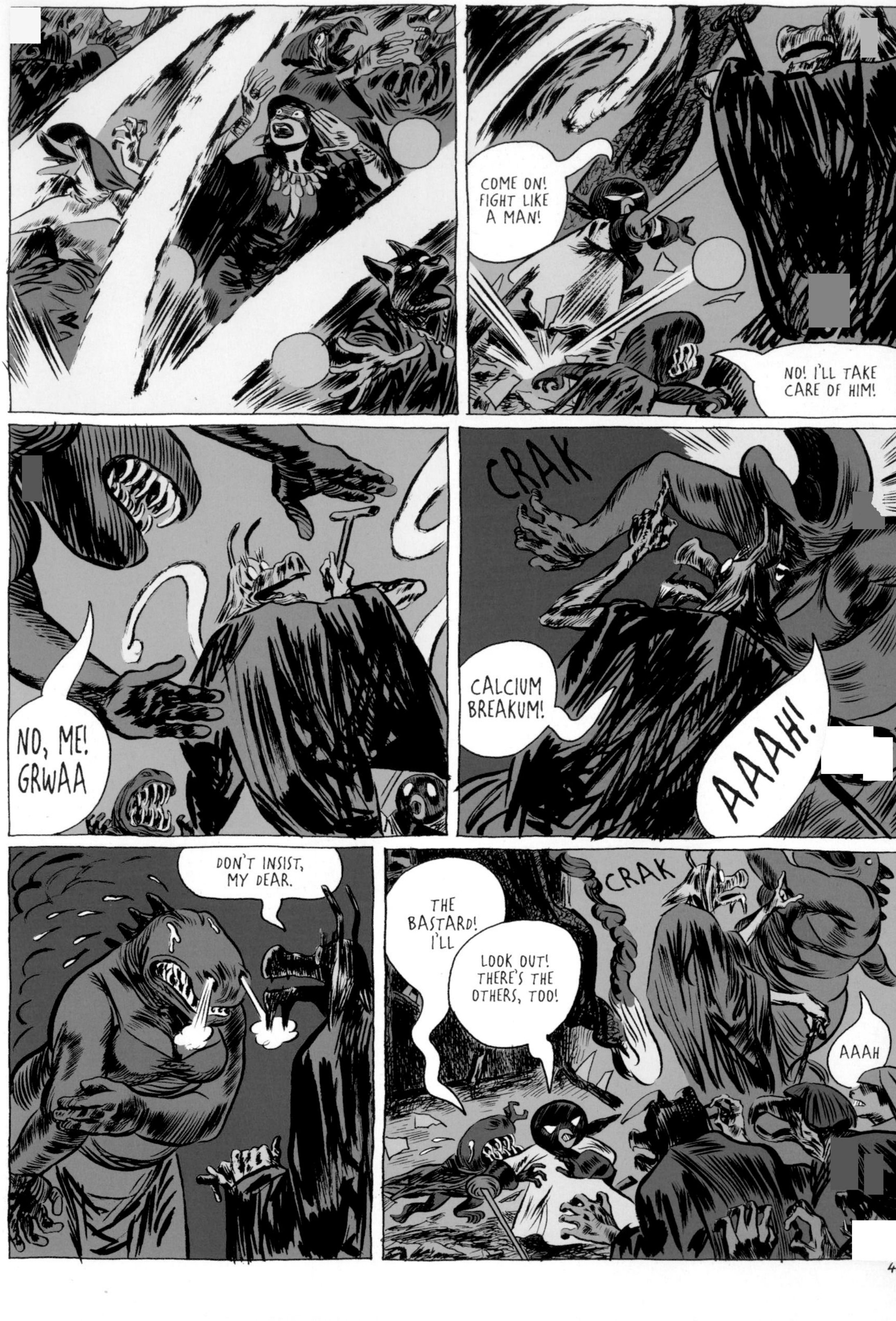
COME ON! FIGHT LIKE A MAN!
NO! I'LL TAKE CARE OF HIM!
NO, ME! GRWAA
CRAK
CALCIUM BREAKUM!
AAAH!
DON'T INSIST, MY DEAR.
CRAK
THE BASTARD! I'LL
LOOK OUT! THERE'S THE OTHERS, TOO!
AAAH

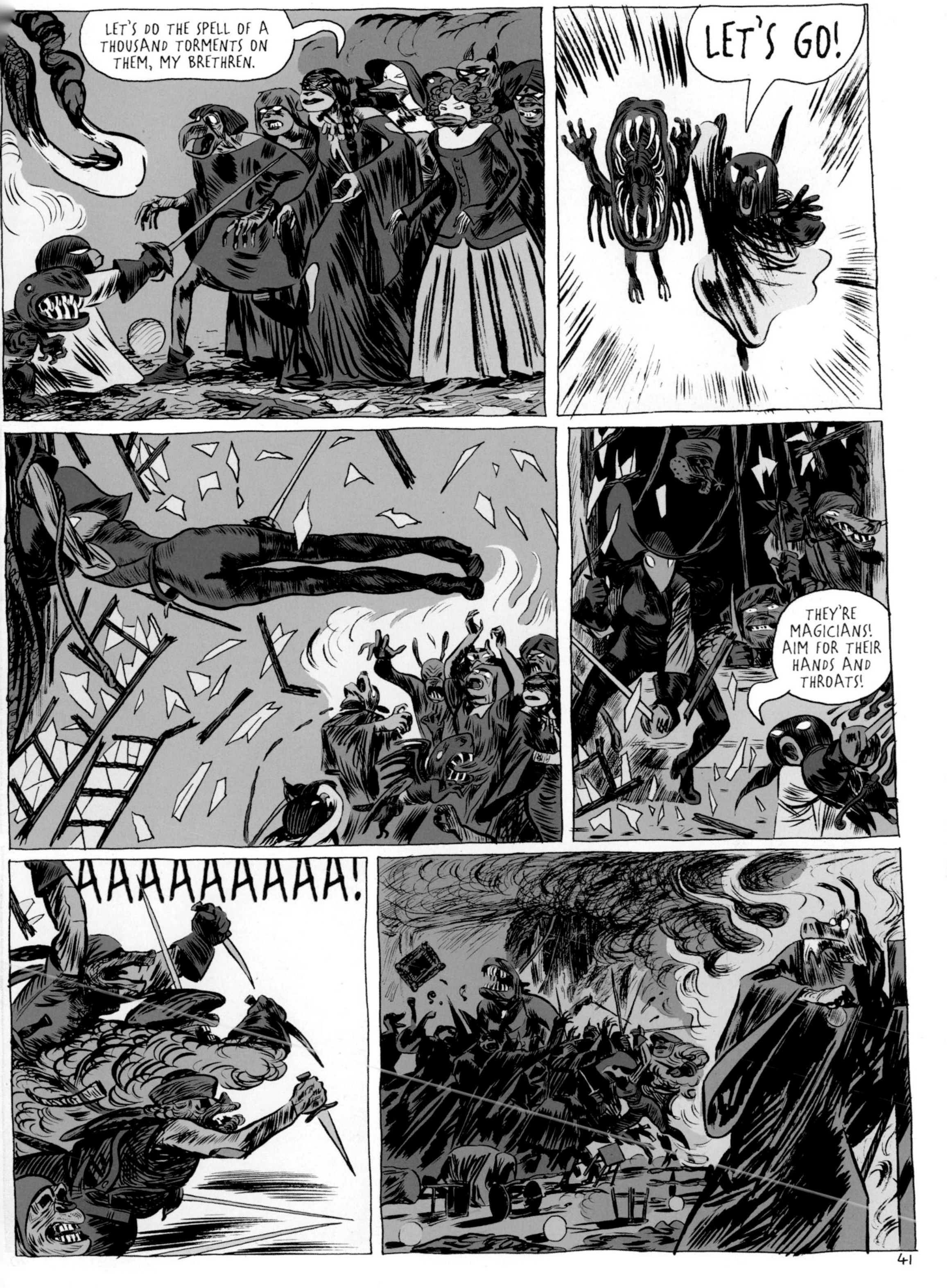
LET'S DO THE SPELL OF A THOUSAND TORMENTS ON THEM, MY BRETHREN.
LET'S GO!
THEY'RE MAGICIANS! AIM FOR THEIR HANDS AND THROATS!
AAAAAAAAAA!

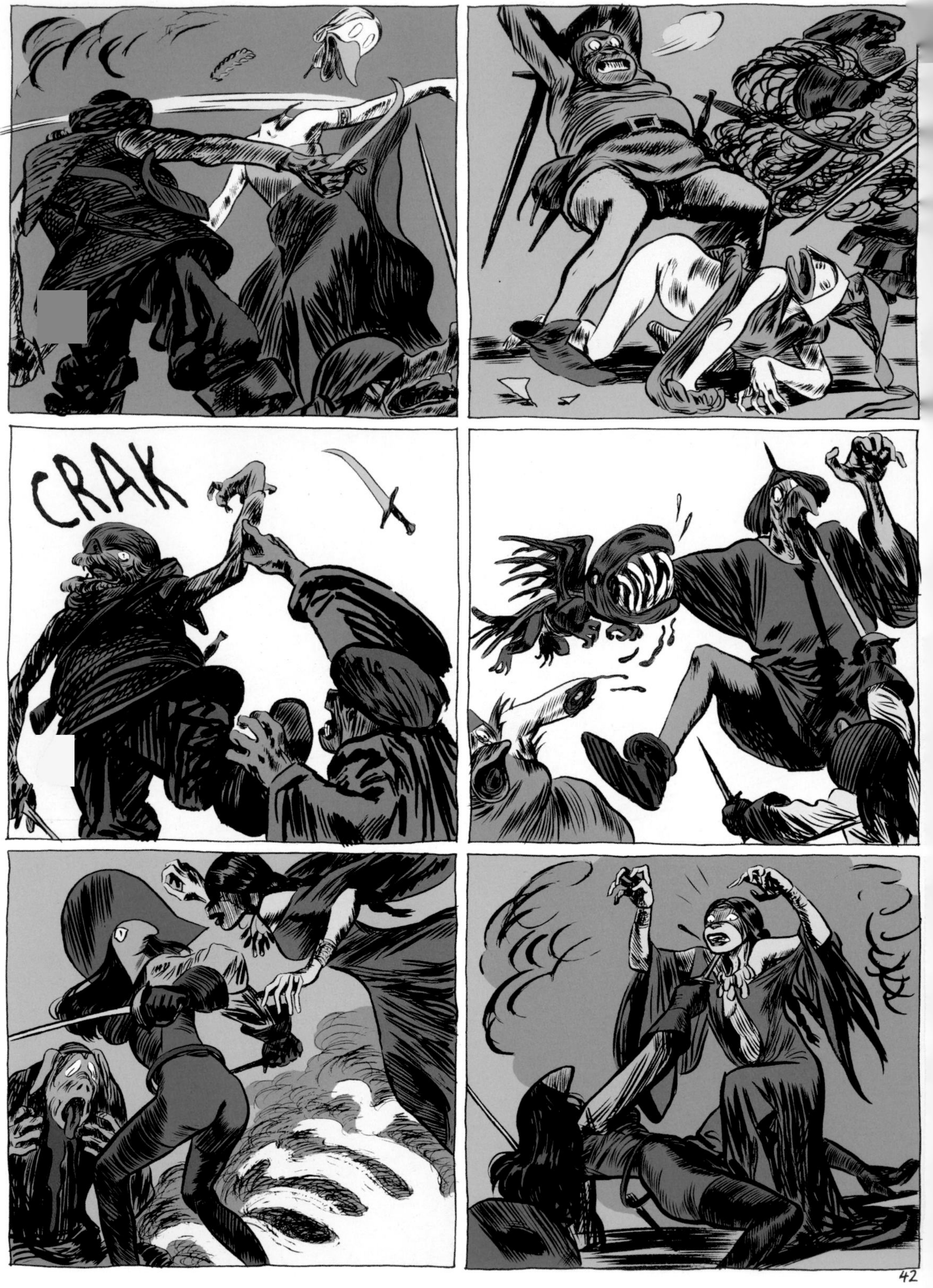
CRAK

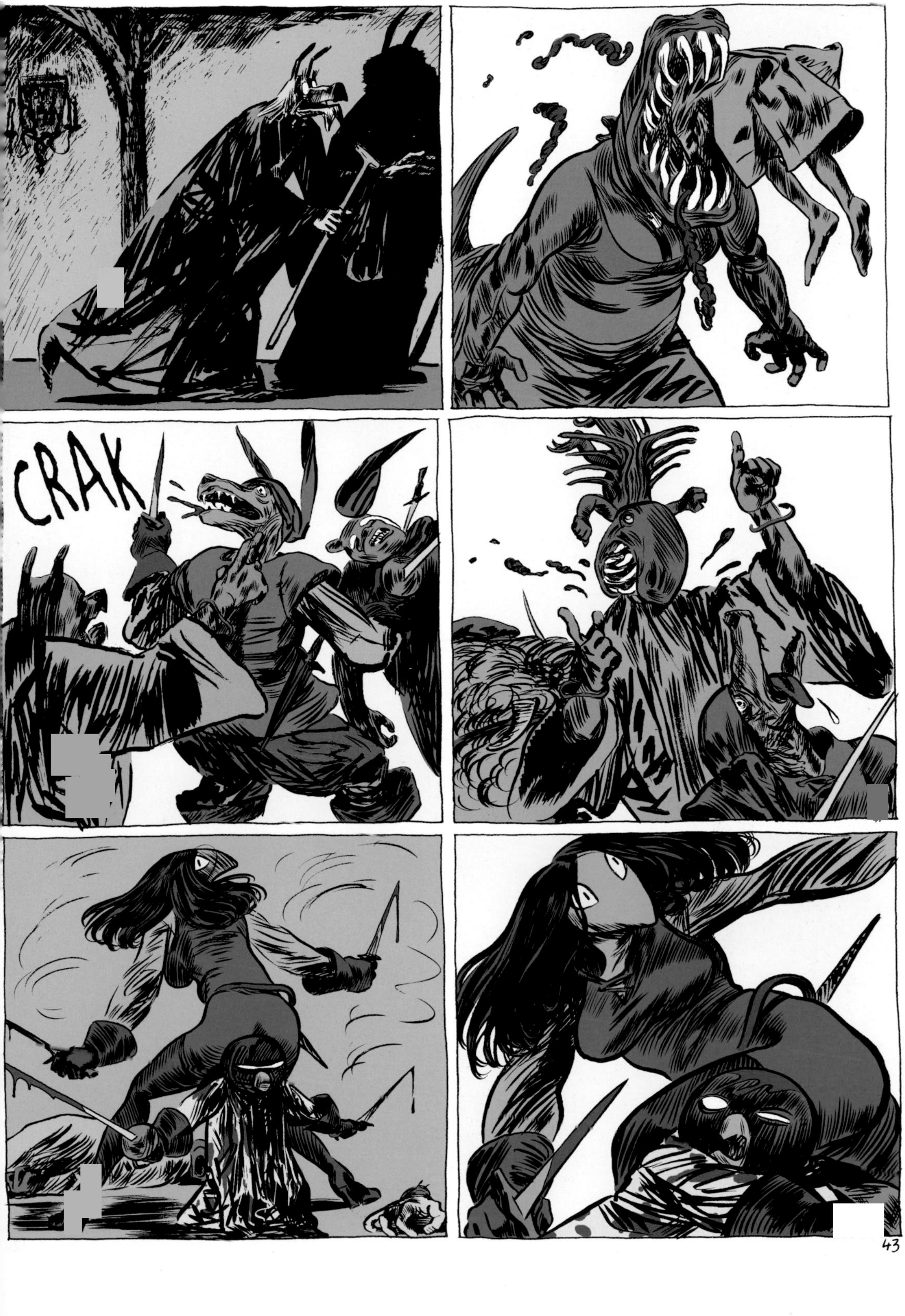
CRAK

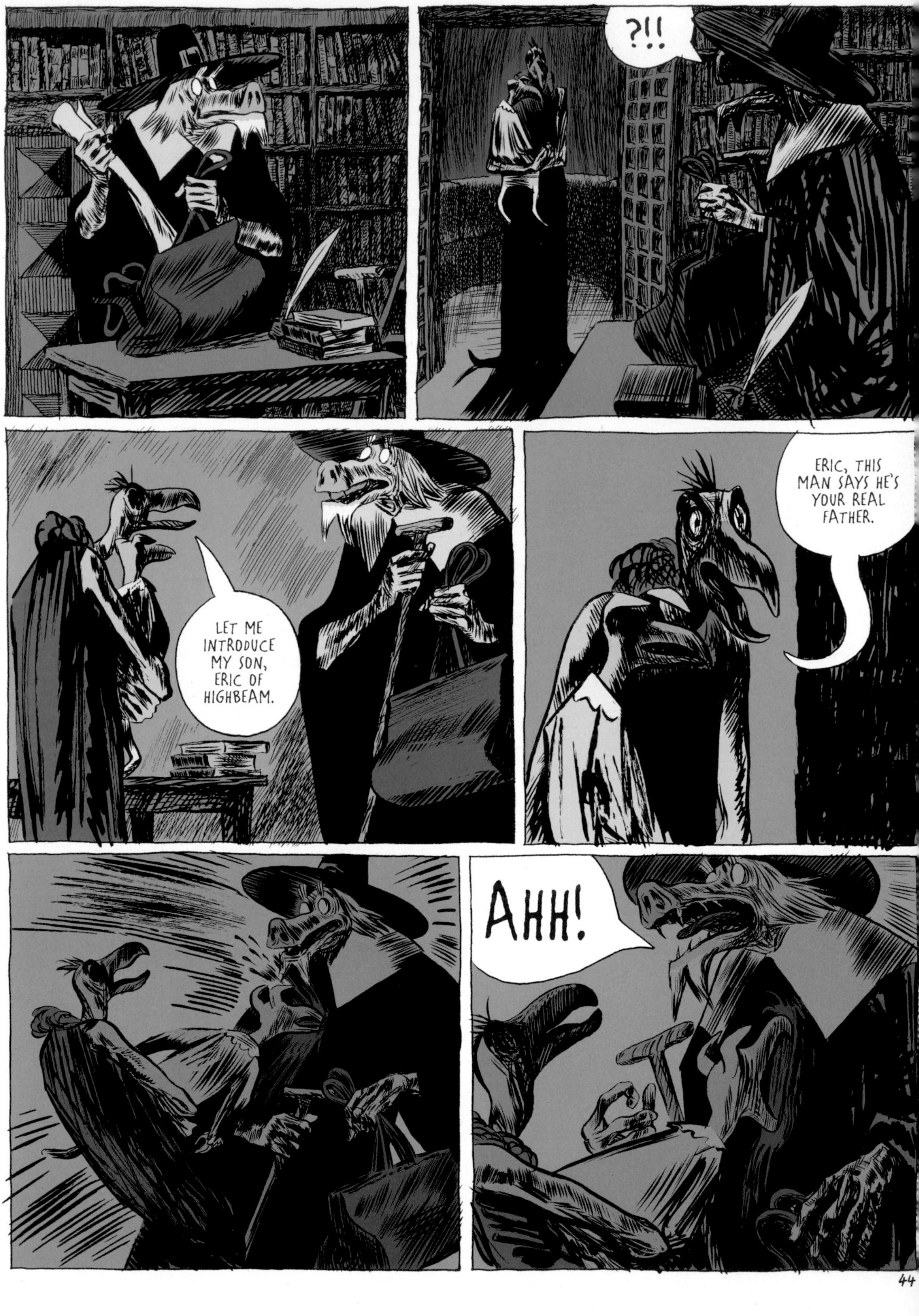
?!!
LET ME INTRODUCE MY SON, ERIC OF HIGHBEAM.
ERIC, THIS MAN SAYS HE'S YOUR REAL FATHER.
AHH!

AAAAAHHHHH!

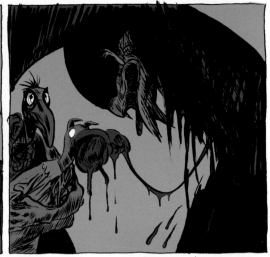

SLEEP, NOW.

SLEEP, MY BABY.

WAS THERE MUCH DAMAGE?

QUITE. WE INTERVENED A LITTLE TOO LATE. THIS MATTER IS BOUND TO GO PUBLIC.

THERE'LL BE A WITCH HUNT ON THE MAGICIANS.

IF I WERE ONE OF THEM, I'D LEAVE TOWN.

45

CASTLE CAVALLERE.

YOU'VE MADE UP YOUR MIND?

YES, SIR, I'M SORRY.

YOU KNOW, IF YOU AGREE TO REMAIN, YOUR SON COULD DO HIS STUDIES. I'D FINANCE EVERYTHING. I'M SURE HE CAN BECOME SOMEONE IMPORTANT.

YES, THERE'S LOTS TO GAIN IN THE CITY FOR AN INTELLIGENT BOY.

THANKS. BUT THE CITY ISN'T FOR US!

AND ALSO, MY SON IS TOO LITTLE FOR ALL THOSE TEMPTATIONS.

SOME OTHER TIME, PERHAPS?

YES, SIR.

GOODBYE, SIR.

Joann Sfar & CHRISTROPHE Blutch

SOLDIERS OF HONOR

Joann SfAR • Lewis TRONDHEIM
Art: BEZIAN
color: WALTER

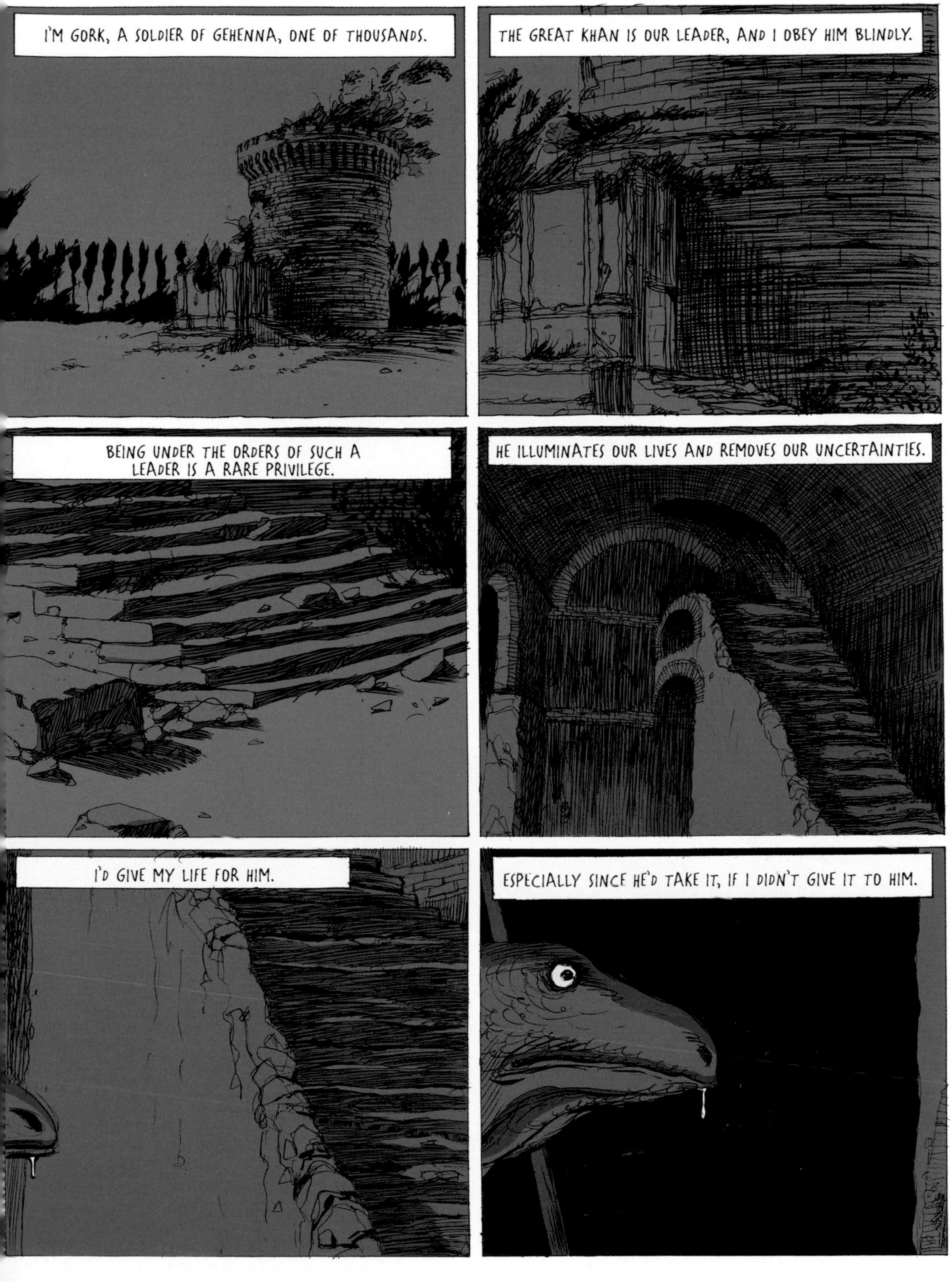
I'M GORK, A SOLDIER OF GEHENNA, ONE OF THOUSANDS.
THE GREAT KHAN IS OUR LEADER, AND I OBEY HIM BLINDLY.
BEING UNDER THE ORDERS OF SUCH A LEADER IS A RARE PRIVILEGE.
HE ILLUMINATES OUR LIVES AND REMOVES OUR UNCERTAINTIES.
I'D GIVE MY LIFE FOR HIM.
ESPECIALLY SINCE HE'D TAKE IT, IF I DIDN'T GIVE IT TO HIM.

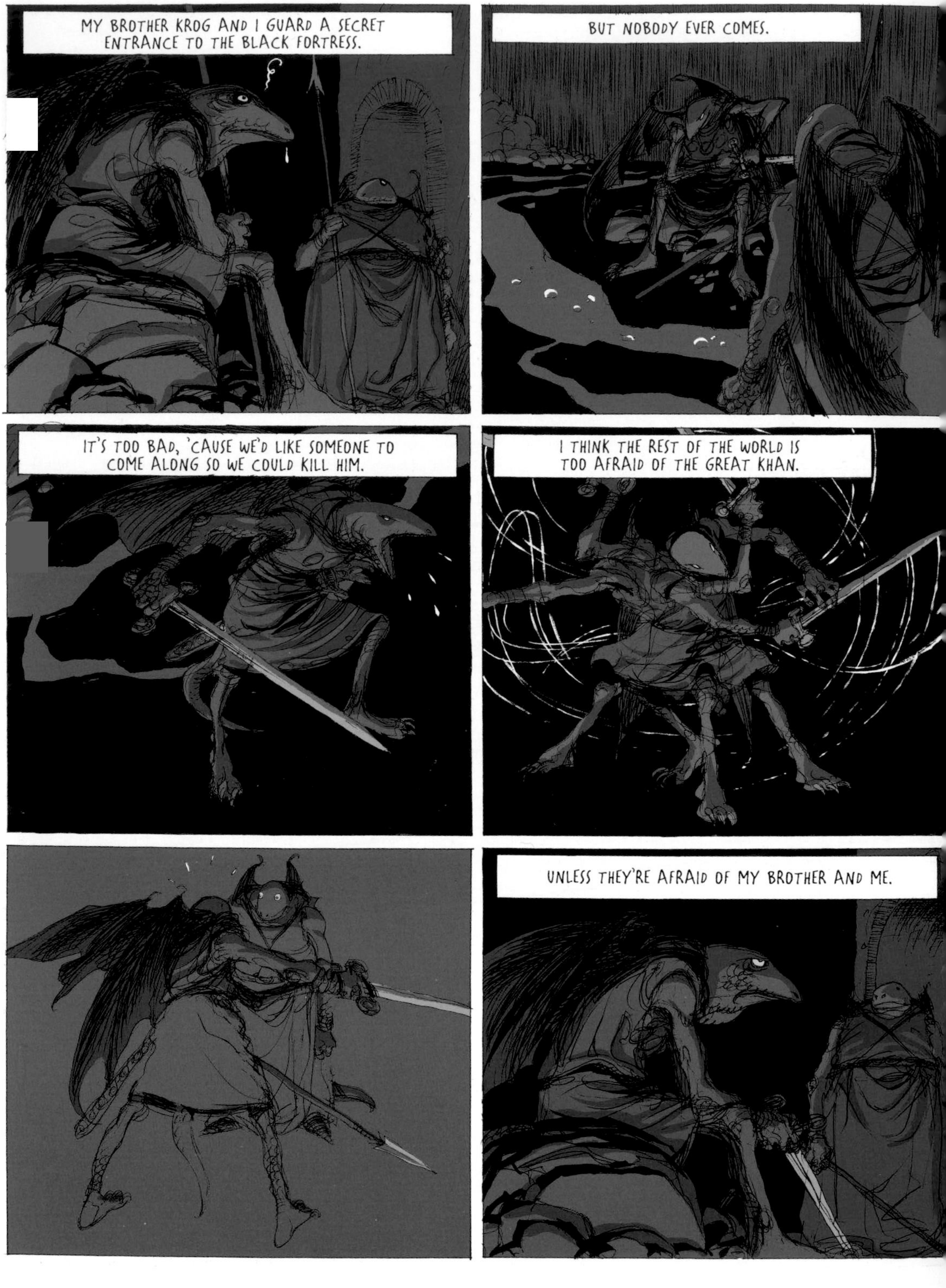
MY BROTHER KROG AND I GUARD A SECRET ENTRANCE TO THE BLACK FORTRESS.
BUT NOBODY EVER COMES.
IT'S TOO BAD, 'CAUSE WE'D LIKE SOMEONE TO COME ALONG SO WE COULD KILL HIM.
I THINK THE REST OF THE WORLD IS TOO AFRAID OF THE GREAT KHAN.
UNLESS THEY'RE AFRAID OF MY BROTHER AND ME.

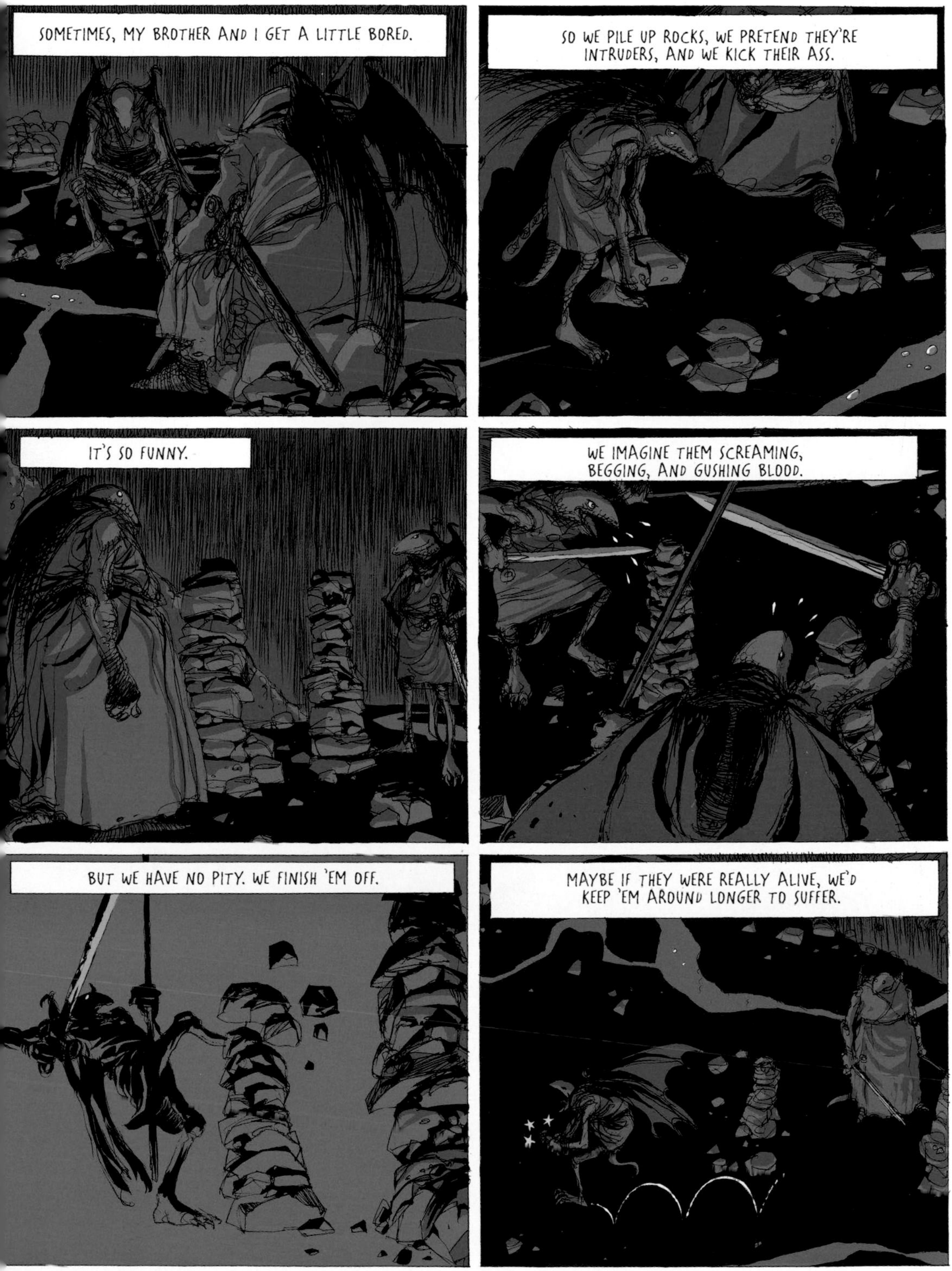
SOMETIMES, MY BROTHER AND I GET A LITTLE BORED.
SO WE PILE UP ROCKS, WE PRETEND THEY'RE INTRUDERS, AND WE KICK THEIR ASS.
IT'S SO FUNNY.
WE IMAGINE THEM SCREAMING, BEGGING, AND GUSHING BLOOD.
BUT WE HAVE NO PITY. WE FINISH 'EM OFF.
MAYBE IF THEY WERE REALLY ALIVE, WE'D KEEP 'EM AROUND LONGER TO SUFFER.

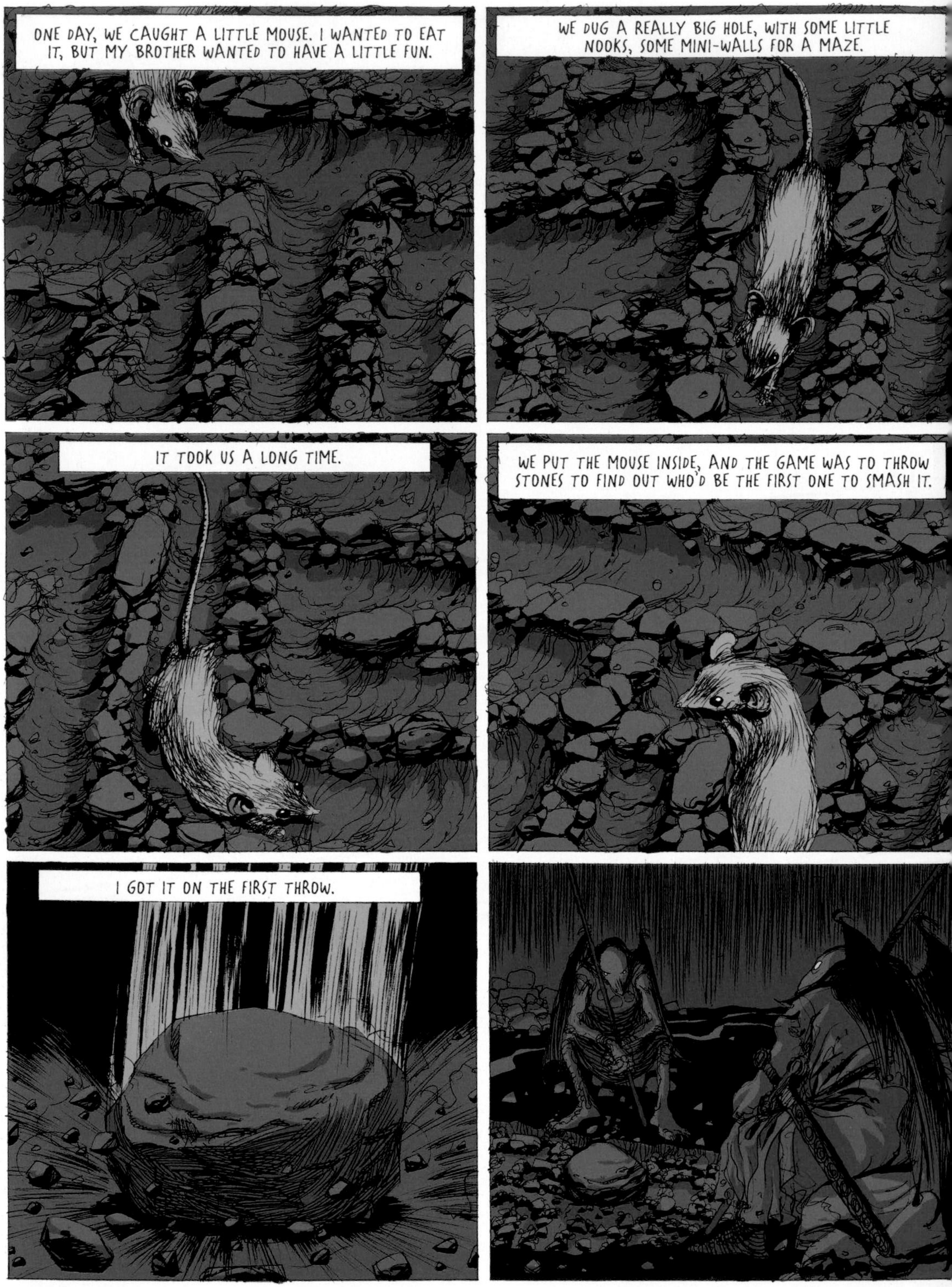
ONE DAY, WE CAUGHT A LITTLE MOUSE. I WANTED TO EAT IT, BUT MY BROTHER WANTED TO HAVE A LITTLE FUN.
WE DUG A REALLY BIG HOLE, WITH SOME LITTLE NOOKS, SOME MINI-WALLS FOR A MAZE.
IT TOOK US A LONG TIME.
WE PUT THE MOUSE INSIDE, AND THE GAME WAS TO THROW STONES TO FIND OUT WHO'D BE THE FIRST ONE TO SMASH IT.
I GOT IT ON THE FIRST THROW.

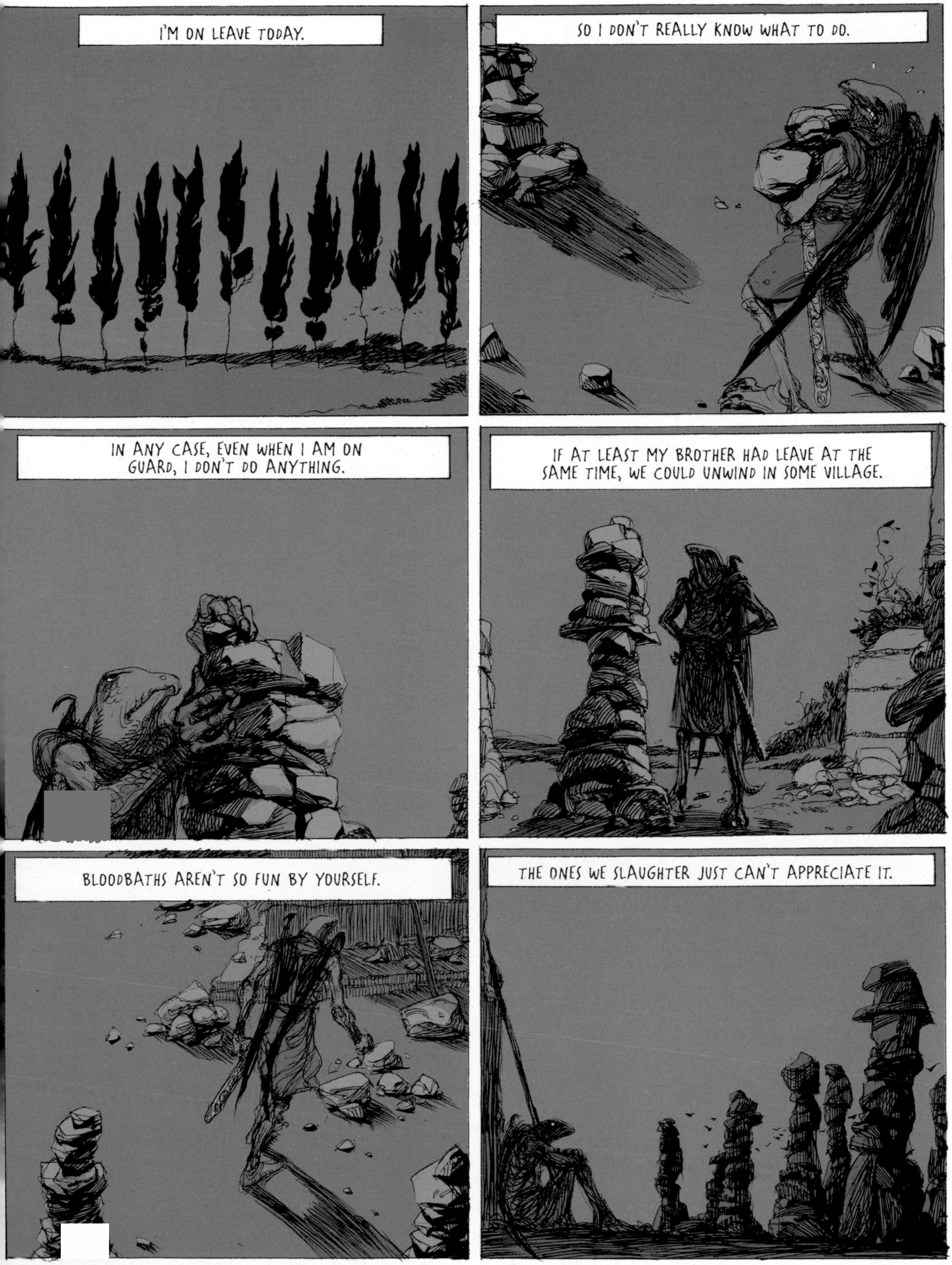
I'M ON LEAVE TODAY.
SO I DON'T REALLY KNOW WHAT TO DO.
IN ANY CASE, EVEN WHEN I AM ON GUARD, I DON'T DO ANYTHING.
IF AT LEAST MY BROTHER HAD LEAVE AT THE SAME TIME, WE COULD UNWIND IN SOME VILLAGE.
BLOODBATHS AREN'T SO FUN BY YOURSELF.
THE ONES WE SLAUGHTER JUST CAN'T APPRECIATE IT.

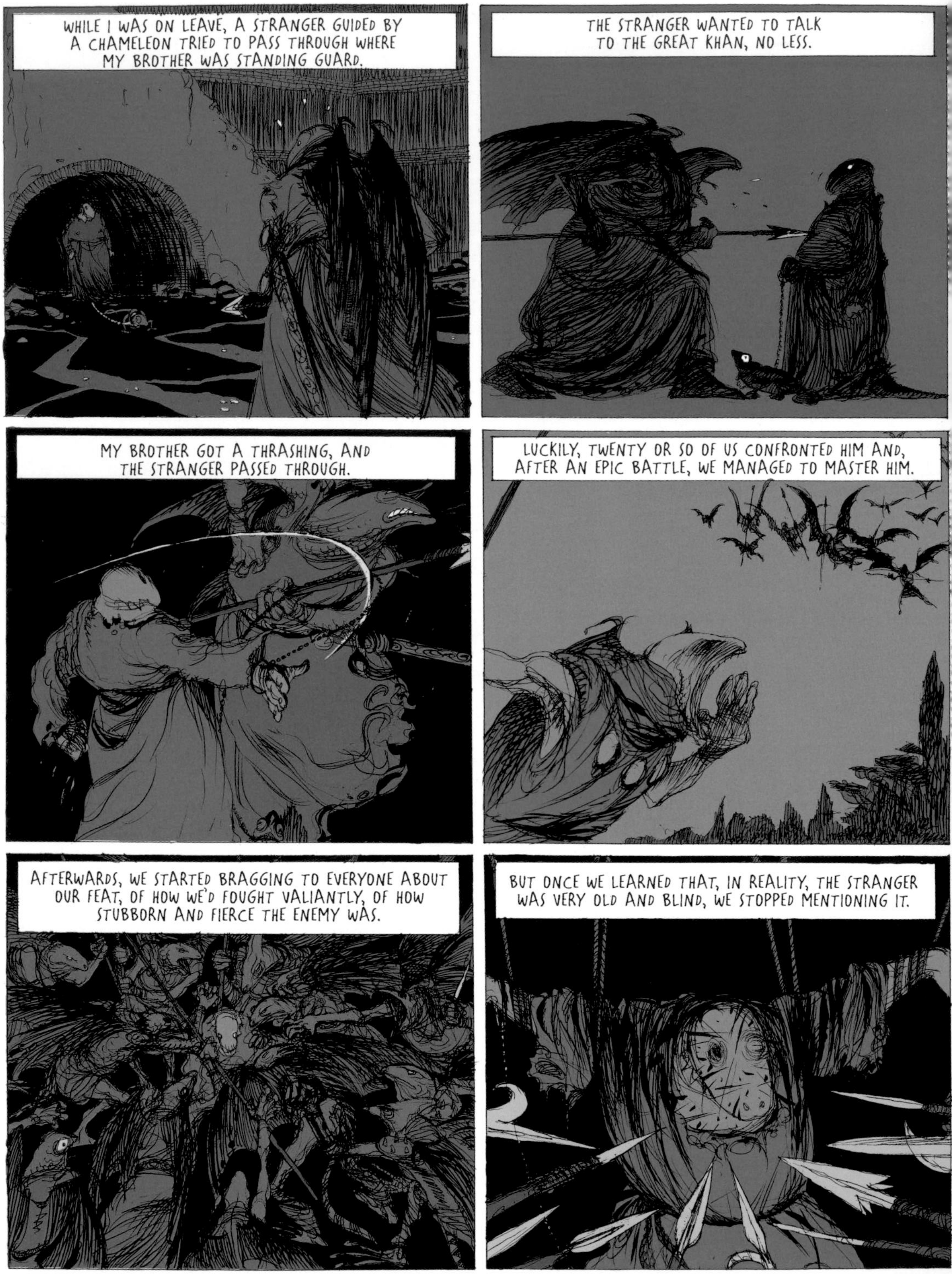
WHILE I WAS ON LEAVE, A STRANGER GUIDED BY A CHAMELEON TRIED TO PASS THROUGH WHERE MY BROTHER WAS STANDING GUARD.
THE STRANGER WANTED TO TALK TO THE GREAT KHAN, NO LESS.
MY BROTHER GOT A THRASHING, AND THE STRANGER PASSED THROUGH.
LUCKILY, TWENTY OR SO OF US CONFRONTED HIM AND, AFTER AN EPIC BATTLE, WE MANAGED TO MASTER HIM.
AFTERWARDS, WE STARTED BRAGGING TO EVERYONE ABOUT OUR FEAT, OF HOW WE'D FOUGHT VALIANTLY, OF HOW STUBBORN AND FIERCE THE ENEMY WAS.
BUT ONCE WE LEARNED THAT, IN REALITY, THE STRANGER WAS VERY OLD AND BLIND, WE STOPPED MENTIONING IT.

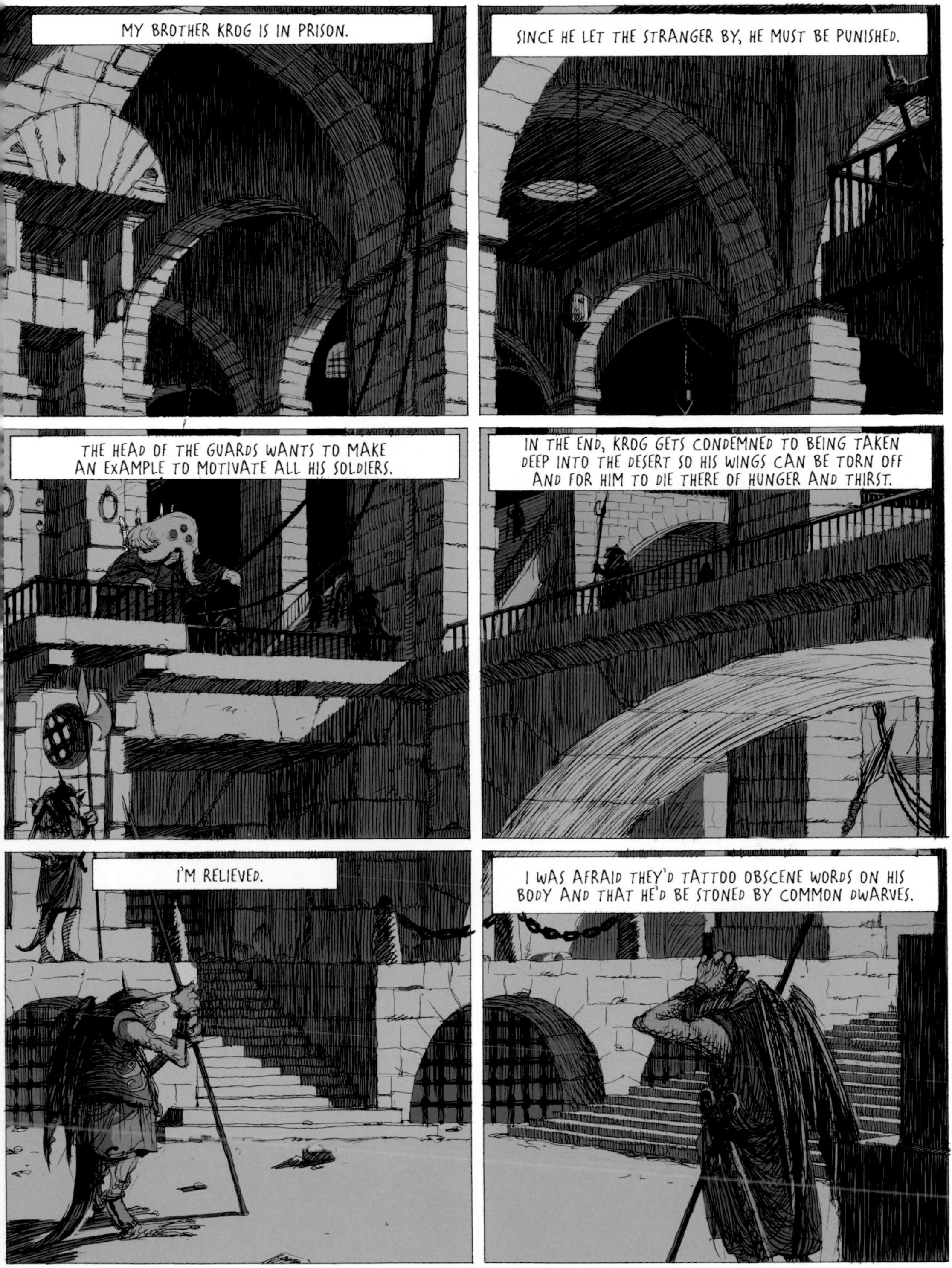

MY BROTHER KROG IS IN PRISON.
SINCE HE LET THE STRANGER BY, HE MUST BE PUNISHED.
THE HEAD OF THE GUARDS WANTS TO MAKE AN EXAMPLE TO MOTIVATE ALL HIS SOLDIERS.
IN THE END, KROG GETS CONDEMNED TO BEING TAKEN DEEP INTO THE DESERT SO HIS WINGS CAN BE TORN OFF AND FOR HIM TO DIE THERE OF HUNGER AND THIRST.
I'M RELIEVED.
I WAS AFRAID THEY'D TATTOO OBSCENE WORDS ON HIS BODY AND THAT HE'D BE STONED BY COMMON DWARVES.

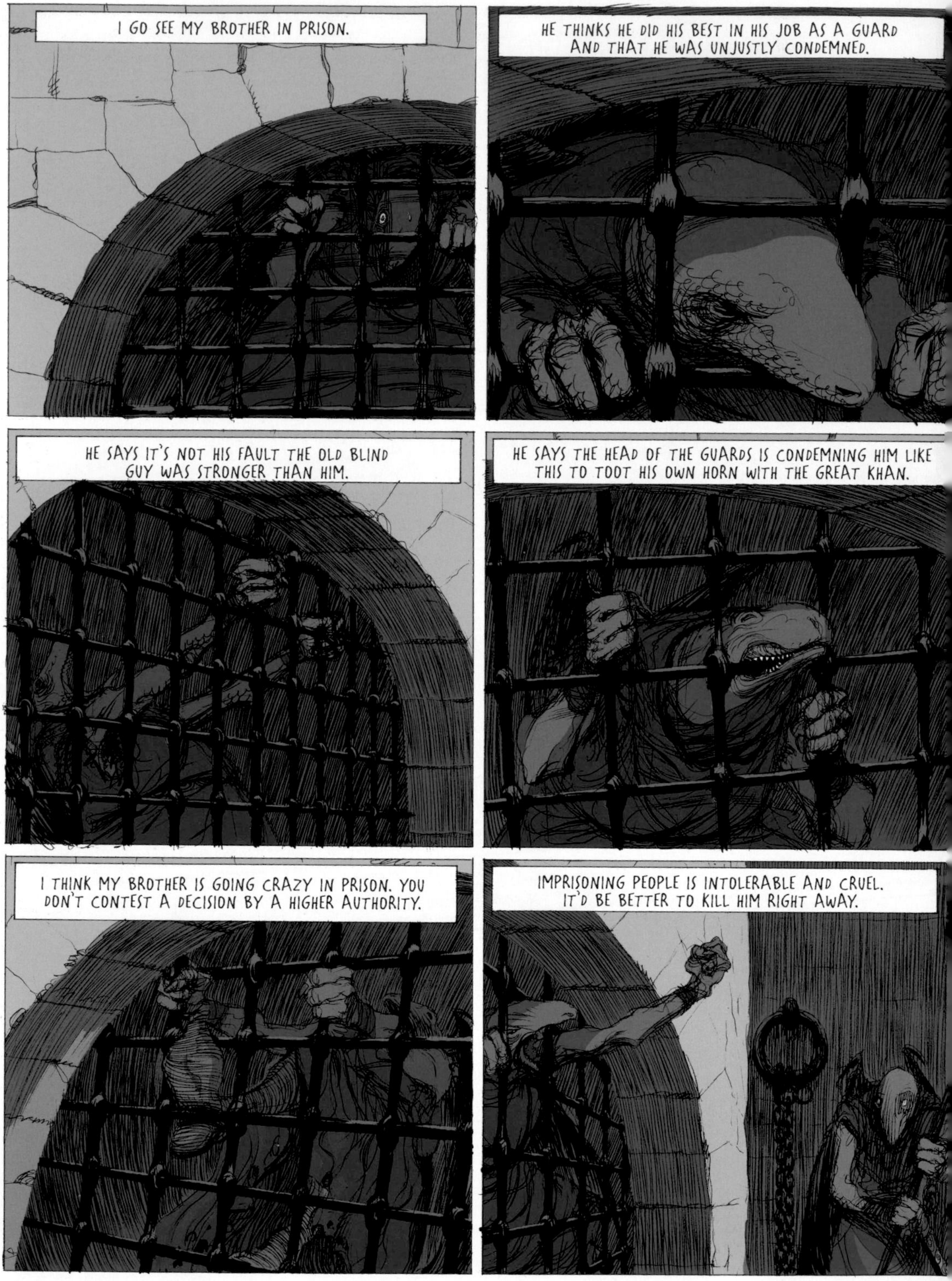
I GO SEE MY BROTHER IN PRISON.
HE THINKS HE DID HIS BEST IN HIS JOB AS A GUARD AND THAT HE WAS UNJUSTLY CONDEMNED.
HE SAYS IT'S NOT HIS FAULT THE OLD BLIND GUY WAS STRONGER THAN HIM.
HE SAYS THE HEAD OF THE GUARDS IS CONDEMNING HIM LIKE THIS TO TOOT HIS OWN HORN WITH THE GREAT KHAN.
I THINK MY BROTHER IS GOING CRAZY IN PRISON. YOU DON'T CONTEST A DECISION BY A HIGHER AUTHORITY.
IMPRISONING PEOPLE IS INTOLERABLE AND CRUEL. IT'D BE BETTER TO KILL HIM RIGHT AWAY.

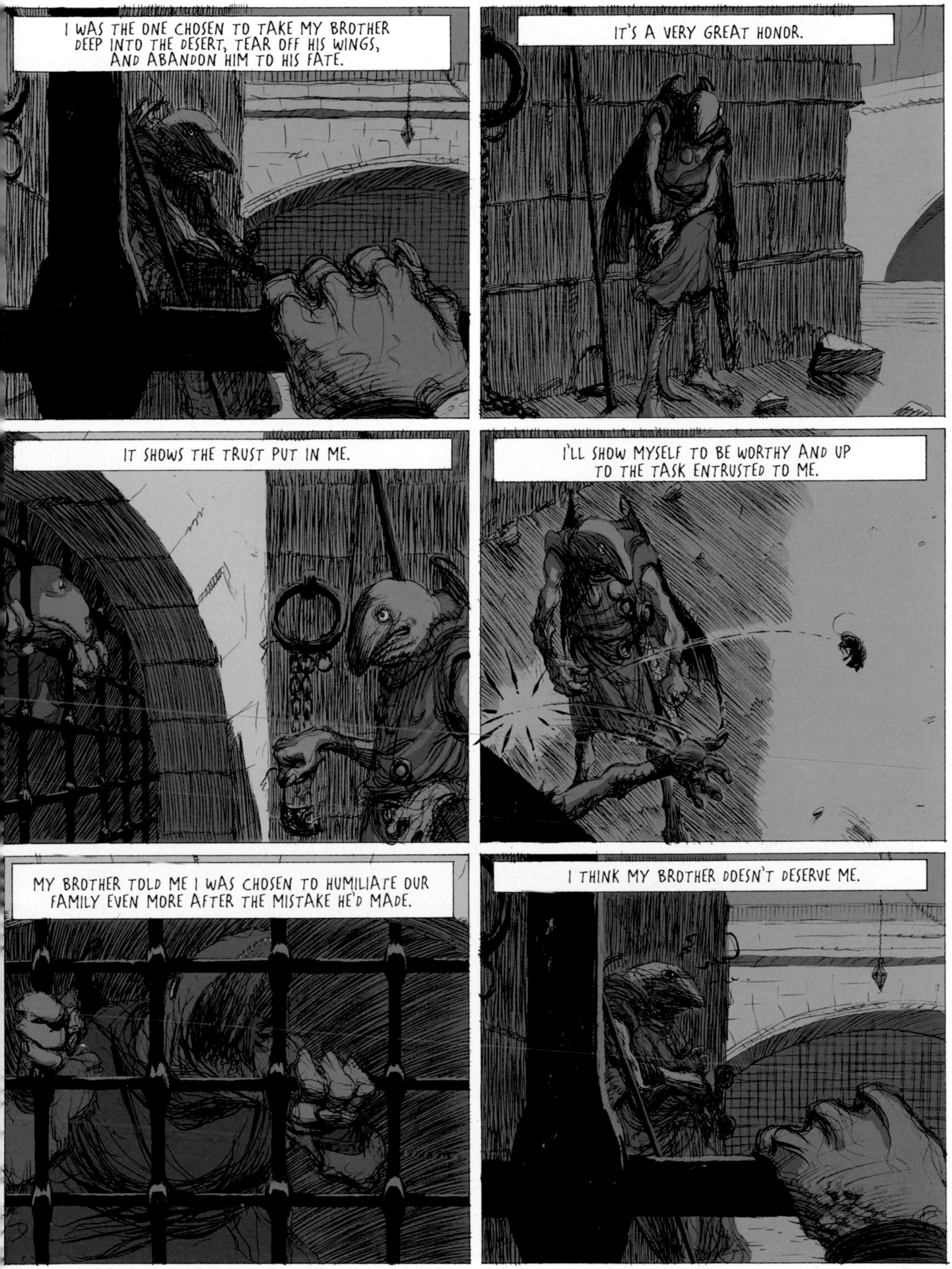
I WAS THE ONE CHOSEN TO TAKE MY BROTHER DEEP INTO THE DESERT, TEAR OFF HIS WINGS, AND ABANDON HIM TO HIS FATE.
IT'S A VERY GREAT HONOR.
IT SHOWS THE TRUST PUT IN ME.
I'LL SHOW MYSELF TO BE WORTHY AND UP TO THE TASK ENTRUSTED TO ME.
MY BROTHER TOLD ME I WAS CHOSEN TO HUMILIATE OUR FAMILY EVEN MORE AFTER THE MISTAKE HE'D MADE.
I THINK MY BROTHER DOESN'T DESERVE ME.

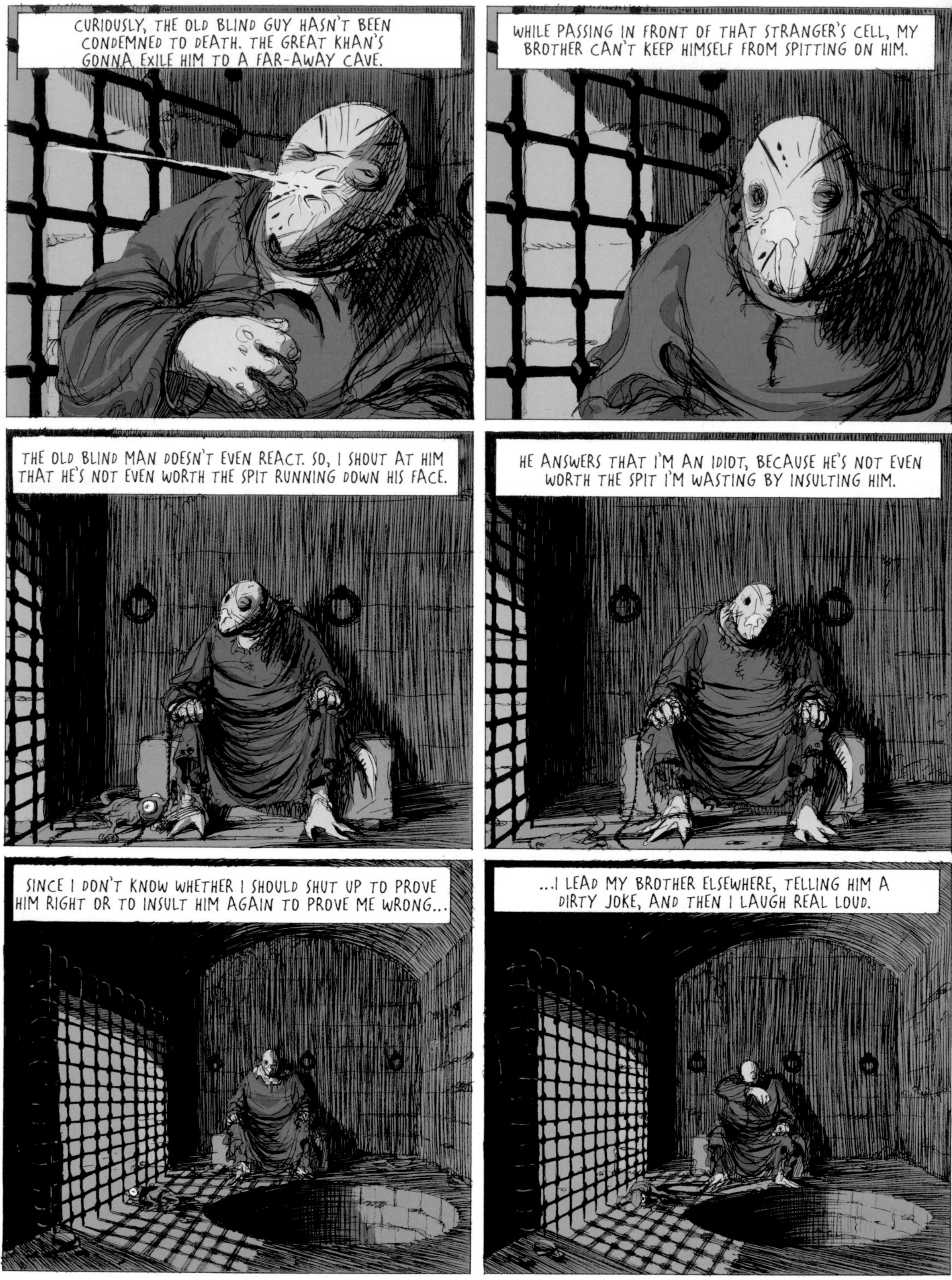
CURIOUSLY, THE OLD BLIND GUY HASN'T BEEN CONDEMNED TO DEATH. THE GREAT KHAN'S GONNA EXILE HIM TO A FAR-AWAY CAVE.
WHILE PASSING IN FRONT OF THAT STRANGER'S CELL, MY BROTHER CAN'T KEEP HIMSELF FROM SPITTING ON HIM.
THE OLD BLIND MAN DOESN'T EVEN REACT. SO, I SHOUT AT HIM THAT HE'S NOT EVEN WORTH THE SPIT RUNNING DOWN HIS FACE.
HE ANSWERS THAT I'M AN IDIOT, BECAUSE HE'S NOT EVEN WORTH THE SPIT I'M WASTING BY INSULTING HIM.
SINCE I DON'T KNOW WHETHER I SHOULD SHUT UP TO PROVE HIM RIGHT OR TO INSULT HIM AGAIN TO PROVE ME WRONG...
...I LEAD MY BROTHER ELSEWHERE, TELLING HIM A DIRTY JOKE, AND THEN I LAUGH REAL LOUD.

KROG AND I LEAVE THE FORTRESS AND HEAD
TOWARDS THE ZONE OF FULL SUNLIGHT.

ON THE WAY, MY BROTHER SUGGESTS A
STOPOVER AT ZEDOTAMAXIM.

HE WANTS TO BUY ME ONE LAST DRINK BEFORE
THE EXECUTION OF THE SENTENCE.

I WONDER IF SUCH A STOP IS REALLY LEGAL.

SO, I EXPLAIN TO HIM THAT, IF HE DRINKS TOO MUCH,
HE RISKS SUFFERING LONGER ONCE HE'S IN THE DESERT.

HE ANSWERS THAT A TRUE WARRIOR MUST
HAVE ENOUGH IN HIS BLADDER TO BE ABLE
TO PISS ON THE CORPSES OF HIS ENEMIES.

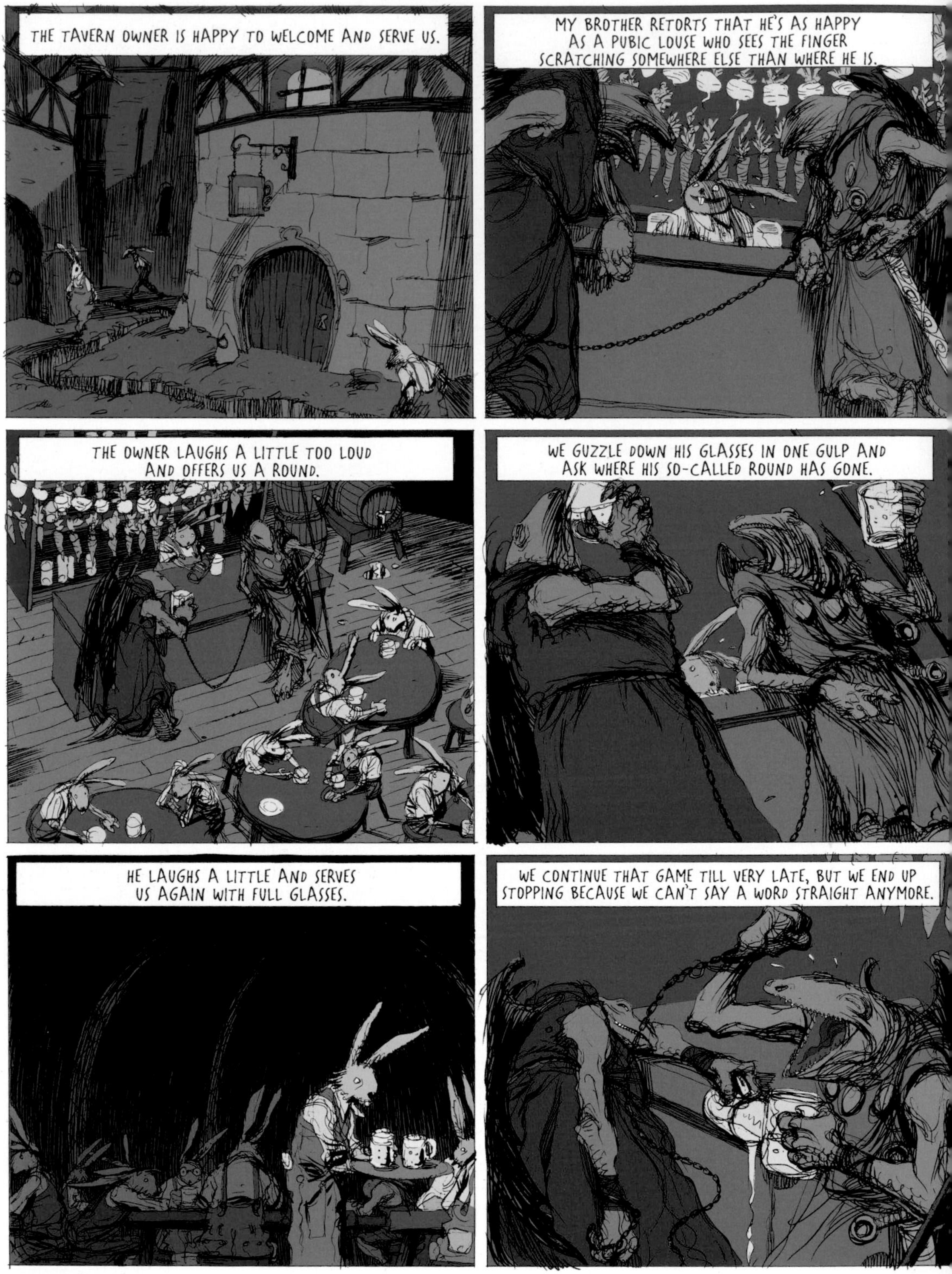
THE TAVERN OWNER IS HAPPY TO WELCOME AND SERVE US.
MY BROTHER RETORTS THAT HE'S AS HAPPY AS A PUBIC LOUSE WHO SEES THE FINGER SCRATCHING SOMEWHERE ELSE THAN WHERE HE IS.
THE OWNER LAUGHS A LITTLE TOO LOUD AND OFFERS US A ROUND.
WE GUZZLE DOWN HIS GLASSES IN ONE GULP AND ASK WHERE HIS SO-CALLED ROUND HAS GONE.
HE LAUGHS A LITTLE AND SERVES US AGAIN WITH FULL GLASSES.
WE CONTINUE THAT GAME TILL VERY LATE, BUT WE END UP STOPPING BECAUSE WE CAN'T SAY A WORD STRAIGHT ANYMORE.

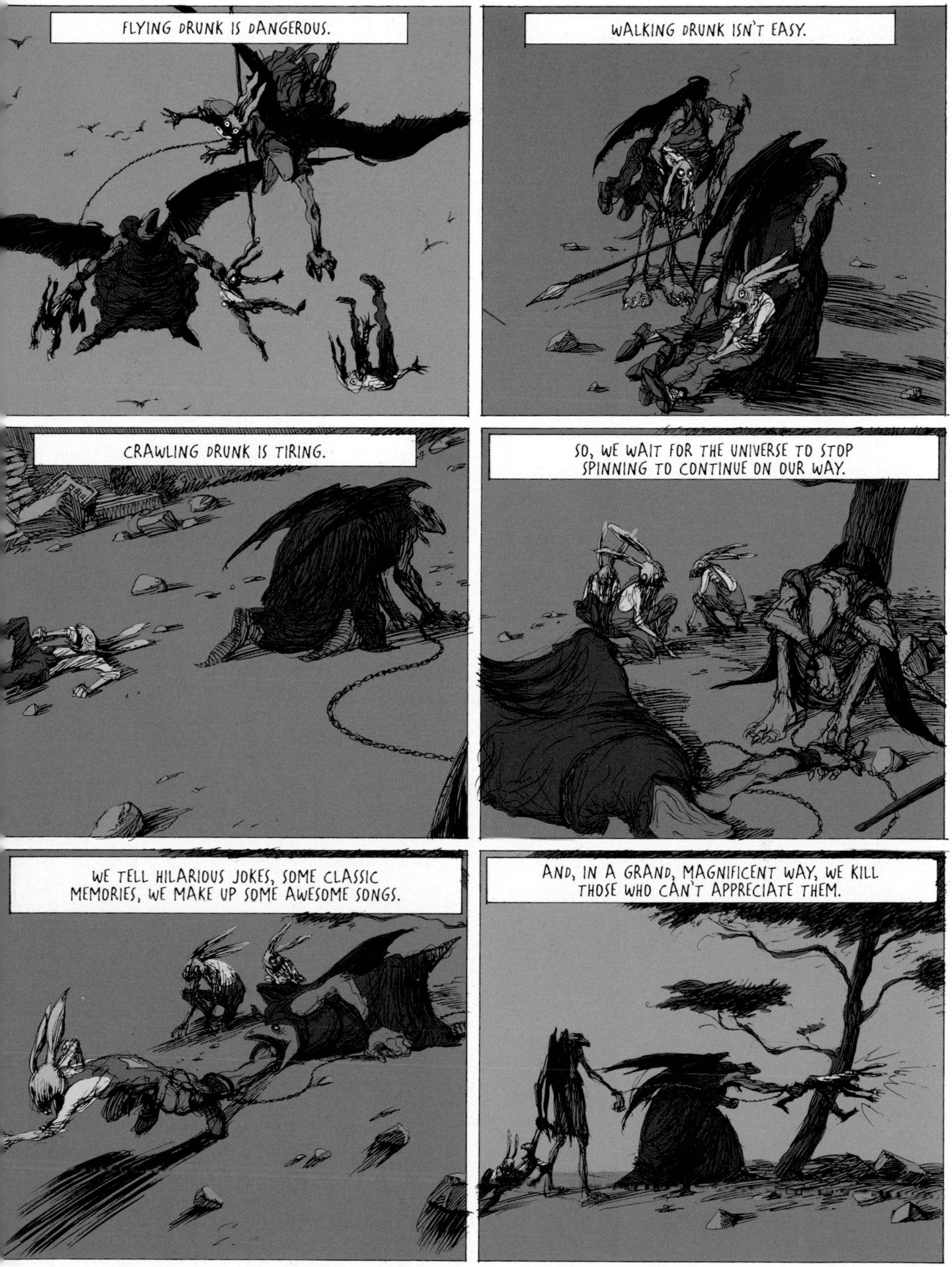
FLYING DRUNK IS DANGEROUS.
WALKING DRUNK ISN'T EASY.
CRAWLING DRUNK IS TIRING.
SO, WE WAIT FOR THE UNIVERSE TO STOP SPINNING TO CONTINUE ON OUR WAY.
WE TELL HILARIOUS JOKES, SOME CLASSIC MEMORIES, WE MAKE UP SOME AWESOME SONGS.
AND, IN A GRAND, MAGNIFICENT WAY, WE KILL THOSE WHO CAN'T APPRECIATE THEM.

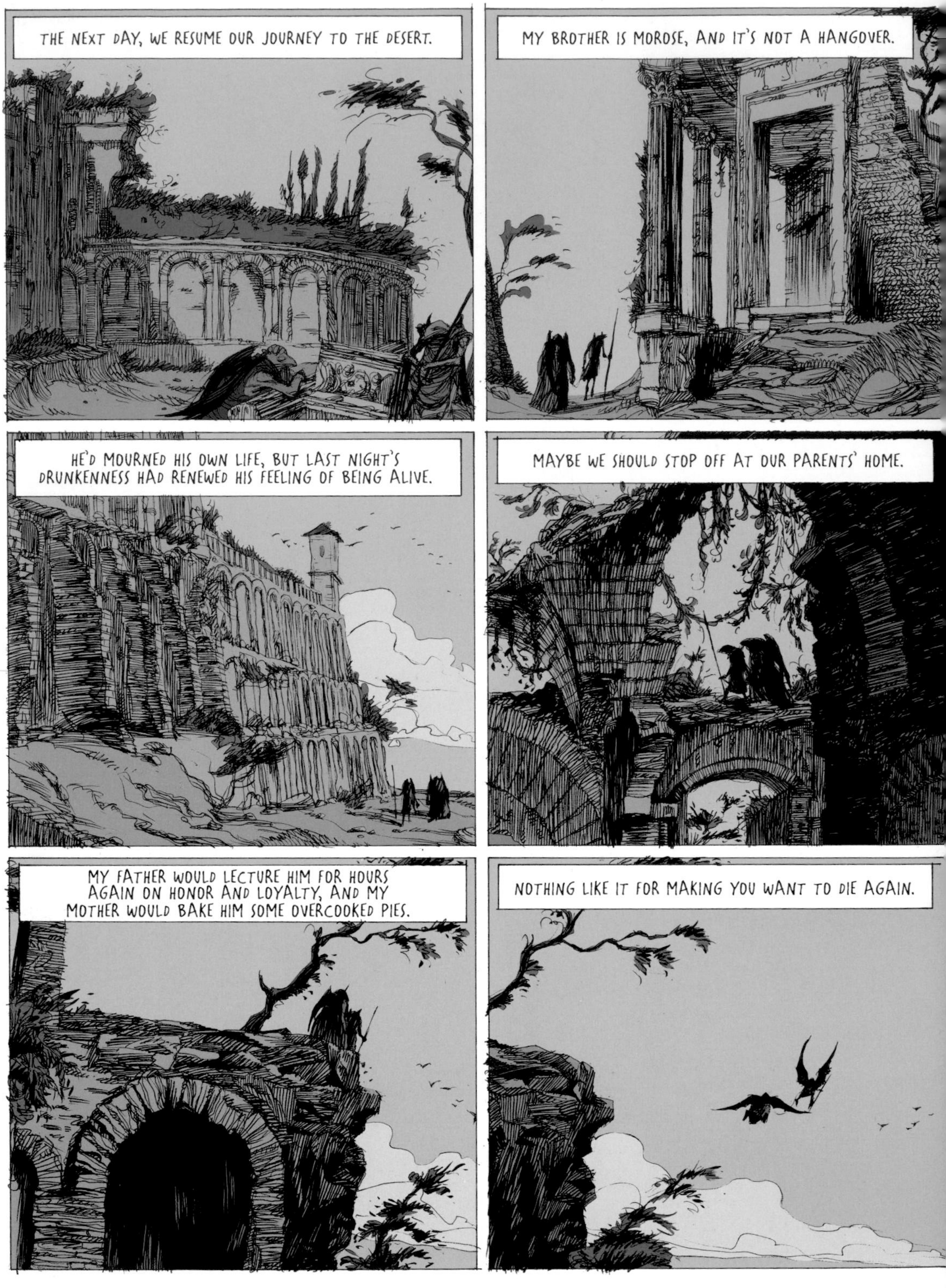
THE NEXT DAY, WE RESUME OUR JOURNEY TO THE DESERT.
MY BROTHER IS MOROSE, AND IT'S NOT A HANGOVER.
HE'D MOURNED HIS OWN LIFE, BUT LAST NIGHT'S DRUNKENNESS HAD RENEWED HIS FEELING OF BEING ALIVE.
MAYBE WE SHOULD STOP OFF AT OUR PARENTS' HOME.
MY FATHER WOULD LECTURE HIM FOR HOURS AGAIN ON HONOR AND LOYALTY, AND MY MOTHER WOULD BAKE HIM SOME OVERCOOKED PIES.
NOTHING LIKE IT FOR MAKING YOU WANT TO DIE AGAIN.

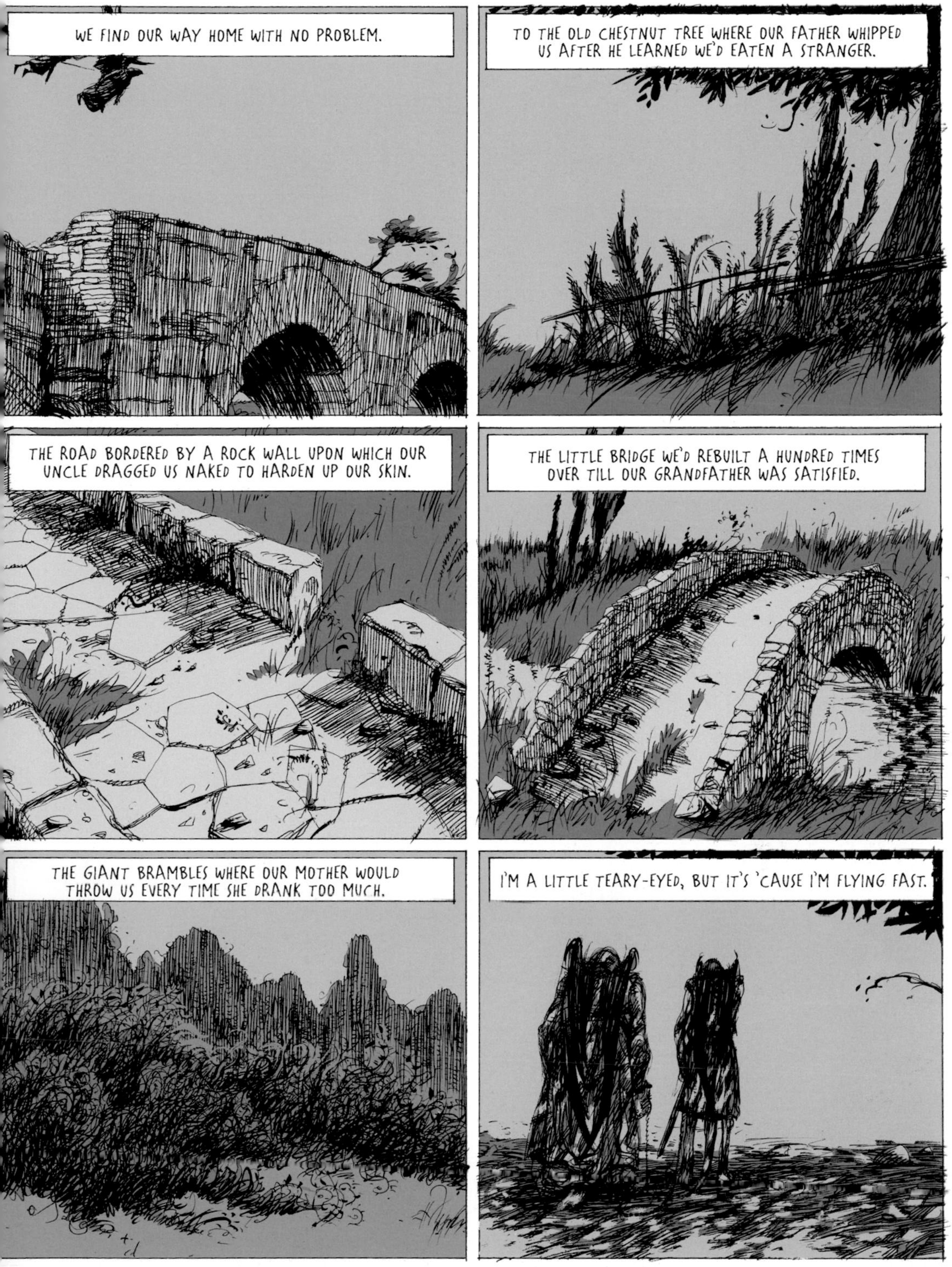
WE FIND OUR WAY HOME WITH NO PROBLEM.
TO THE OLD CHESTNUT TREE WHERE OUR FATHER WHIPPED US AFTER HE LEARNED WE'D EATEN A STRANGER.
THE ROAD BORDERED BY A ROCK WALL UPON WHICH OUR UNCLE DRAGGED US NAKED TO HARDEN UP OUR SKIN.
THE LITTLE BRIDGE WE'D REBUILT A HUNDRED TIMES OVER TILL OUR GRANDFATHER WAS SATISFIED.
THE GIANT BRAMBLES WHERE OUR MOTHER WOULD THROW US EVERY TIME SHE DRANK TOO MUCH.
I'M A LITTLE TEARY-EYED, BUT IT'S 'CAUSE I'M FLYING FAST.

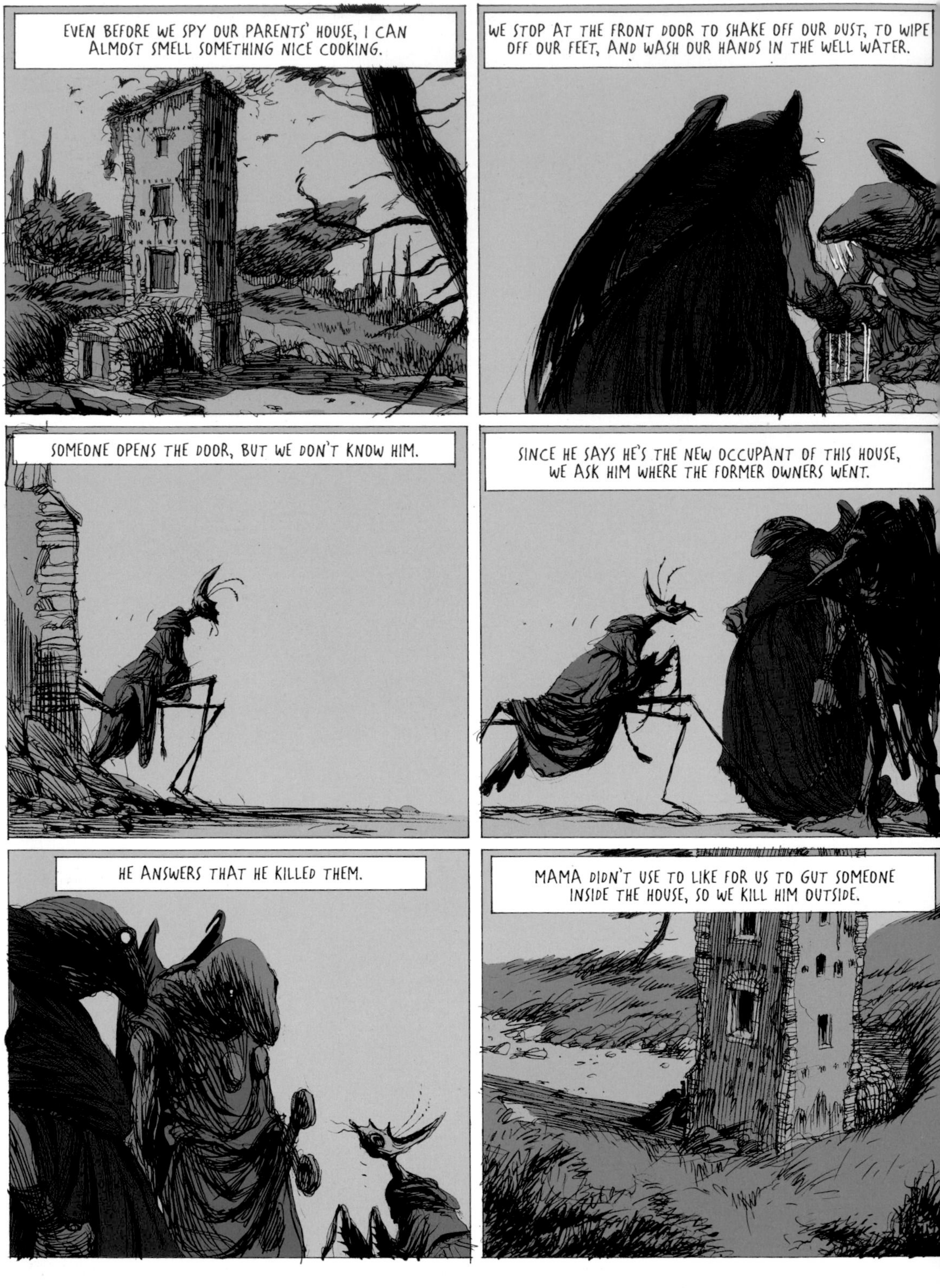
EVEN BEFORE WE SPY OUR PARENTS' HOUSE, I CAN ALMOST SMELL SOMETHING NICE COOKING.
WE STOP AT THE FRONT DOOR TO SHAKE OFF OUR DUST, TO WIPE OFF OUR FEET, AND WASH OUR HANDS IN THE WELL WATER.
SOMEONE OPENS THE DOOR, BUT WE DON'T KNOW HIM.
SINCE HE SAYS HE'S THE NEW OCCUPANT OF THIS HOUSE, WE ASK HIM WHERE THE FORMER OWNERS WENT.
HE ANSWERS THAT HE KILLED THEM.
MAMA DIDN'T USE TO LIKE FOR US TO GUT SOMEONE INSIDE THE HOUSE, SO WE KILL HIM OUTSIDE.

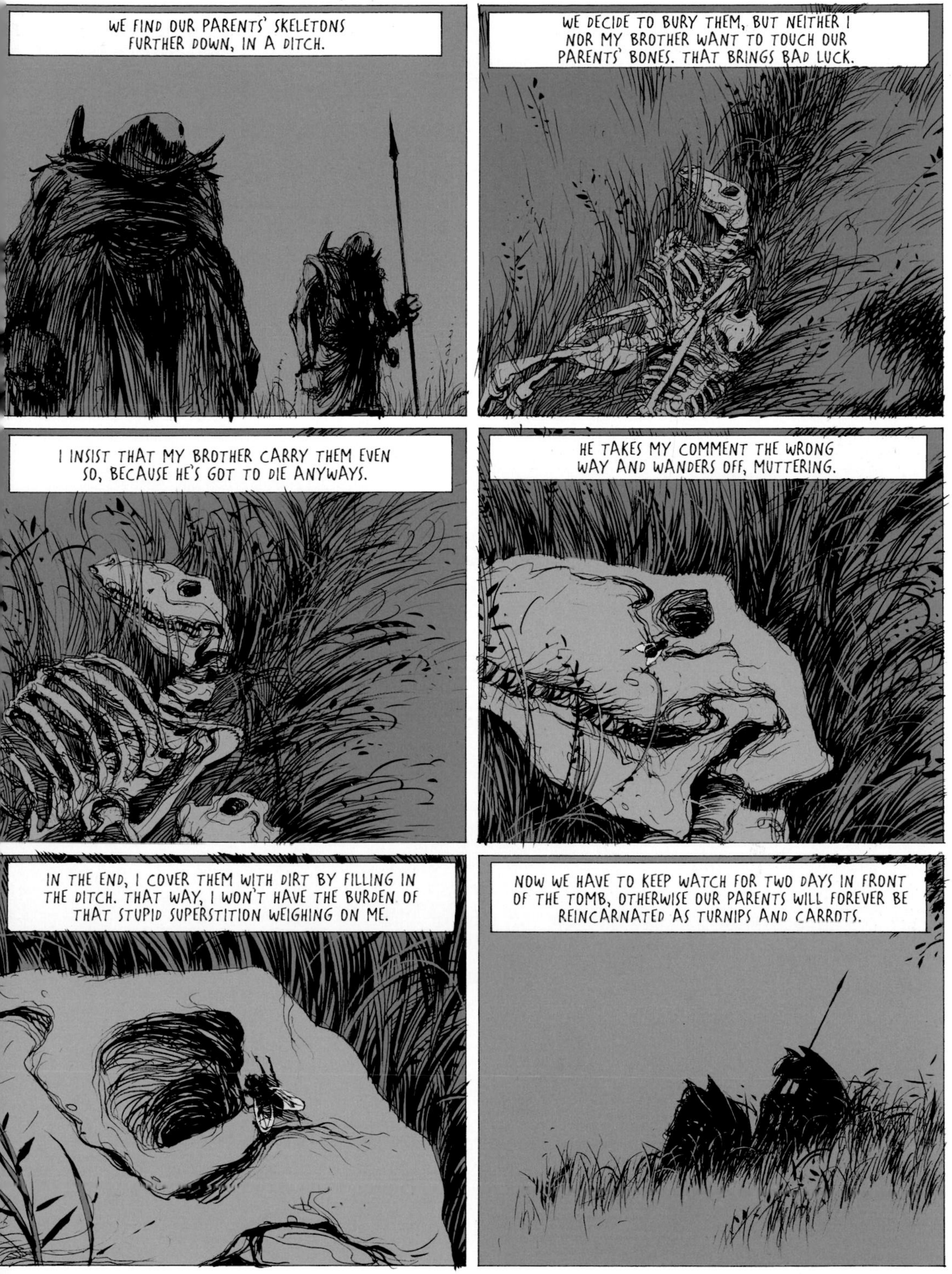
WE FIND OUR PARENTS' SKELETONS FURTHER DOWN, IN A DITCH.
WE DECIDE TO BURY THEM, BUT NEITHER I NOR MY BROTHER WANT TO TOUCH OUR PARENTS' BONES. THAT BRINGS BAD LUCK.
I INSIST THAT MY BROTHER CARRY THEM EVEN SO, BECAUSE HE'S GOT TO DIE ANYWAYS.
HE TAKES MY COMMENT THE WRONG WAY AND WANDERS OFF, MUTTERING.
IN THE END, I COVER THEM WITH DIRT BY FILLING IN THE DITCH. THAT WAY, I WON'T HAVE THE BURDEN OF THAT STUPID SUPERSTITION WEIGHING ON ME.
NOW WE HAVE TO KEEP WATCH FOR TWO DAYS IN FRONT OF THE TOMB, OTHERWISE OUR PARENTS WILL FOREVER BE REINCARNATED AS TURNIPS AND CARROTS.

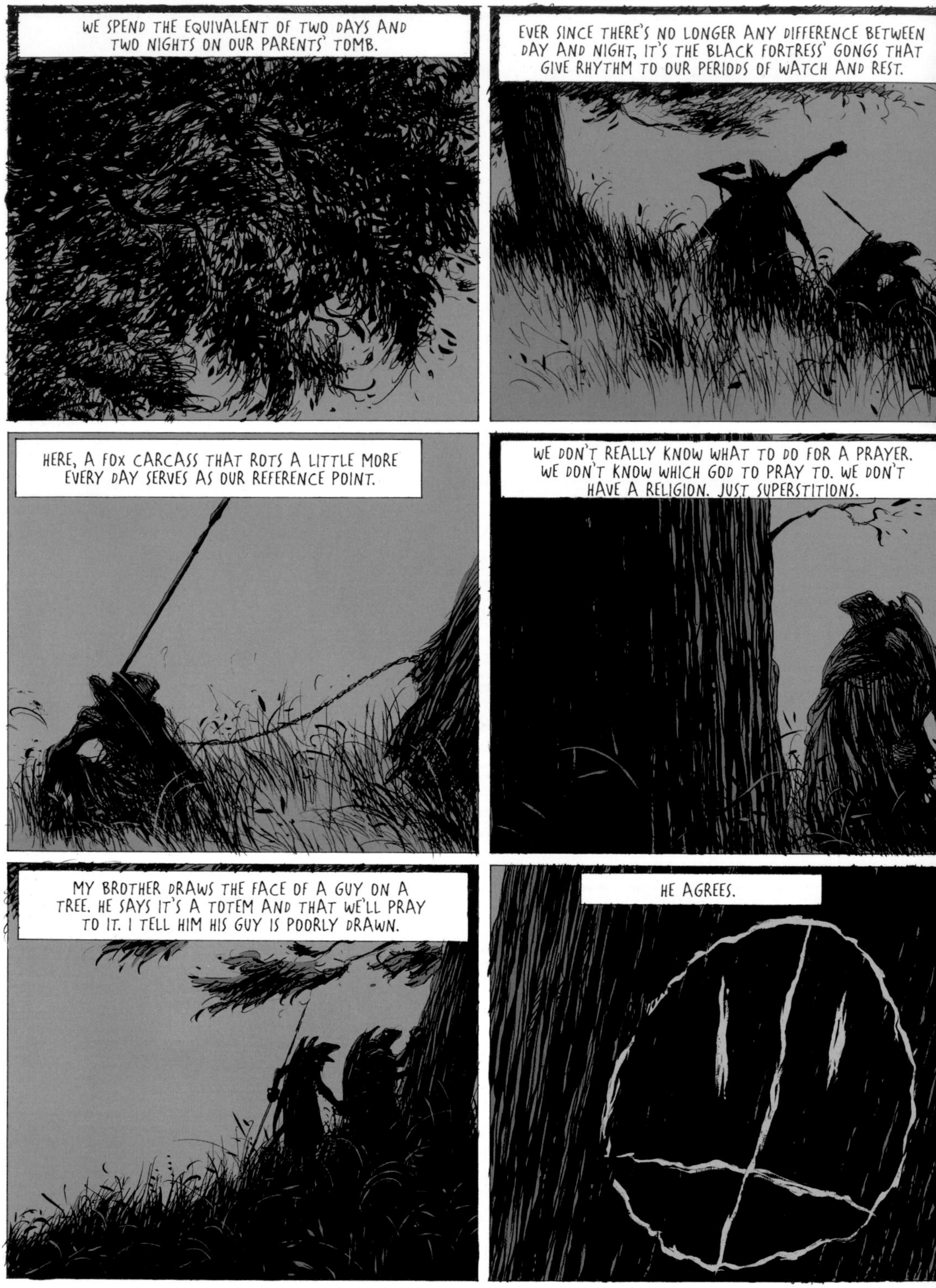
WE SPEND THE EQUIVALENT OF TWO DAYS AND TWO NIGHTS ON OUR PARENTS' TOMB.
EVER SINCE THERE'S NO LONGER ANY DIFFERENCE BETWEEN DAY AND NIGHT, IT'S THE BLACK FORTRESS' GONGS THAT GIVE RHYTHM TO OUR PERIODS OF WATCH AND REST.
HERE, A FOX CARCASS THAT ROTS A LITTLE MORE EVERY DAY SERVES AS OUR REFERENCE POINT.
WE DON'T REALLY KNOW WHAT TO DO FOR A PRAYER. WE DON'T KNOW WHICH GOD TO PRAY TO. WE DON'T HAVE A RELIGION. JUST SUPERSTITIONS.
MY BROTHER DRAWS THE FACE OF A GUY ON A TREE. HE SAYS IT'S A TOTEM AND THAT WE'LL PRAY TO IT. I TELL HIM HIS GUY IS POORLY DRAWN.
HE AGREES.

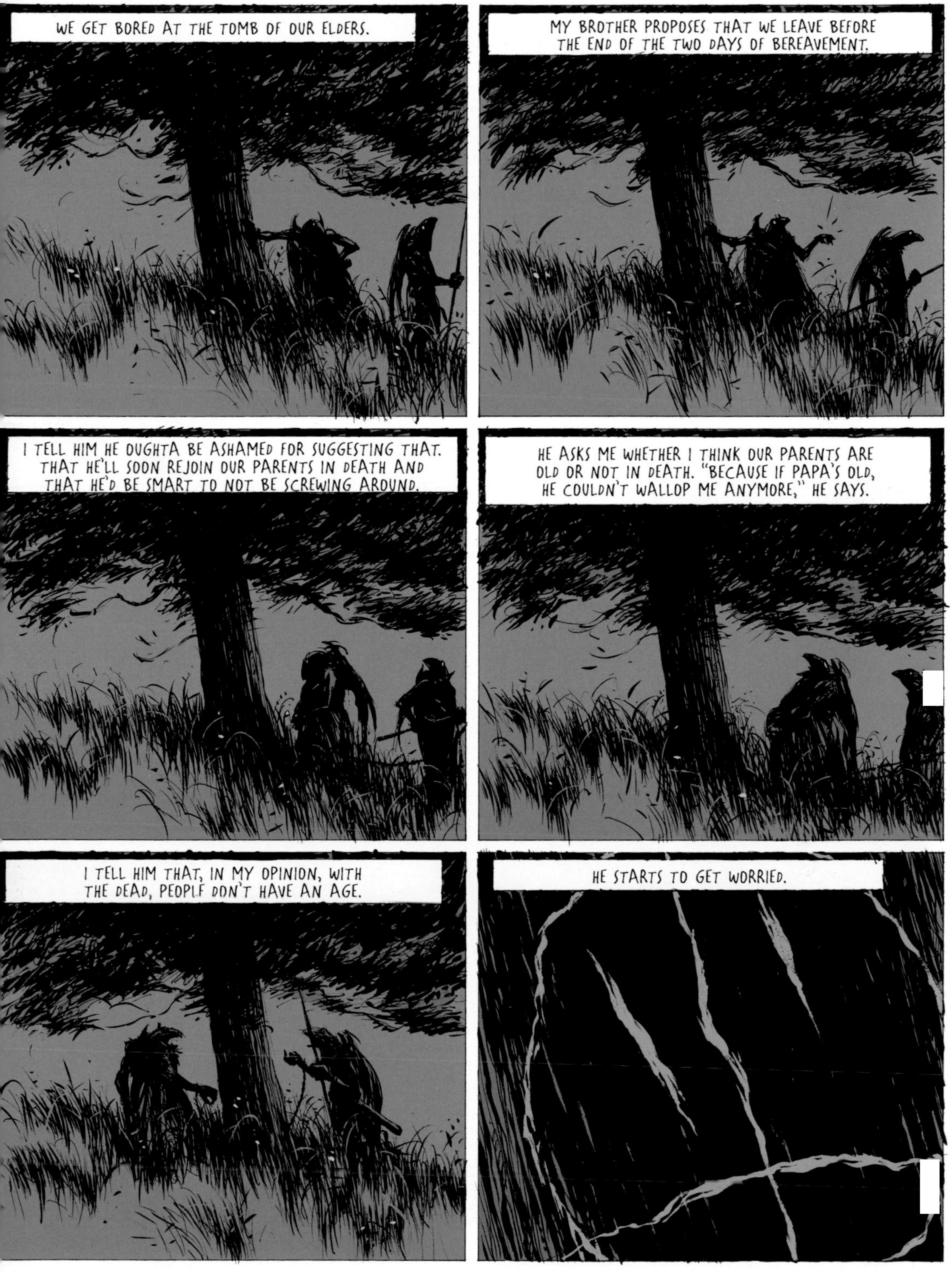
WE GET BORED AT THE TOMB OF OUR ELDERS.
MY BROTHER PROPOSES THAT WE LEAVE BEFORE THE END OF THE TWO DAYS OF BEREAVEMENT.
I TELL HIM HE OUGHTA BE ASHAMED FOR SUGGESTING THAT. THAT HE'LL SOON REJOIN OUR PARENTS IN DEATH AND THAT HE'D BE SMART TO NOT BE SCREWING AROUND.
HE ASKS ME WHETHER I THINK OUR PARENTS ARE OLD OR NOT IN DEATH. "BECAUSE IF PAPA'S OLD, HE COULDN'T WALLOP ME ANYMORE," HE SAYS.
I TELL HIM THAT, IN MY OPINION, WITH THE DEAD, PEOPLE DON'T HAVE AN AGE.
HE STARTS TO GET WORRIED.

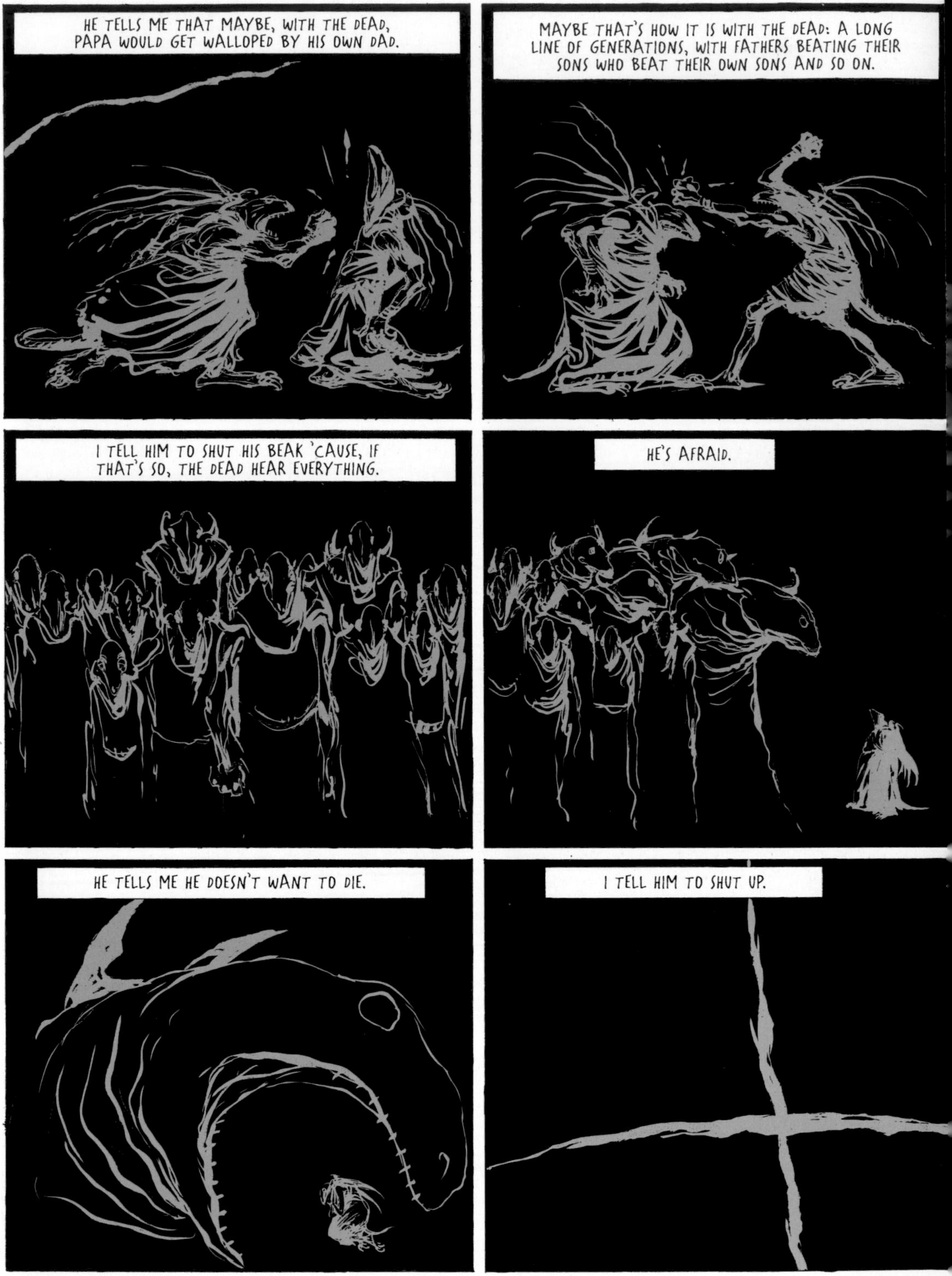
HE TELLS ME THAT MAYBE, WITH THE DEAD, PAPA WOULD GET WALLOPED BY HIS OWN DAD.
MAYBE THAT'S HOW IT IS WITH THE DEAD: A LONG LINE OF GENERATIONS, WITH FATHERS BEATING THEIR SONS WHO BEAT THEIR OWN SONS AND SO ON.
I TELL HIM TO SHUT HIS BEAK 'CAUSE, IF THAT'S SO, THE DEAD HEAR EVERYTHING.
HE'S AFRAID.
HE TELLS ME HE DOESN'T WANT TO DIE.
I TELL HIM TO SHUT UP.

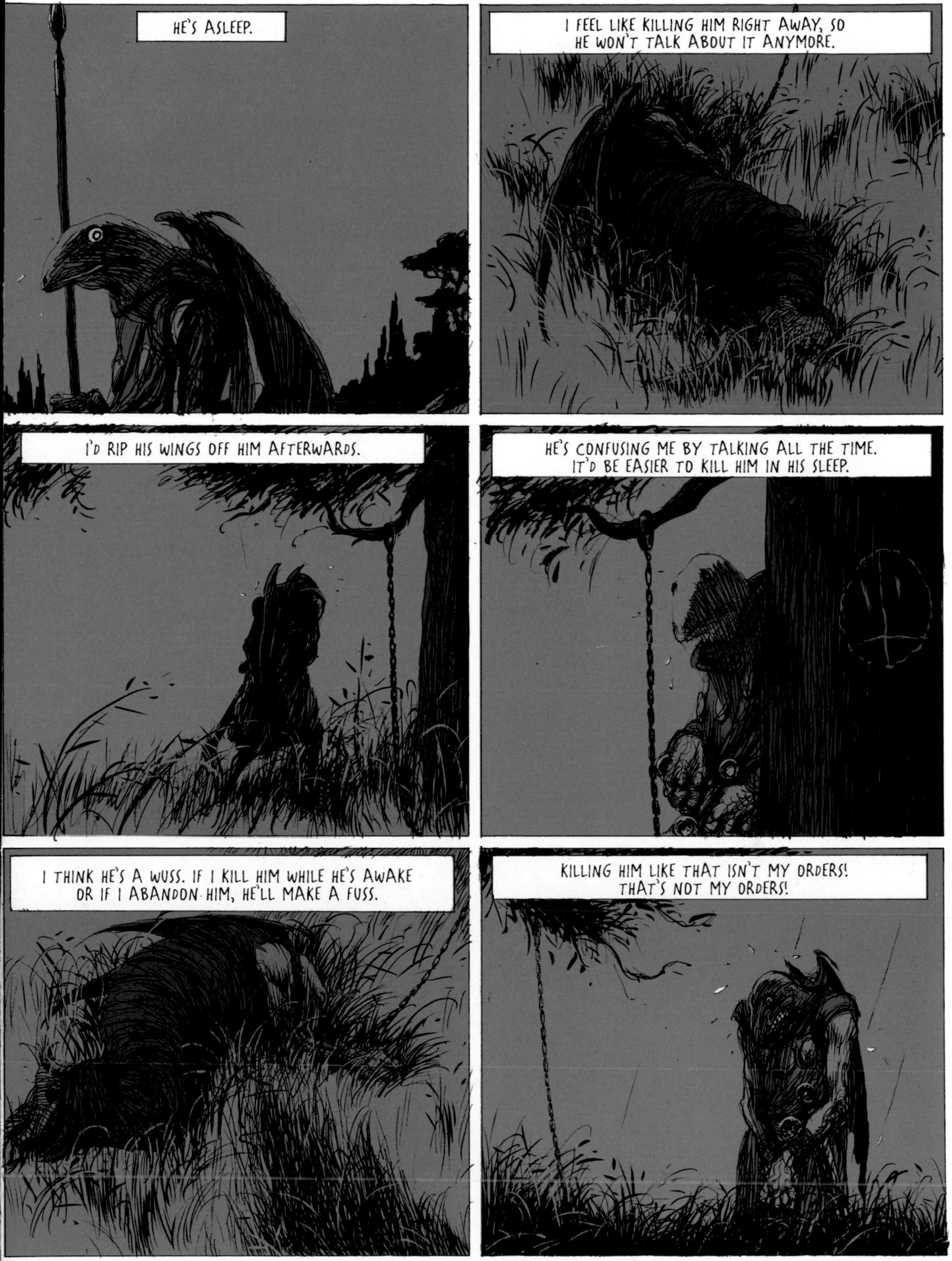
HE'S ASLEEP.
I FEEL LIKE KILLING HIM RIGHT AWAY, SO HE WON'T TALK ABOUT IT ANYMORE.
I'D RIP HIS WINGS OFF HIM AFTERWARDS.
HE'S CONFUSING ME BY TALKING ALL THE TIME. IT'D BE EASIER TO KILL HIM IN HIS SLEEP.
I THINK HE'S A WUSS. IF I KILL HIM WHILE HE'S AWAKE OR IF I ABANDON HIM, HE'LL MAKE A FUSS.
KILLING HIM LIKE THAT ISN'T MY ORDERS! THAT'S NOT MY ORDERS!

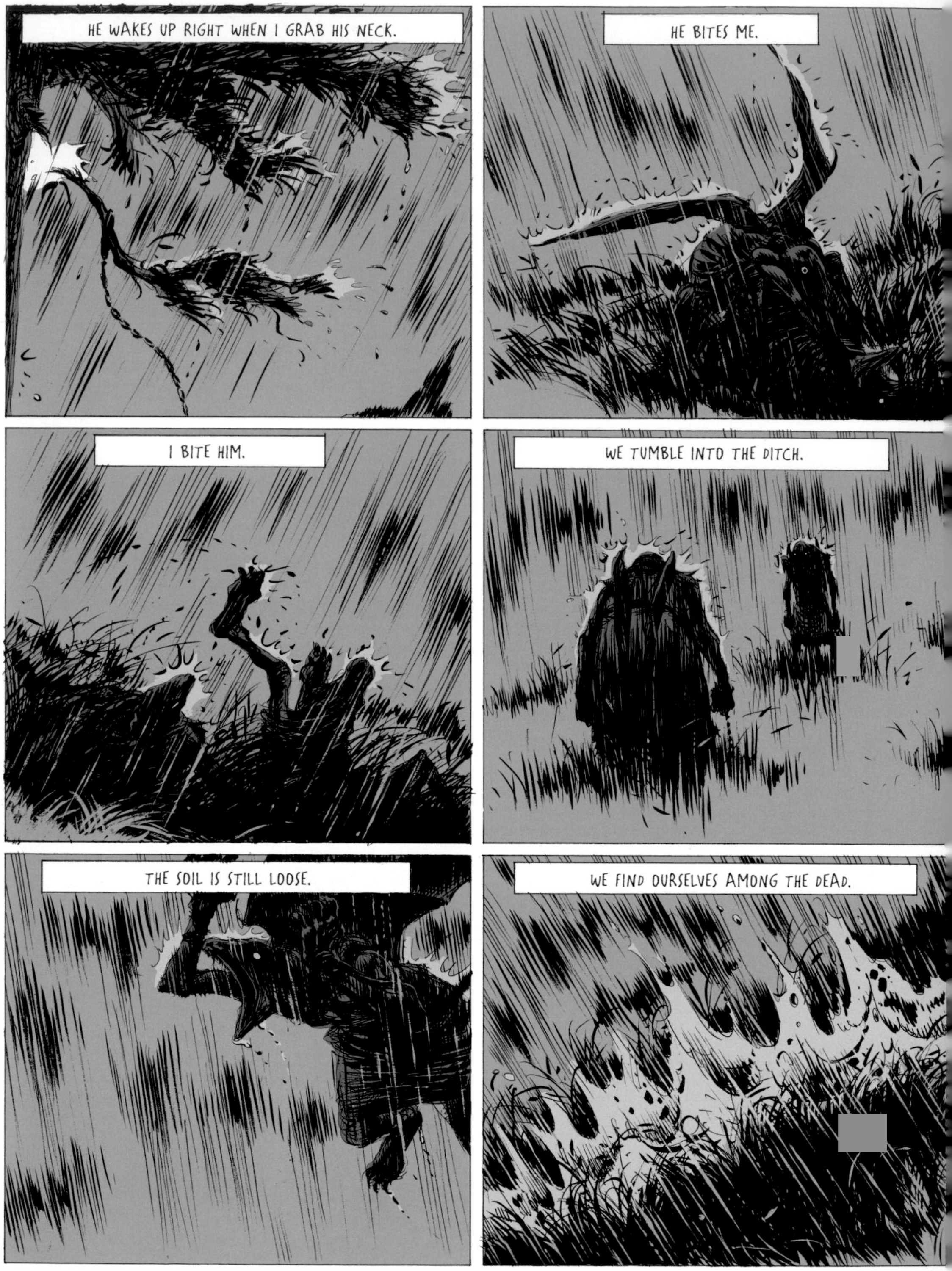
HE WAKES UP RIGHT WHEN I GRAB HIS NECK.
HE BITES ME.
I BITE HIM.
WE TUMBLE INTO THE DITCH.
THE SOIL IS STILL LOOSE.
WE FIND OURSELVES AMONG THE DEAD.

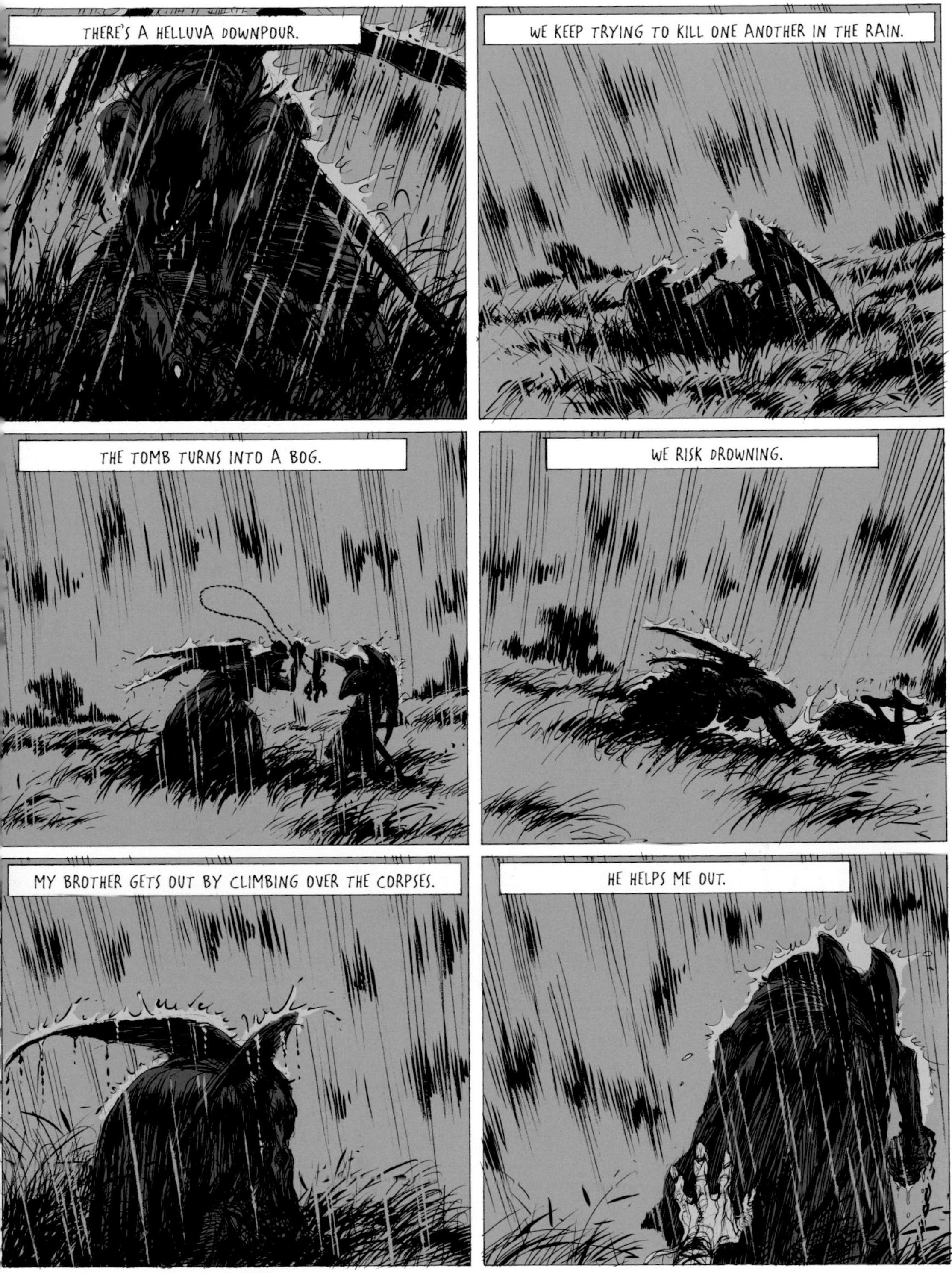
THERE'S A HELLUVA DOWNPOUR.
WE KEEP TRYING TO KILL ONE ANOTHER IN THE RAIN.
THE TOMB TURNS INTO A BOG.
WE RISK DROWNING.
MY BROTHER GETS OUT BY CLIMBING OVER THE CORPSES.
HE HELPS ME OUT.

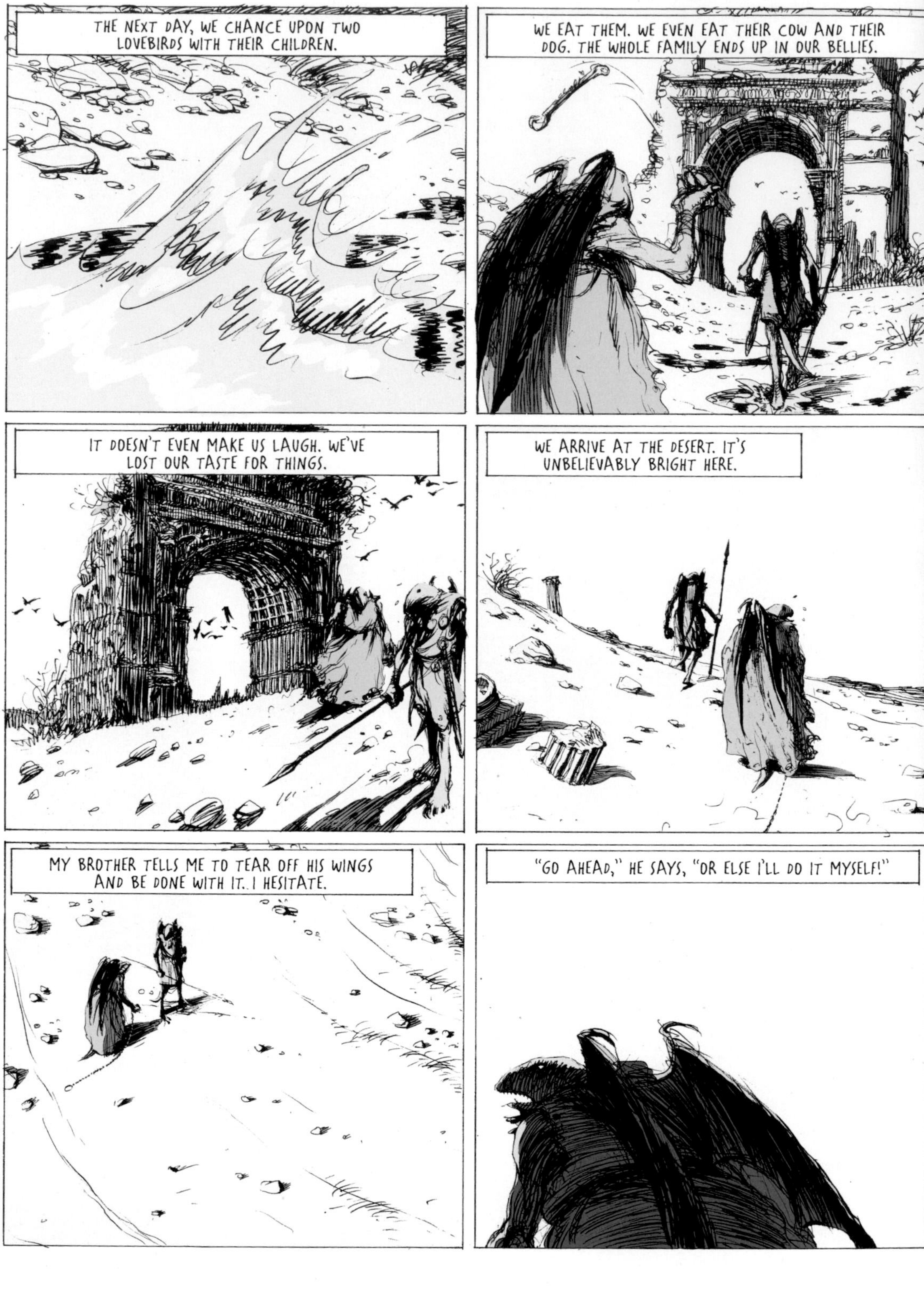
THE NEXT DAY, WE CHANCE UPON TWO LOVEBIRDS WITH THEIR CHILDREN.
WE EAT THEM. WE EVEN EAT THEIR COW AND THEIR DOG. THE WHOLE FAMILY ENDS UP IN OUR BELLIES.
IT DOESN'T EVEN MAKE US LAUGH. WE'VE LOST OUR TASTE FOR THINGS.
WE ARRIVE AT THE DESERT. IT'S UNBELIEVABLY BRIGHT HERE.
MY BROTHER TELLS ME TO TEAR OFF HIS WINGS AND BE DONE WITH IT. I HESITATE.
"GO AHEAD," HE SAYS, "OR ELSE I'LL DO IT MYSELF!"

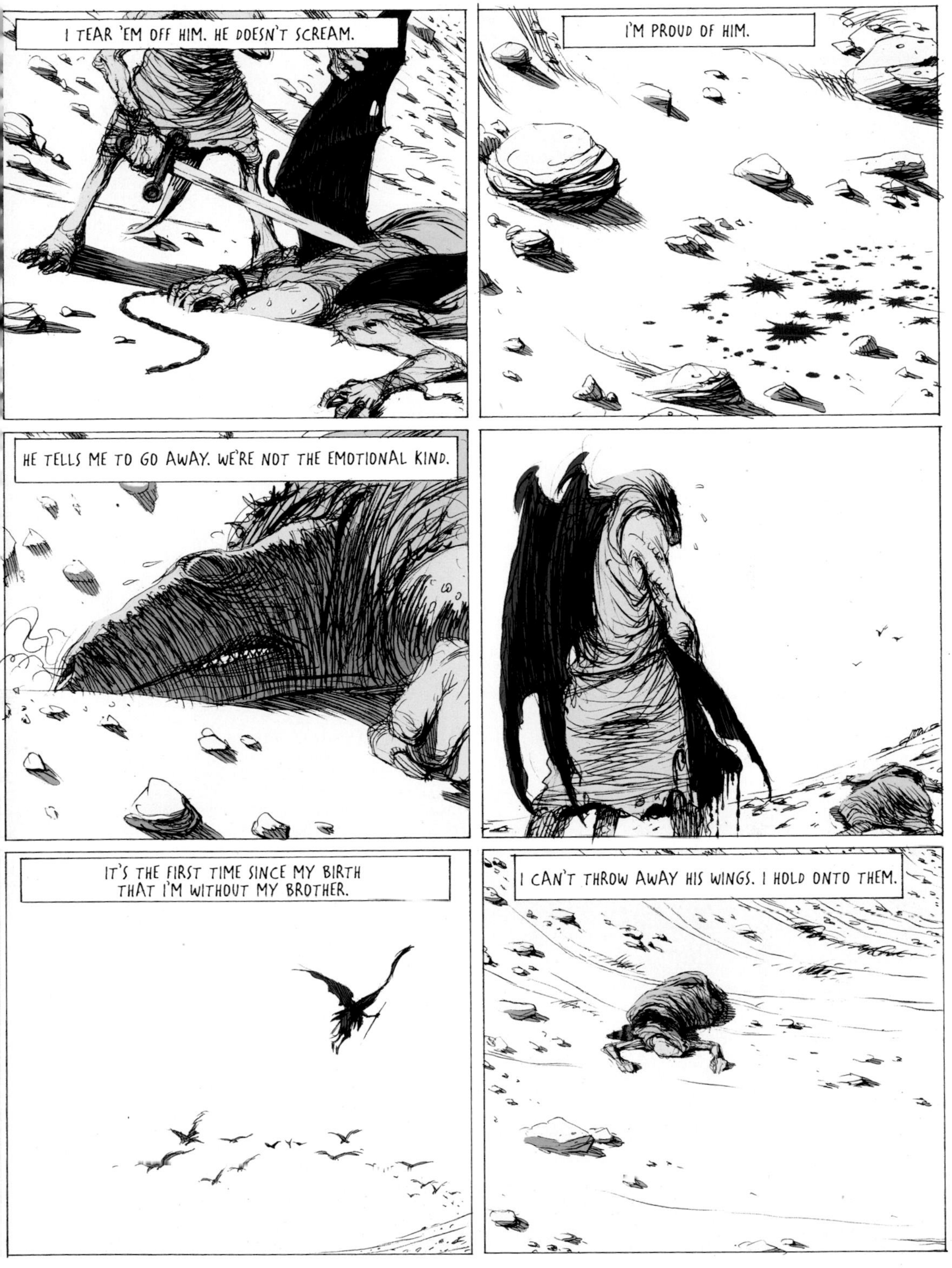
I TEAR 'EM OFF HIM. HE DOESN'T SCREAM.
I'M PROUD OF HIM.
HE TELLS ME TO GO AWAY. WE'RE NOT THE EMOTIONAL KIND.
IT'S THE FIRST TIME SINCE MY BIRTH THAT I'M WITHOUT MY BROTHER.
I CAN'T THROW AWAY HIS WINGS. I HOLD ONTO THEM.

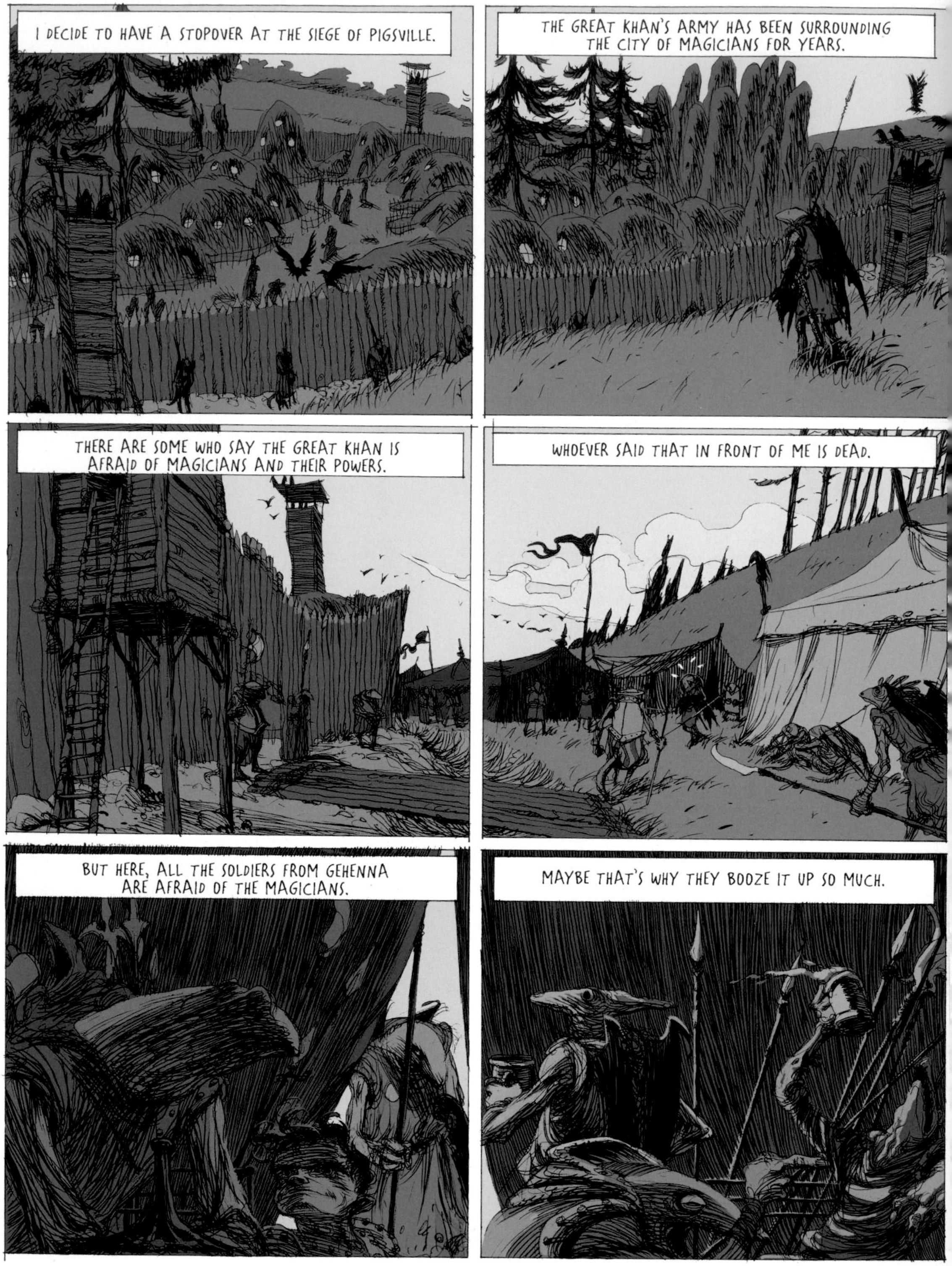
I DECIDE TO HAVE A STOPOVER AT THE SIEGE OF PIGSVILLE.
THE GREAT KHAN'S ARMY HAS BEEN SURROUNDING THE CITY OF MAGICIANS FOR YEARS.
THERE ARE SOME WHO SAY THE GREAT KHAN IS AFRAID OF MAGICIANS AND THEIR POWERS.
WHOEVER SAID THAT IN FRONT OF ME IS DEAD.
BUT HERE, ALL THE SOLDIERS FROM GEHENNA ARE AFRAID OF THE MAGICIANS.
MAYBE THAT'S WHY THEY BOOZE IT UP SO MUCH.

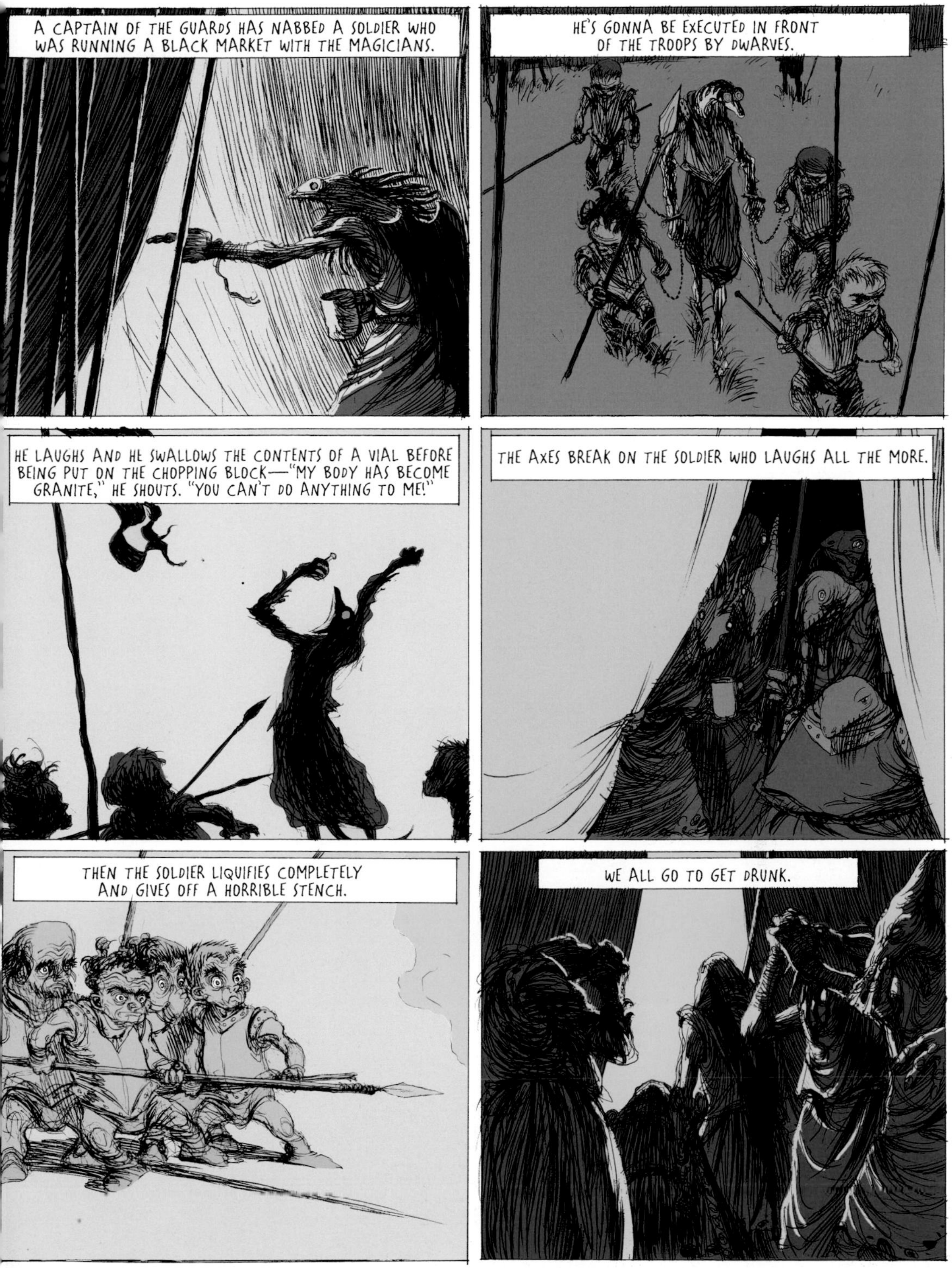
A CAPTAIN OF THE GUARDS HAS NABBED A SOLDIER WHO WAS RUNNING A BLACK MARKET WITH THE MAGICIANS.
HE'S GONNA BE EXECUTED IN FRONT OF THE TROOPS BY DWARVES.
HE LAUGHS AND HE SWALLOWS THE CONTENTS OF A VIAL BEFORE BEING PUT ON THE CHOPPING BLOCK—"MY BODY HAS BECOME GRANITE," HE SHOUTS. "YOU CAN'T DO ANYTHING TO ME!"
THE AXES BREAK ON THE SOLDIER WHO LAUGHS ALL THE MORE.
THEN THE SOLDIER LIQUIFIES COMPLETELY AND GIVES OFF A HORRIBLE STENCH.
WE ALL GO TO GET DRUNK.

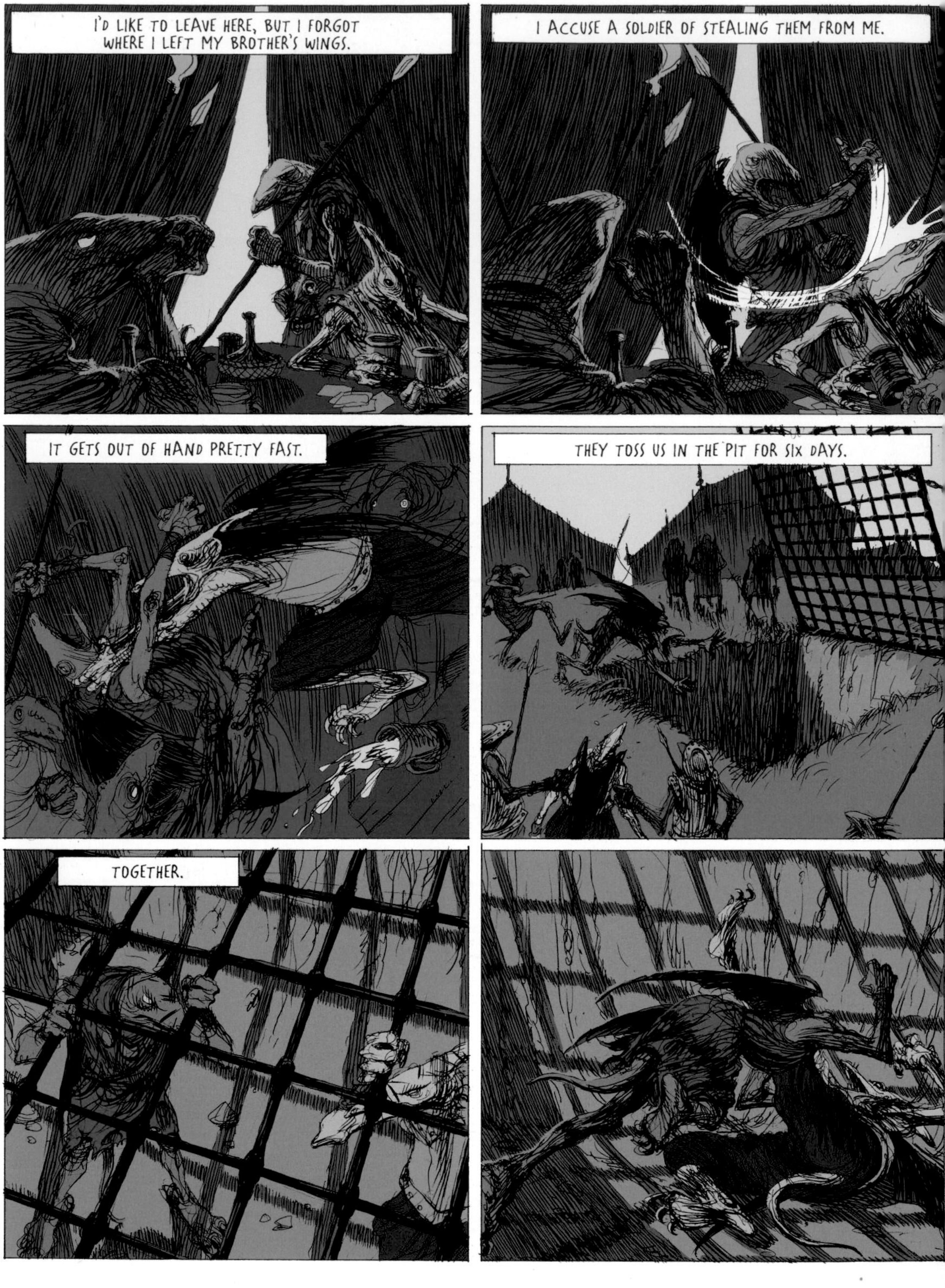
I'D LIKE TO LEAVE HERE, BUT I FORGOT WHERE I LEFT MY BROTHER'S WINGS.
I ACCUSE A SOLDIER OF STEALING THEM FROM ME.
IT GETS OUT OF HAND PRETTY FAST.
THEY TOSS US IN THE PIT FOR SIX DAYS.
TOGETHER.

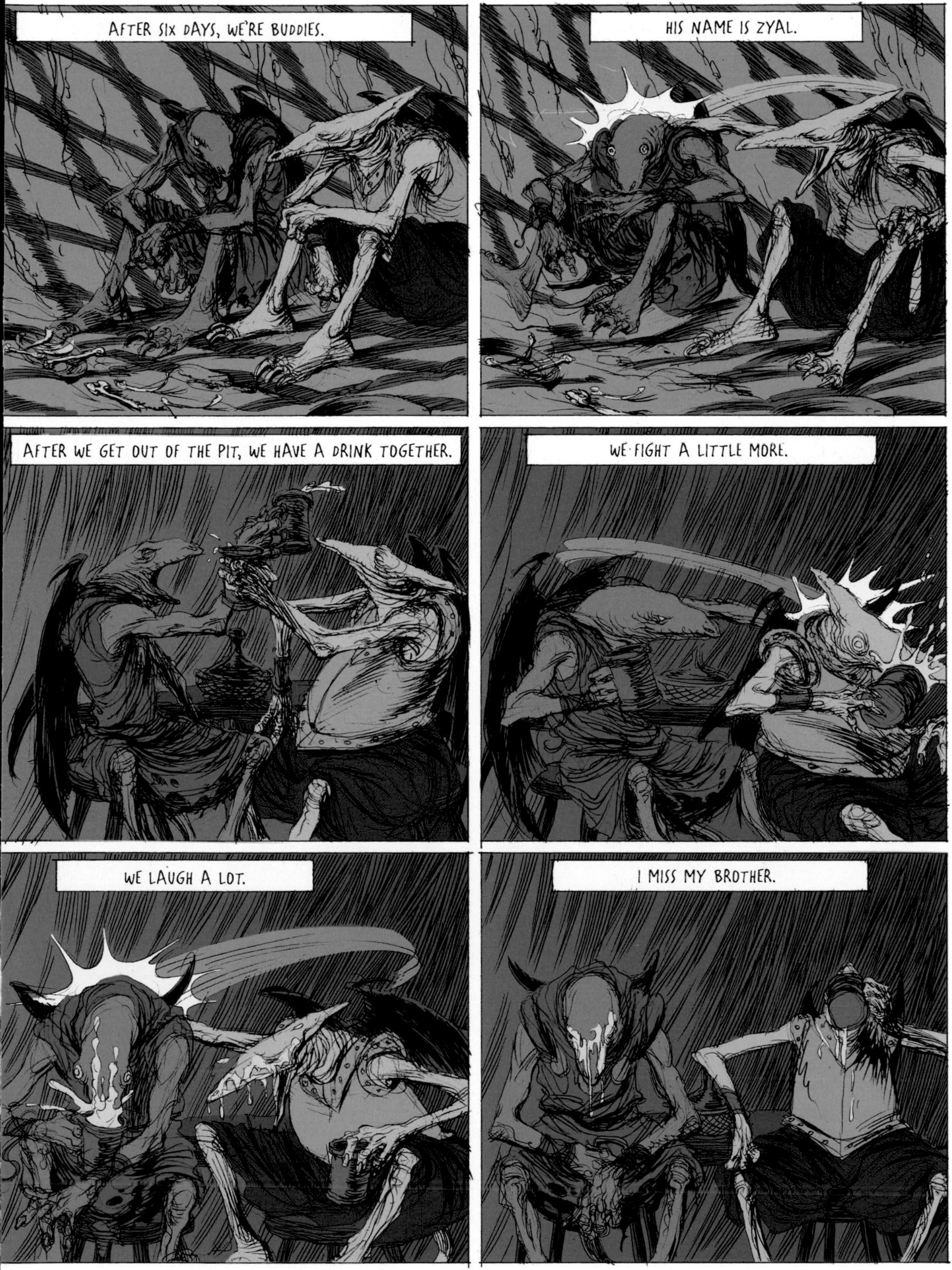
AFTER SIX DAYS, WE'RE BUDDIES.
HIS NAME IS ZYAL.
AFTER WE GET OUT OF THE PIT, WE HAVE A DRINK TOGETHER.
WE FIGHT A LITTLE MORE.
WE LAUGH A LOT.
I MISS MY BROTHER.

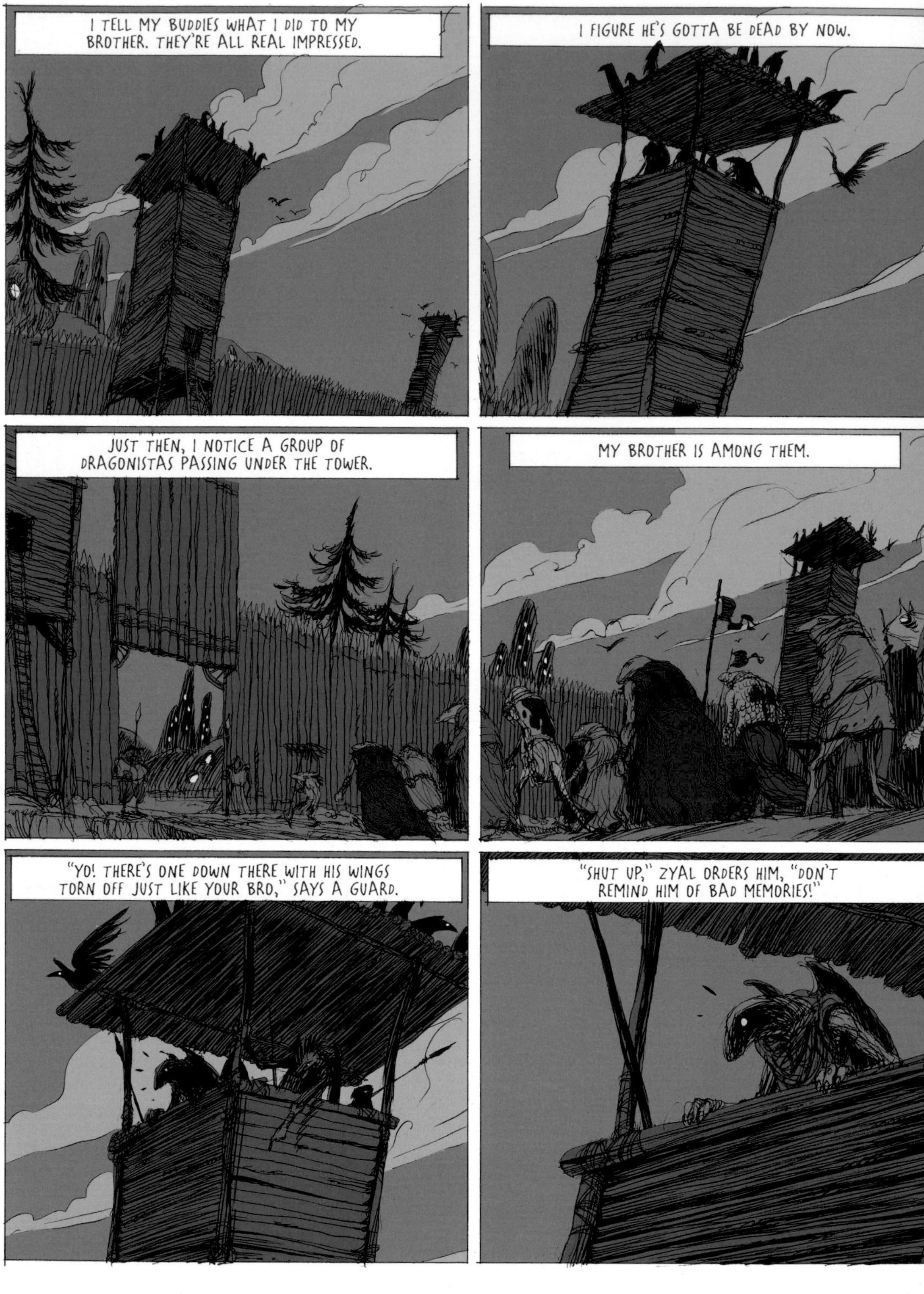
I TELL MY BUDDIES WHAT I DID TO MY BROTHER. THEY'RE ALL REAL IMPRESSED.
I FIGURE HE'S GOTTA BE DEAD BY NOW.
JUST THEN, I NOTICE A GROUP OF DRAGONISTAS PASSING UNDER THE TOWER.
MY BROTHER IS AMONG THEM.
"YO! THERE'S ONE DOWN THERE WITH HIS WINGS TORN OFF JUST LIKE YOUR BRO," SAYS A GUARD.
"SHUT UP," ZYAL ORDERS HIM, "DON'T REMIND HIM OF BAD MEMORIES!"

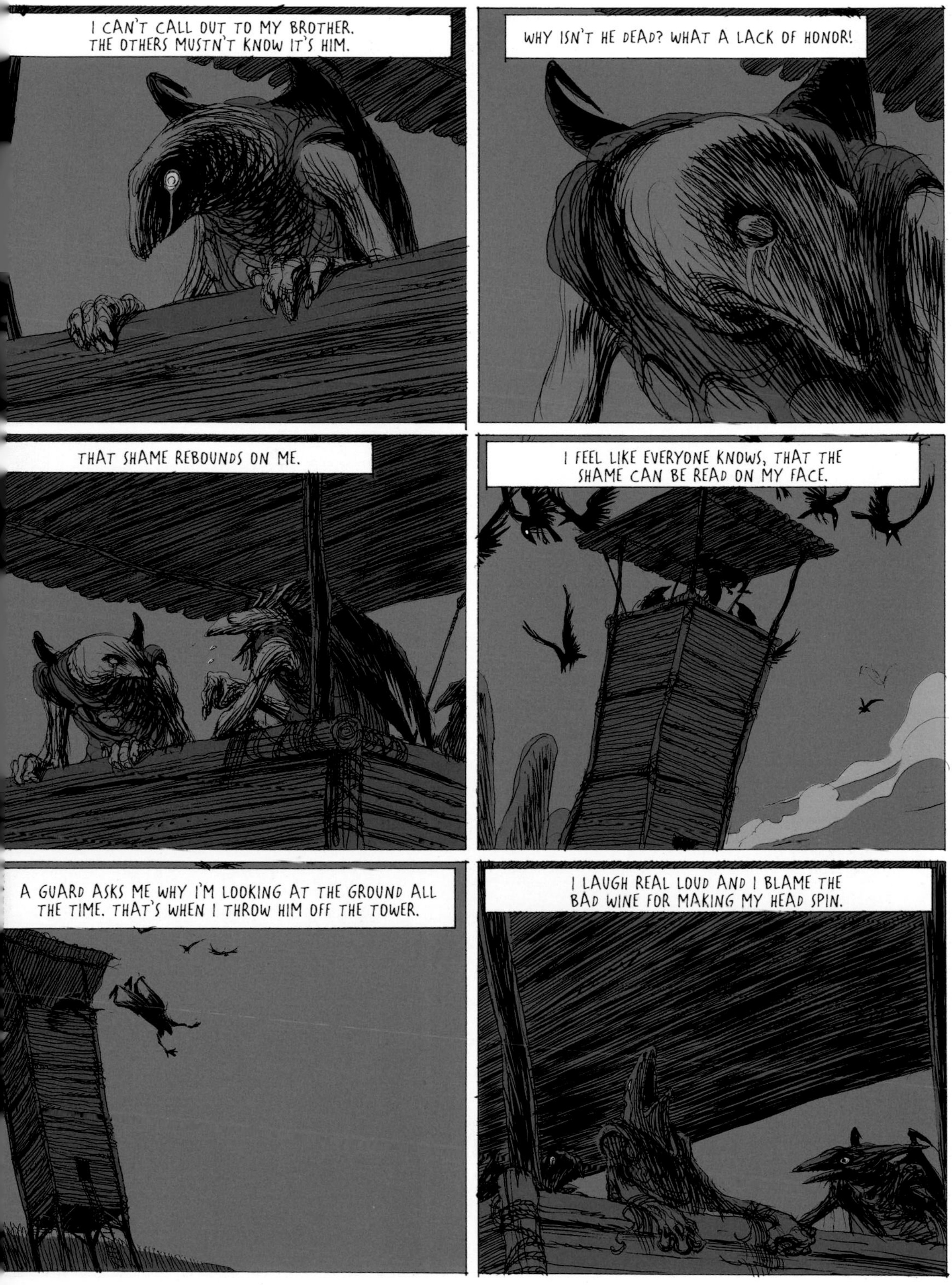
I CAN'T CALL OUT TO MY BROTHER. THE OTHERS MUSTN'T KNOW IT'S HIM.
WHY ISN'T HE DEAD? WHAT A LACK OF HONOR!
THAT SHAME REBOUNDS ON ME.
I FEEL LIKE EVERYONE KNOWS, THAT THE SHAME CAN BE READ ON MY FACE.
A GUARD ASKS ME WHY I'M LOOKING AT THE GROUND ALL THE TIME. THAT'S WHEN I THROW HIM OFF THE TOWER.
I LAUGH REAL LOUD AND I BLAME THE BAD WINE FOR MAKING MY HEAD SPIN.

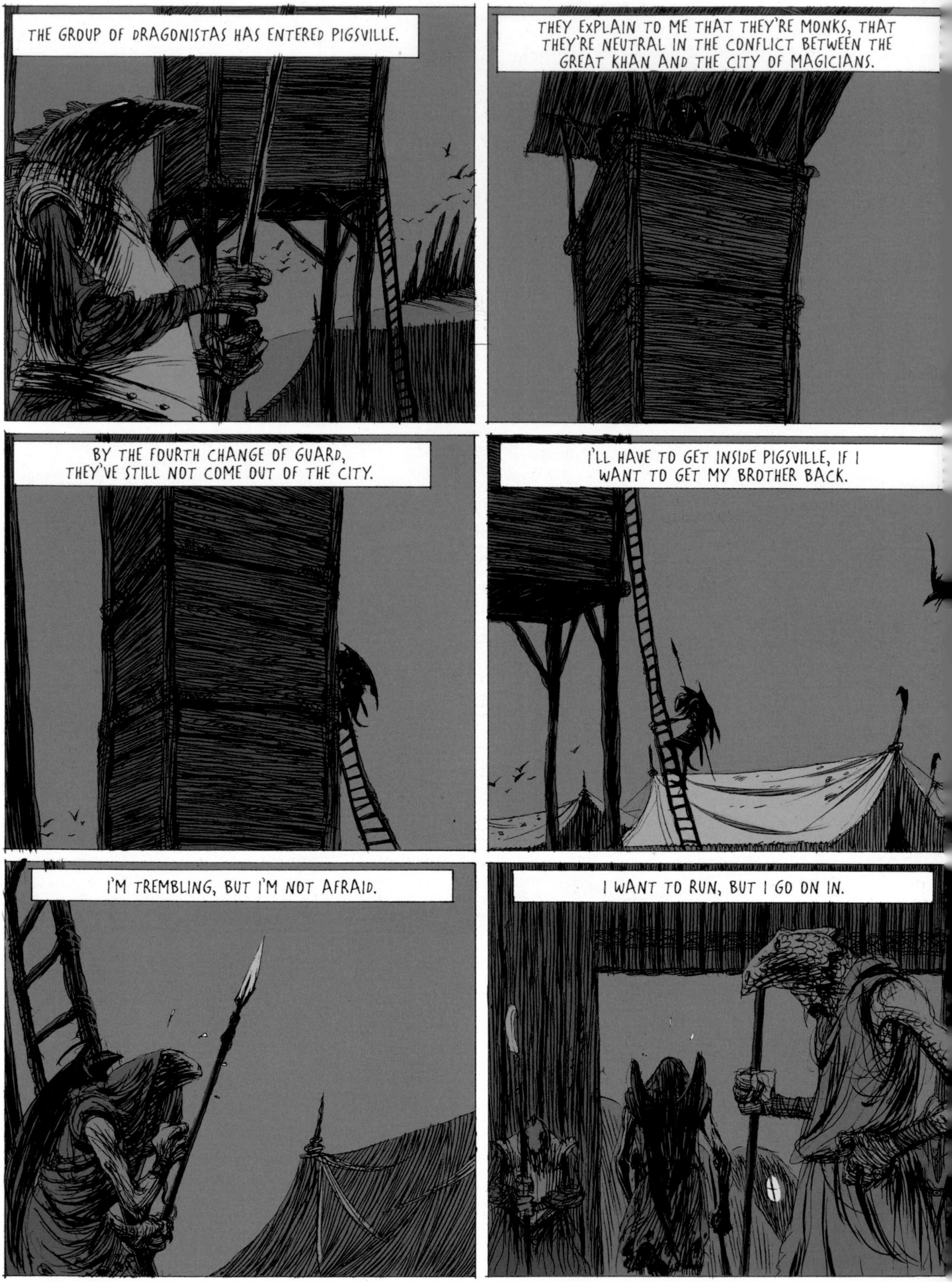
THE GROUP OF DRAGONISTAS HAS ENTERED PIGSVILLE.
THEY EXPLAIN TO ME THAT THEY'RE MONKS, THAT THEY'RE NEUTRAL IN THE CONFLICT BETWEEN THE GREAT KHAN AND THE CITY OF MAGICIANS.
BY THE FOURTH CHANGE OF GUARD, THEY'VE STILL NOT COME OUT OF THE CITY.
I'LL HAVE TO GET INSIDE PIGSVILLE, IF I WANT TO GET MY BROTHER BACK.
I'M TREMBLING, BUT I'M NOT AFRAID.
I WANT TO RUN, BUT I GO ON IN.

EVERYONE'S SO STRANGE IN THIS CITY, I PASS BY UNSEEN. SORCERERS, POTIONS, AND SMOKE EVERYWHERE. I HATE IT.

I PASS A MAGICIAN WHO TRANSFORMS PISS INTO DRINKABLE WATER. SINCE THE SIEGE OF PIGSVILLE HAS LASTED A LONG TIME, HE'S GOT LOTS OF CUSTOMERS.

NEAR ME, IN AN UNDERGROUND TAVERN, A SLIMY CREATURE EATS ITS OWN ARM. THE ARM GROWS BACK IMMEDIATELY. MAGICIANS ADAPT TO ALL SITUATIONS.

PEOPLE SPEAK TO ME. I ACT LIKE I DON'T KNOW HOW TO TALK.

I SMELL THE ODOR OF PEOPLE OF MY KIND. THE DRAGONISTAS ARE THERE, IN THE BACK OF THE ROOM. A DOZEN FELLOWS WEARING TRADITIONAL GARB. THEIR LEADER IS SOME LITTLE OLD GUY.

I CALCULATE MY CHANCES OF MESSING 'EM ALL UP TO GET MY BROTHER BACK. THEN, HAVING FIGURED IT OUT, I SIT DOWN AT A TABLE AND ORDER SOMETHING TO DRINK.

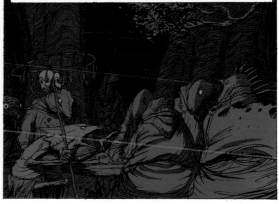

THE OLD GUY MAKES SOME GESTURES UNKNOWN TO ME.

A SMALL EXPLOSION OF BLUE LIGHT OCCURS NOT FAR FROM ME, AMID A GROUP OF MAGICIANS.

ONE OF THE MAGICIANS KNOCKS OVER HIS BEER. HE ACCUSES ONE OF HIS COLLEAGUES OF CAUSING THE EXPLOSION.

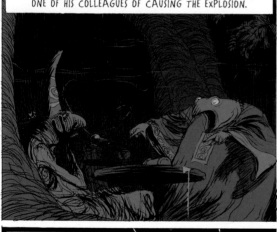

IT DEGENERATES INTO A MAGIC DUEL.

THEY DO MAGIC SPELLS ON EACH OTHER FROM AFAR.

IT DOESN'T HAVE THE SAME CLASS AS A BEAUTIFUL AX-FIGHT.

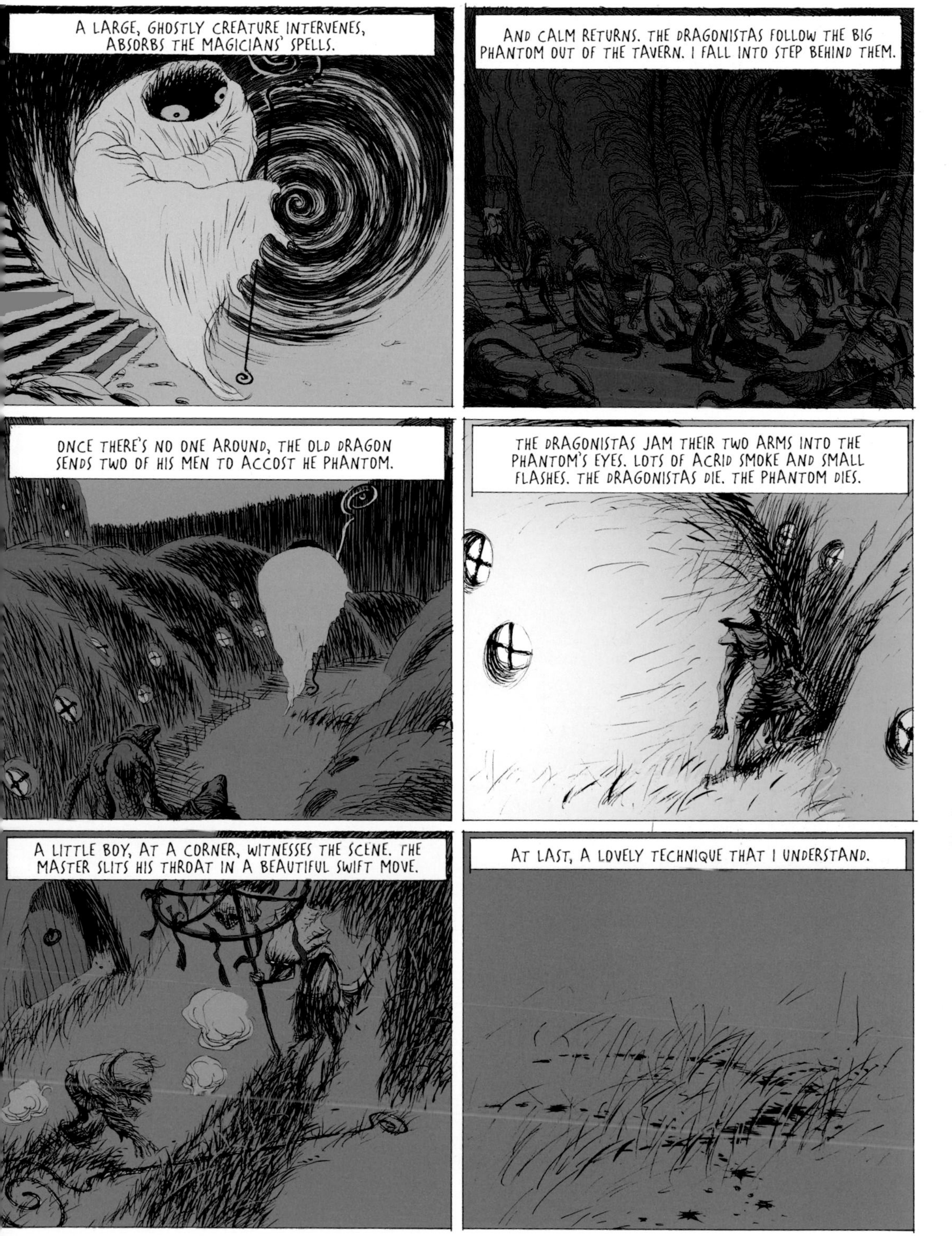
A LARGE, GHOSTLY CREATURE INTERVENES, ABSORBS THE MAGICIANS' SPELLS.
AND CALM RETURNS. THE DRAGONISTAS FOLLOW THE BIG PHANTOM OUT OF THE TAVERN. I FALL INTO STEP BEHIND THEM.
ONCE THERE'S NO ONE AROUND, THE OLD DRAGON SENDS TWO OF HIS MEN TO ACCOST HE PHANTOM.
THE DRAGONISTAS JAM THEIR TWO ARMS INTO THE PHANTOM'S EYES. LOTS OF ACRID SMOKE AND SMALL FLASHES. THE DRAGONISTAS DIE. THE PHANTOM DIES.
A LITTLE BOY, AT A CORNER, WITNESSES THE SCENE. THE MASTER SLITS HIS THROAT IN A BEAUTIFUL SWIFT MOVE.
AT LAST, A LOVELY TECHNIQUE THAT I UNDERSTAND.

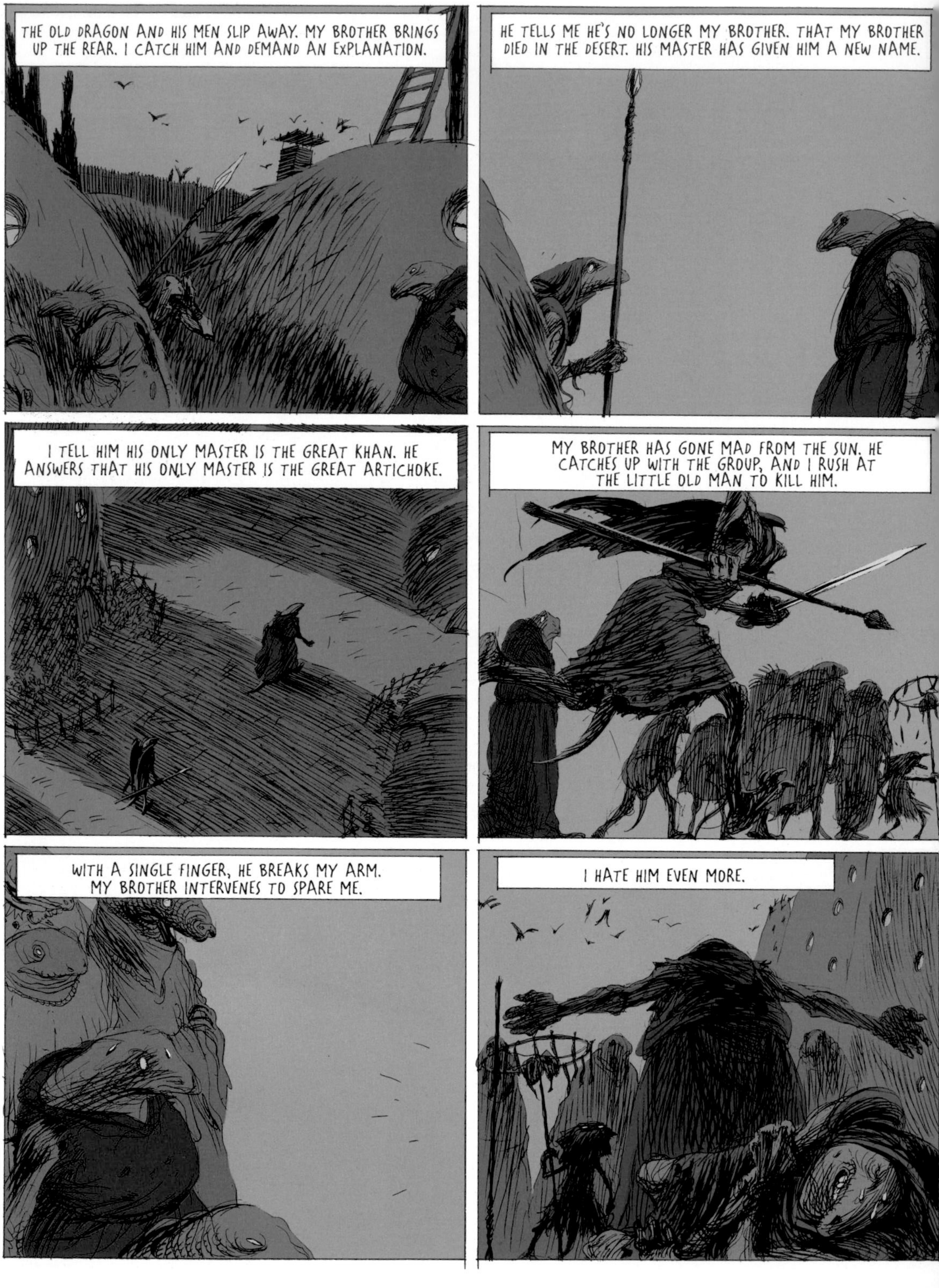
THE OLD DRAGON AND HIS MEN SLIP AWAY. MY BROTHER BRINGS UP THE REAR. I CATCH HIM AND DEMAND AN EXPLANATION.
HE TELLS ME HE'S NO LONGER MY BROTHER. THAT MY BROTHER DIED IN THE DESERT. HIS MASTER HAS GIVEN HIM A NEW NAME.
I TELL HIM HIS ONLY MASTER IS THE GREAT KHAN. HE ANSWERS THAT HIS ONLY MASTER IS THE GREAT ARTICHOKE.
MY BROTHER HAS GONE MAD FROM THE SUN. HE CATCHES UP WITH THE GROUP, AND I RUSH AT THE LITTLE OLD MAN TO KILL HIM.
WITH A SINGLE FINGER, HE BREAKS MY ARM. MY BROTHER INTERVENES TO SPARE ME.
I HATE HIM EVEN MORE.

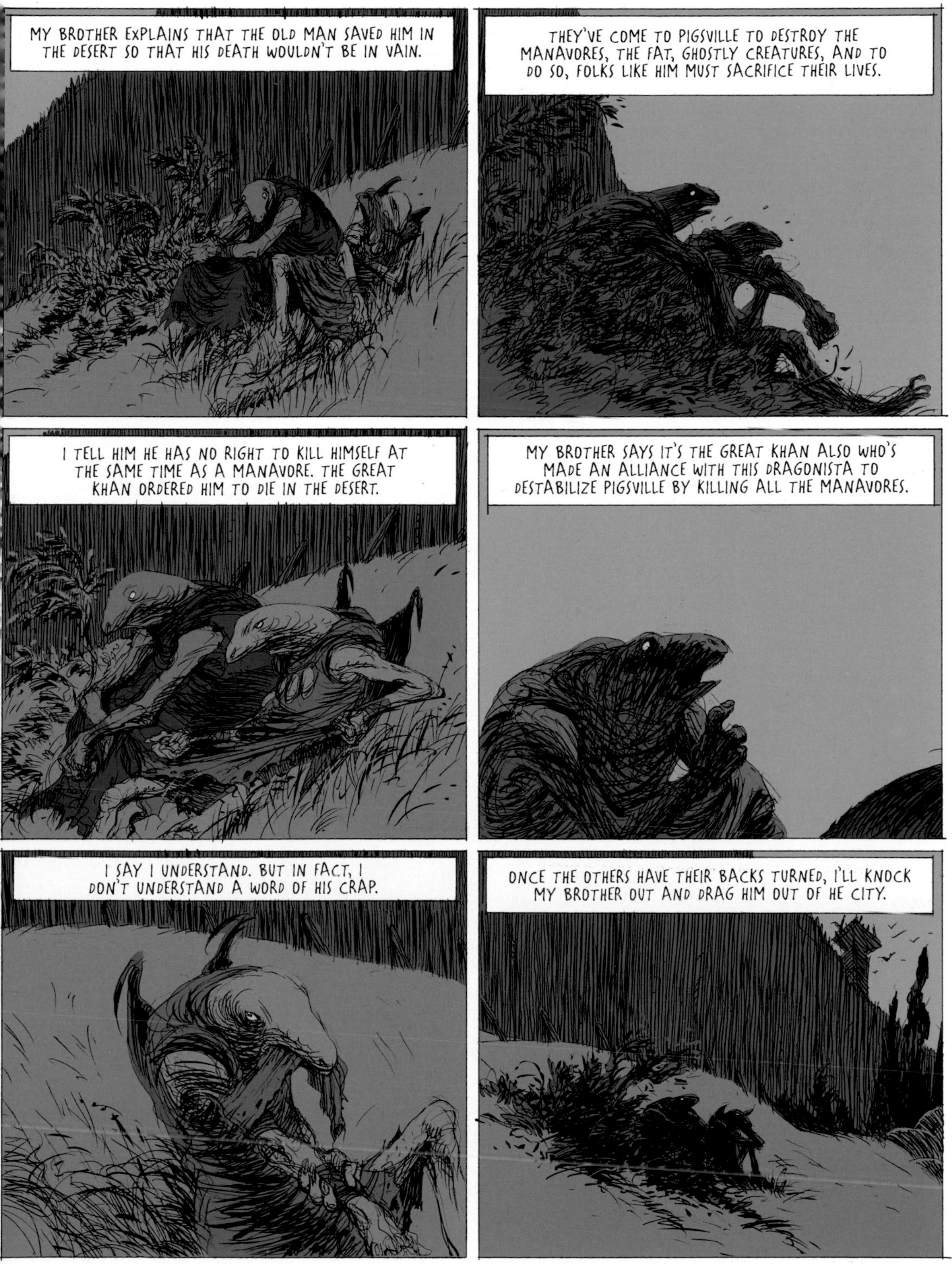
MY BROTHER EXPLAINS THAT THE OLD MAN SAVED HIM IN THE DESERT SO THAT HIS DEATH WOULDN'T BE IN VAIN.
THEY'VE COME TO PIGSVILLE TO DESTROY THE MANAVORES, THE FAT, GHOSTLY CREATURES, AND TO DO SO, FOLKS LIKE HIM MUST SACRIFICE THEIR LIVES.
I TELL HIM HE HAS NO RIGHT TO KILL HIMSELF AT THE SAME TIME AS A MANAVORE. THE GREAT KHAN ORDERED HIM TO DIE IN THE DESERT.
MY BROTHER SAYS IT'S THE GREAT KHAN ALSO WHO'S MADE AN ALLIANCE WITH THIS DRAGONISTA TO DESTABILIZE PIGSVILLE BY KILLING ALL THE MANAVORES.
I SAY I UNDERSTAND. BUT IN FACT, I DON'T UNDERSTAND A WORD OF HIS CRAP.
ONCE THE OTHERS HAVE THEIR BACKS TURNED, I'LL KNOCK MY BROTHER OUT AND DRAG HIM OUT OF HE CITY.

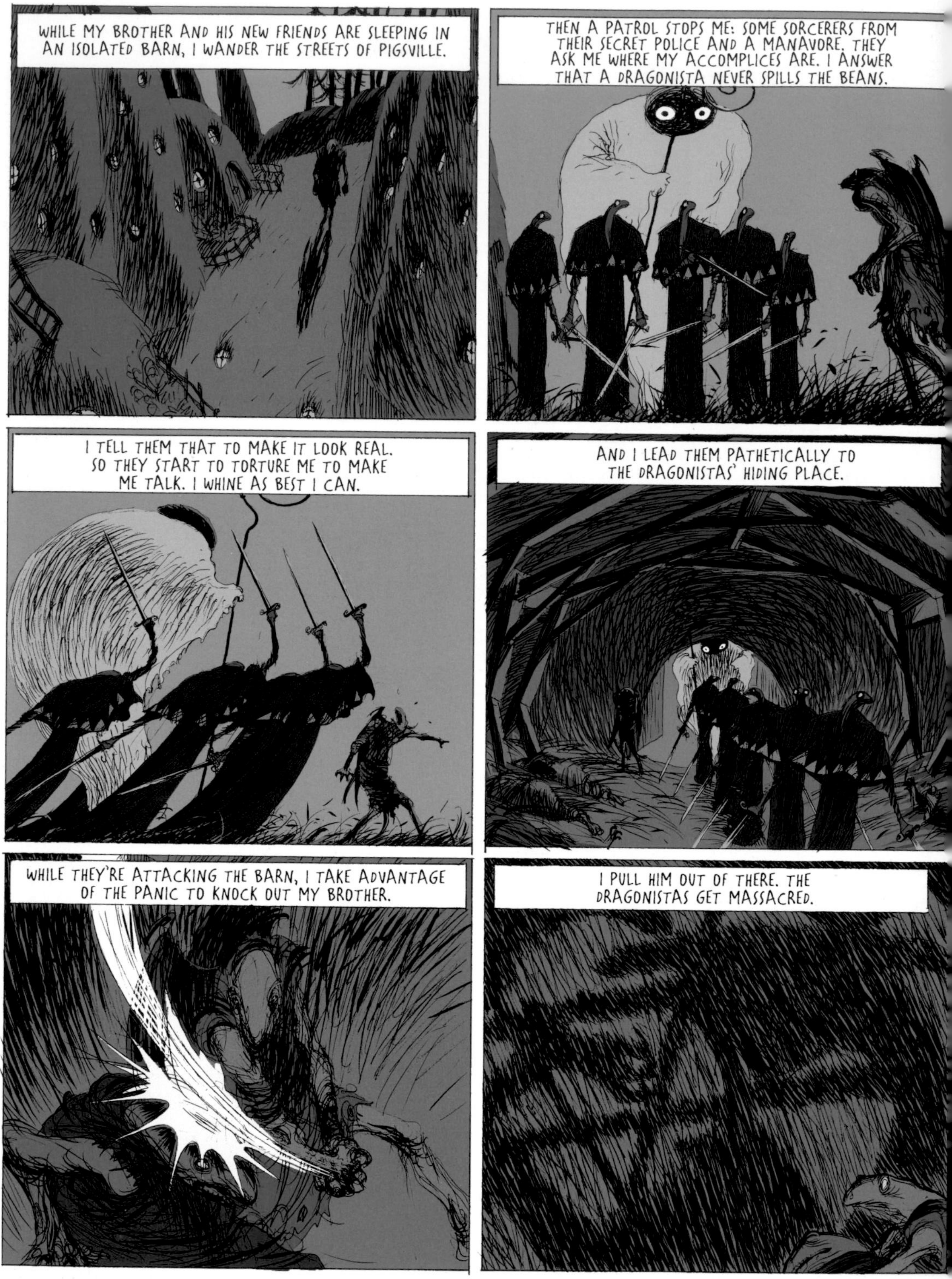
WHILE MY BROTHER AND HIS NEW FRIENDS ARE SLEEPING IN AN ISOLATED BARN, I WANDER THE STREETS OF PIGSVILLE.
THEN A PATROL STOPS ME: SOME SORCERERS FROM THEIR SECRET POLICE AND A MANAVORE. THEY ASK ME WHERE MY ACCOMPLICES ARE. I ANSWER THAT A DRAGONISTA NEVER SPILLS THE BEANS.
I TELL THEM THAT TO MAKE IT LOOK REAL. SO THEY START TO TORTURE ME TO MAKE ME TALK. I WHINE AS BEST I CAN.
AND I LEAD THEM PATHETICALLY TO THE DRAGONISTAS' HIDING PLACE.
WHILE THEY'RE ATTACKING THE BARN, I TAKE ADVANTAGE OF THE PANIC TO KNOCK OUT MY BROTHER.
I PULL HIM OUT OF THERE. THE DRAGONISTAS GET MASSACRED.

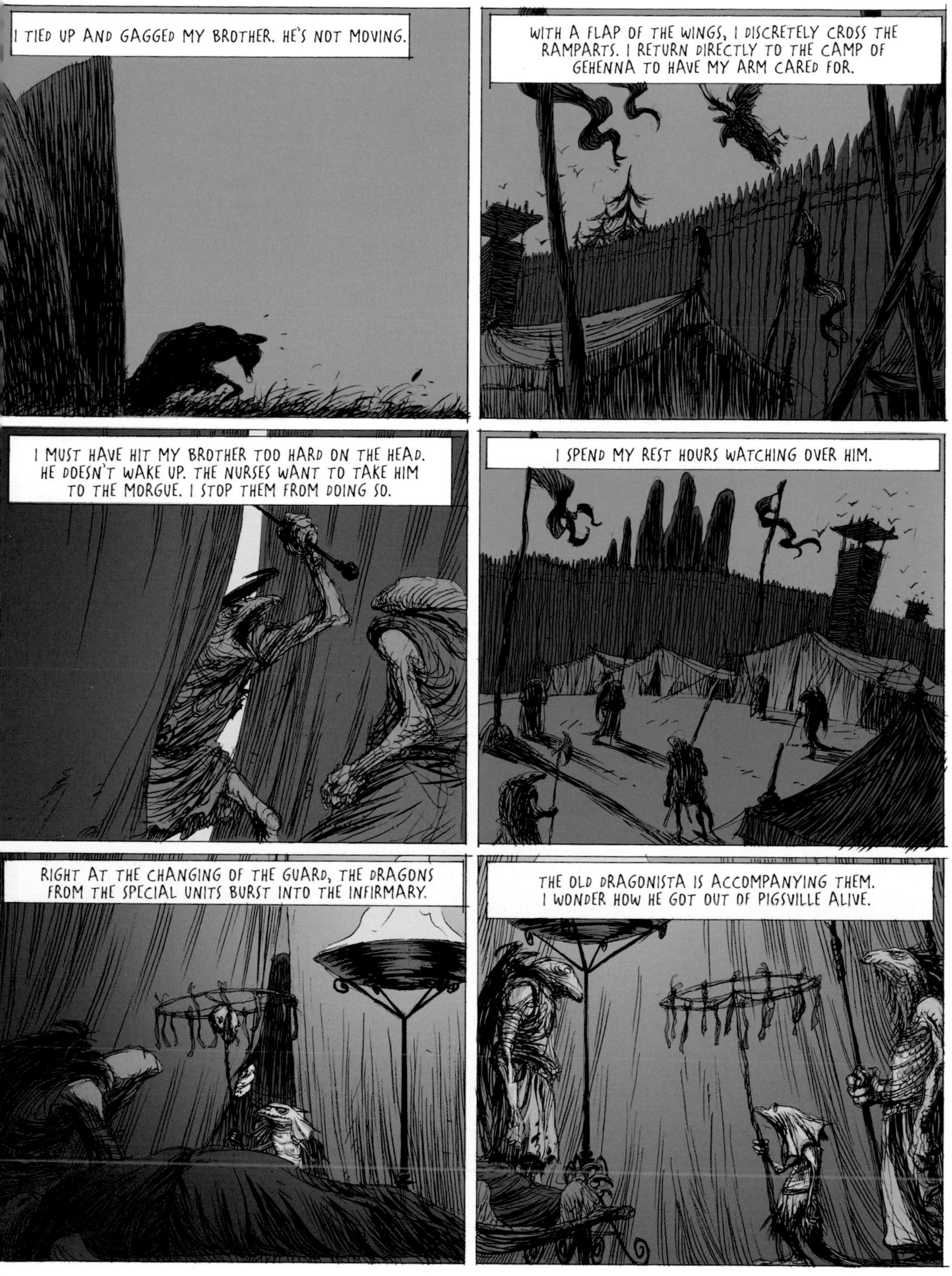
I TIED UP AND GAGGED MY BROTHER. HE'S NOT MOVING.
WITH A FLAP OF THE WINGS, I DISCRETELY CROSS THE RAMPARTS. I RETURN DIRECTLY TO THE CAMP OF GEHENNA TO HAVE MY ARM CARED FOR.
I MUST HAVE HIT MY BROTHER TOO HARD ON THE HEAD. HE DOESN'T WAKE UP. THE NURSES WANT TO TAKE HIM TO THE MORGUE. I STOP THEM FROM DOING SO.
I SPEND MY REST HOURS WATCHING OVER HIM.
RIGHT AT THE CHANGING OF THE GUARD, THE DRAGONS FROM THE SPECIAL UNITS BURST INTO THE INFIRMARY.
THE OLD DRAGONISTA IS ACCOMPANYING THEM. I WONDER HOW HE GOT OUT OF PIGSVILLE ALIVE.

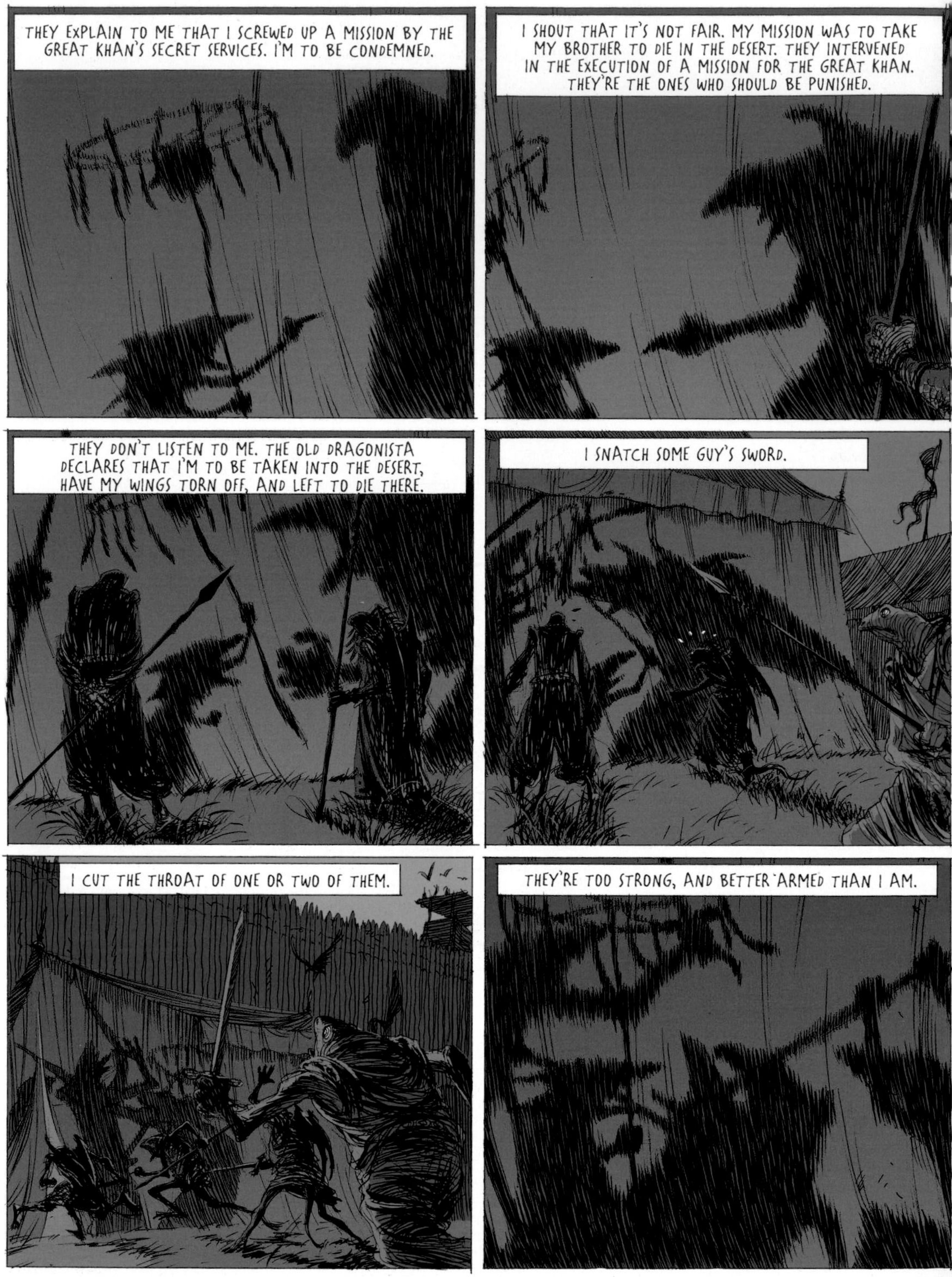
THEY EXPLAIN TO ME THAT I SCREWED UP A MISSION BY THE GREAT KHAN'S SECRET SERVICES. I'M TO BE CONDEMNED.
I SHOUT THAT IT'S NOT FAIR. MY MISSION WAS TO TAKE MY BROTHER TO DIE IN THE DESERT. THEY INTERVENED IN THE EXECUTION OF A MISSION FOR THE GREAT KHAN. THEY'RE THE ONES WHO SHOULD BE PUNISHED.
THEY DON'T LISTEN TO ME. THE OLD DRAGONISTA DECLARES THAT I'M TO BE TAKEN INTO THE DESERT, HAVE MY WINGS TORN OFF, AND LEFT TO DIE THERE.
I SNATCH SOME GUY'S SWORD.
I CUT THE THROAT OF ONE OR TWO OF THEM.
THEY'RE TOO STRONG, AND BETTER ARMED THAN I AM.

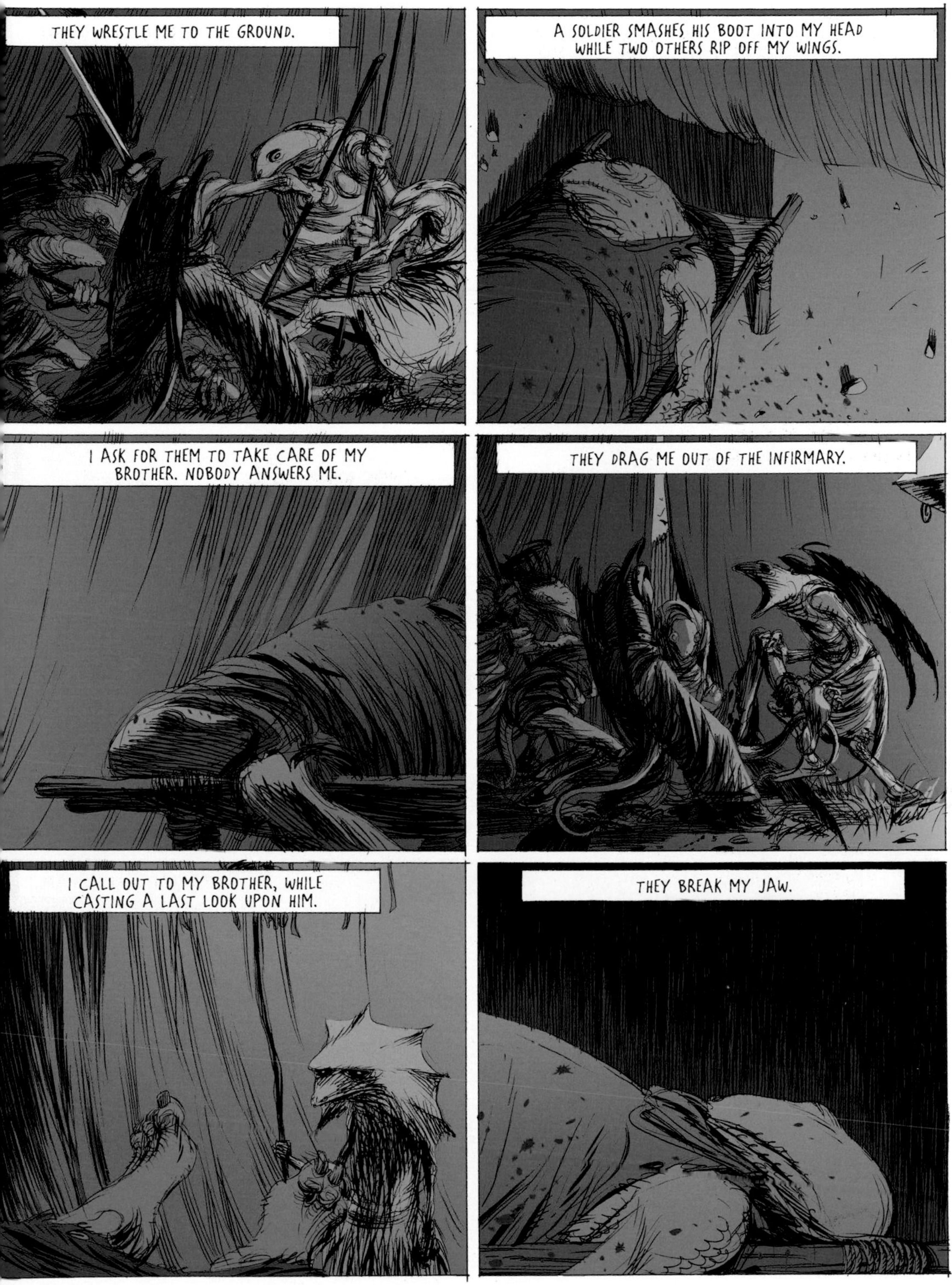
THEY WRESTLE ME TO THE GROUND.
A SOLDIER SMASHES HIS BOOT INTO MY HEAD WHILE TWO OTHERS RIP OFF MY WINGS.
I ASK FOR THEM TO TAKE CARE OF MY BROTHER. NOBODY ANSWERS ME.
THEY DRAG ME OUT OF THE INFIRMARY.
I CALL OUT TO MY BROTHER, WHILE CASTING A LAST LOOK UPON HIM.
THEY BREAK MY JAW.

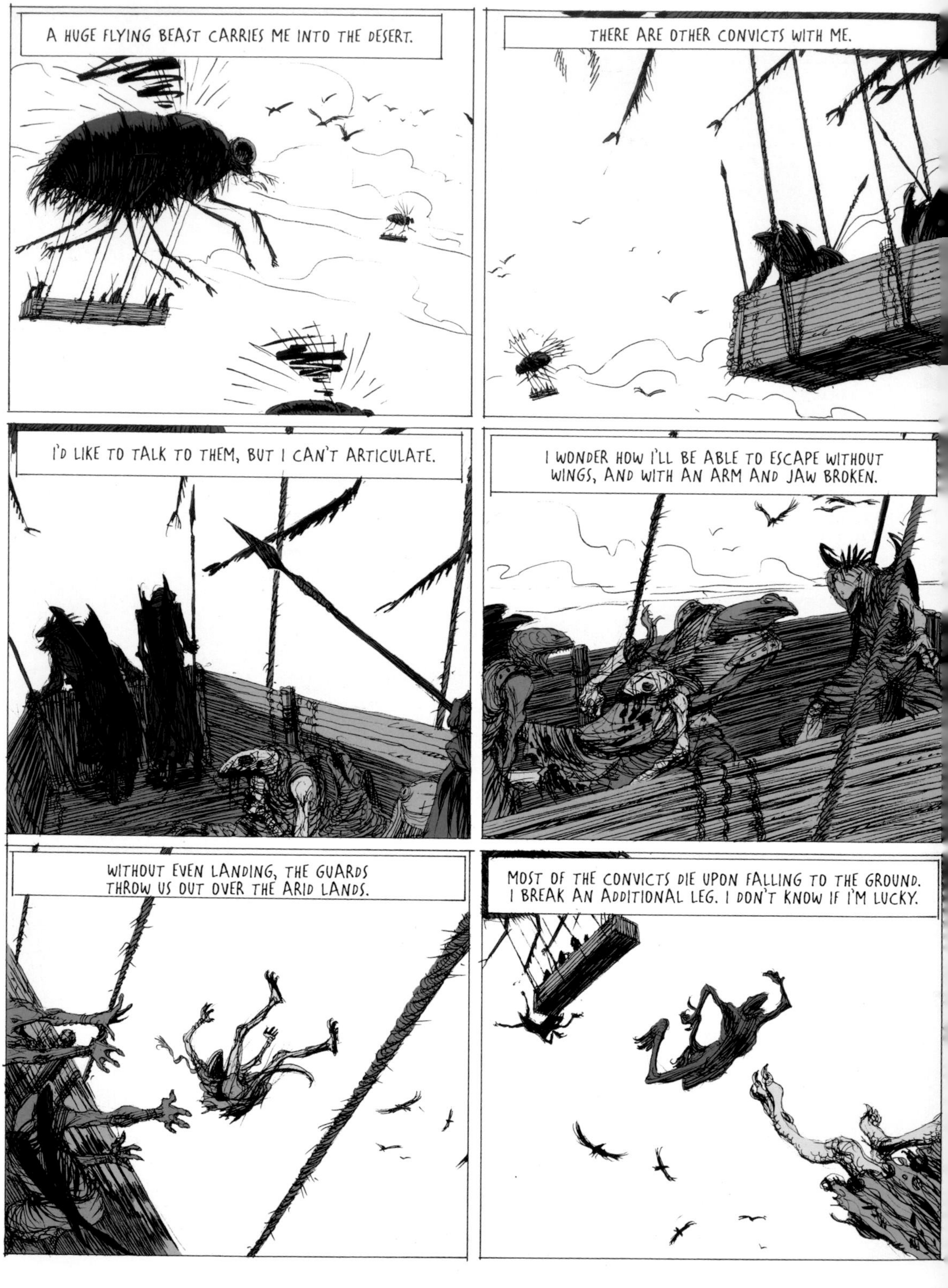
A HUGE FLYING BEAST CARRIES ME INTO THE DESERT.
THERE ARE OTHER CONVICTS WITH ME.
I'D LIKE TO TALK TO THEM, BUT I CAN'T ARTICULATE.
I WONDER HOW I'LL BE ABLE TO ESCAPE WITHOUT WINGS, AND WITH AN ARM AND JAW BROKEN.
WITHOUT EVEN LANDING, THE GUARDS THROW US OUT OVER THE ARID LANDS.
MOST OF THE CONVICTS DIE UPON FALLING TO THE GROUND. I BREAK AN ADDITIONAL LEG. I DON'T KNOW IF I'M LUCKY.

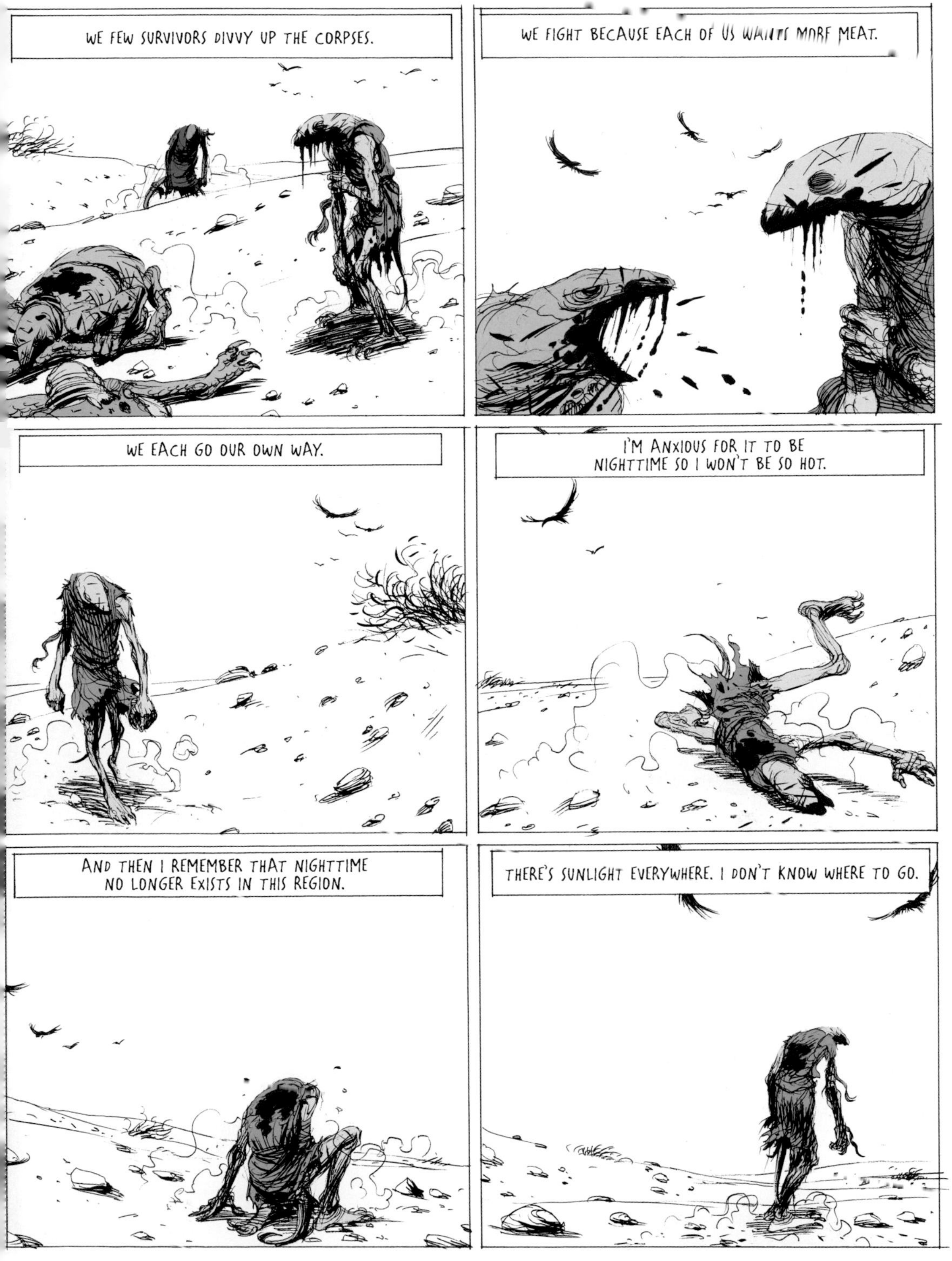
WE FEW SURVIVORS DIVVY UP THE CORPSES.
WE FIGHT BECAUSE EACH OF US WANTS MORE MEAT.
WE EACH GO OUR OWN WAY.
I'M ANXIOUS FOR IT TO BE NIGHTTIME SO I WON'T BE SO HOT.
AND THEN I REMEMBER THAT NIGHTTIME NO LONGER EXISTS IN THIS REGION.
THERE'S SUNLIGHT EVERYWHERE. I DON'T KNOW WHERE TO GO.

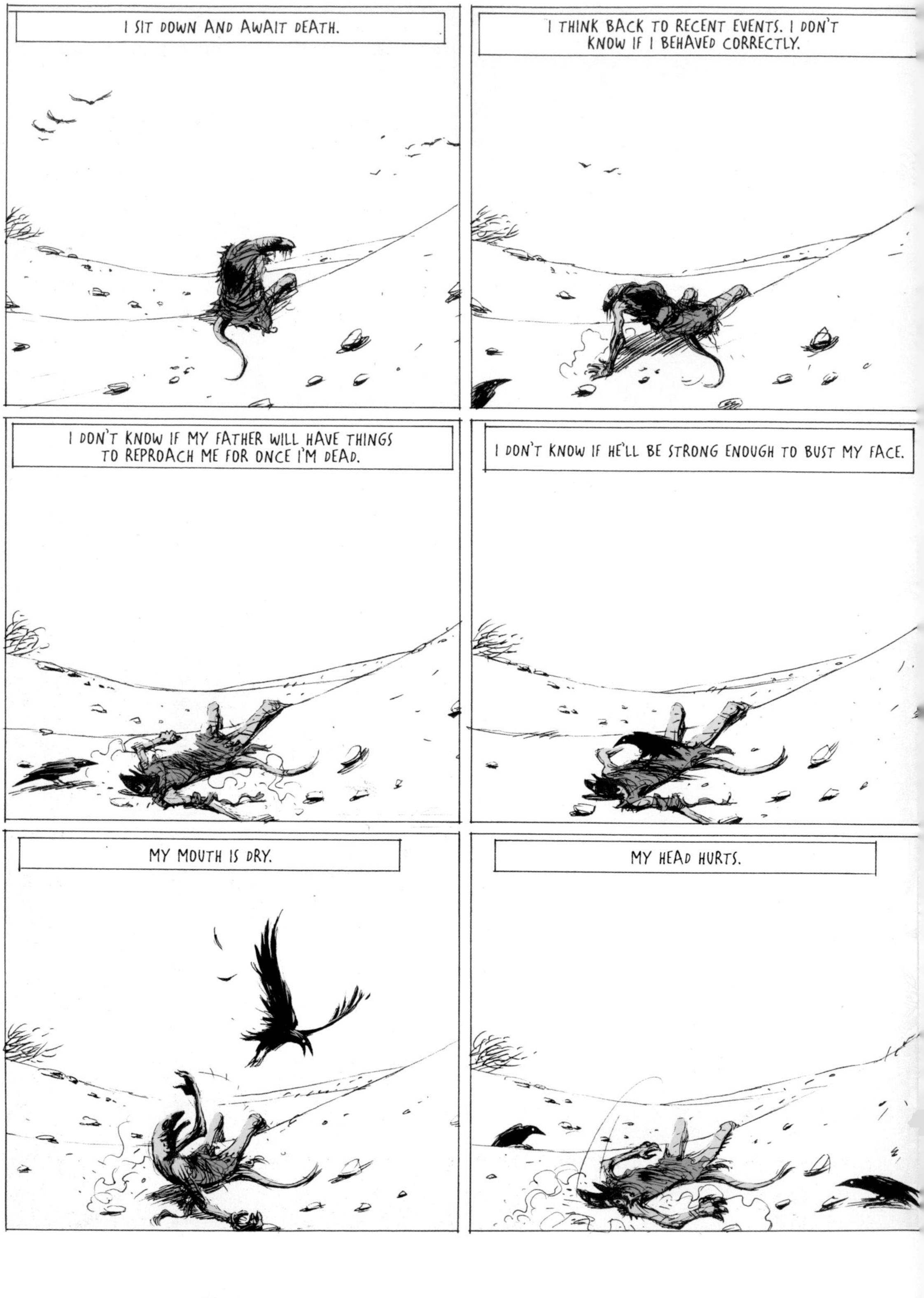
I SIT DOWN AND AWAIT DEATH.
I THINK BACK TO RECENT EVENTS. I DON'T KNOW IF I BEHAVED CORRECTLY.
I DON'T KNOW IF MY FATHER WILL HAVE THINGS TO REPROACH ME FOR ONCE I'M DEAD.
I DON'T KNOW IF HE'LL BE STRONG ENOUGH TO BUST MY FACE.
MY MOUTH IS DRY.
MY HEAD HURTS.

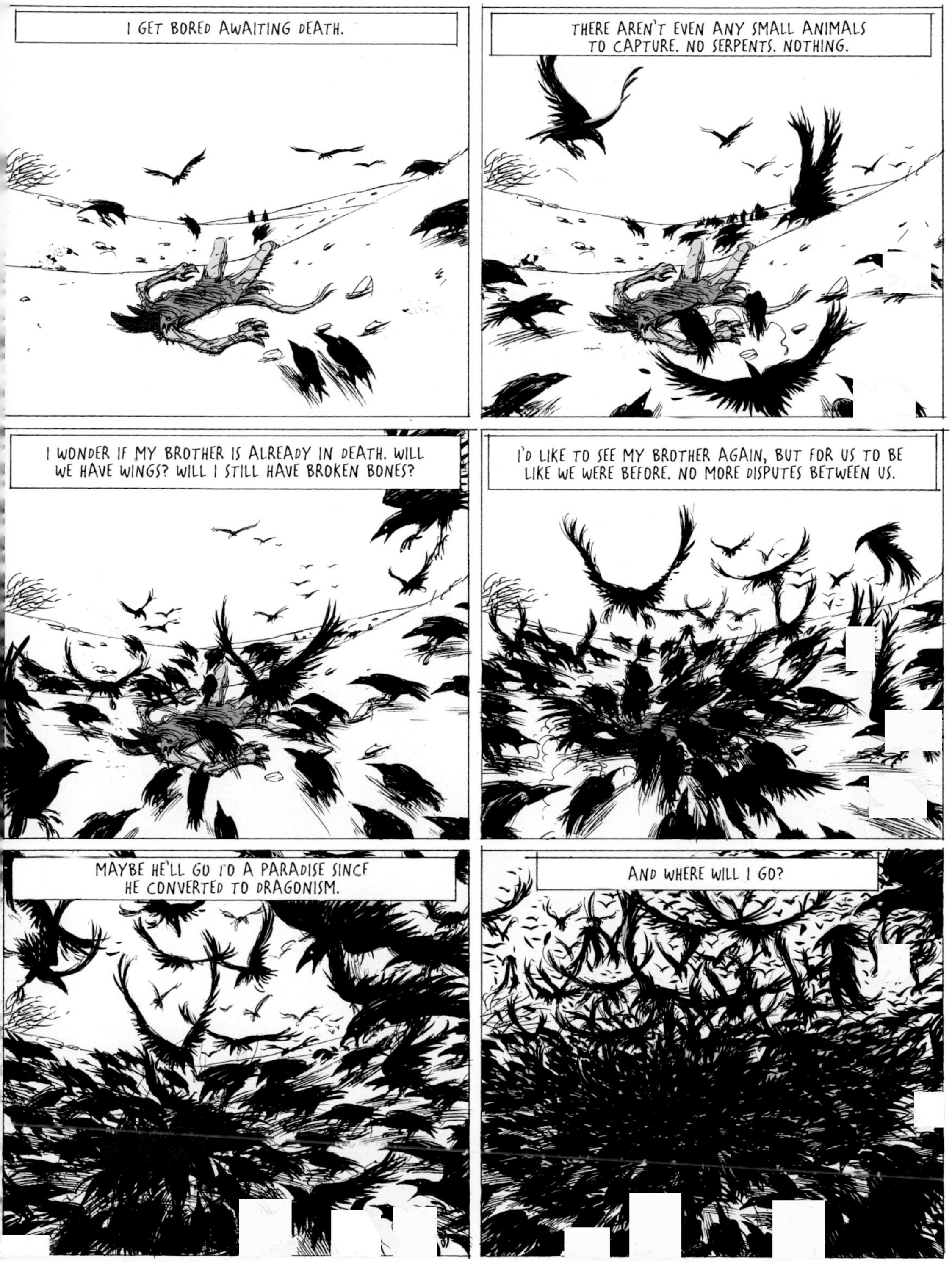
I GET BORED AWAITING DEATH.
THERE AREN'T EVEN ANY SMALL ANIMALS TO CAPTURE. NO SERPENTS. NOTHING.
I WONDER IF MY BROTHER IS ALREADY IN DEATH. WILL WE HAVE WINGS? WILL I STILL HAVE BROKEN BONES?
I'D LIKE TO SEE MY BROTHER AGAIN, BUT FOR US TO BE LIKE WE WERE BEFORE. NO MORE DISPUTES BETWEEN US.
MAYBE HE'LL GO TO A PARADISE SINCE HE CONVERTED TO DRAGONISM.
AND WHERE WILL I GO?

Joann Sfar & LEWIS TRONDHEIM